AFRICAN DEVELOPMENT

AFRICAN DEVELOPMENT

Making Sense of the Issues and Actors

Todd J. Moss

LYNNE
RIENNER
PUBLISHERS

BOULDER
LONDON

Published in the United States of America in 2007 by
Lynne Rienner Publishers, Inc.
1800 30th Street, Boulder, Colorado 80301
www.rienner.com

and in the United Kingdom by
Lynne Rienner Publishers, Inc.
3 Henrietta Street, Covent Garden, London WC2E 8LU

Library of Congress Cataloging-in-Publication Data
Moss, Todd J., 1970–
    African development : making sense of the issues and actors / Todd J. Moss.
    Includes bibliographical references and index.
    ISBN-13: 978-1-58826-496-1 (hardcover : alk. paper)
    ISBN-13: 978-1-58826-472-5 (pbk. : alk. paper)
    1. Africa—Economic conditions—1960– 2. Africa—Economic policy.
3. Economic assistance—Africa. 4. Economic development. I. Title.
HC800.M6775 2007
338.96—dc22

                                                        2006033589

British Cataloguing in Publication Data
A Cataloguing in Publication record for this book
is available from the British Library.

Printed and bound in the United States of America

The paper used in this publication meets the requirements
of the American National Standard for Permanence of
Paper for Printed Library Materials Z39.48-1992.

5   4   3

For Gabriel, Leo, and Max

Contents

Tables and Figures

Tables

Figures

Acknowledgments

I AM ESPECIALLY THANKFUL TO MARKUS GOLDSTEIN, WHOSE help began a decade ago when he rescued me from the sweltering Ghanaian sun and welcomed me into the sanctuary of his office in Legon. Today he is my great friend and my collaborator on Chapter 10.

I am grateful for insights from my energetic and thoughtful colleagues at the Center for Global Development and many former colleagues who have all indirectly influenced this book. For helpful comments and advice on early draft chapters, I thank Kaysie Brown, Michael Clemens, David Cowan, Kim Elliott, Bill Fanjoy, Piers Haben, Charles Kenny, Maureen Lewis, Joshua Nadel, Stewart Patrick, Vijaya Ramachandran, Anneliese Simmons, Harsha Thirumurthy, Nicolas van de Walle, Jeremy Weinstein, and two anonymous reviewers. I am especially appreciative of Nancy Birdsall for her encouragement on the book and for creating an environment with the right balance of passion, rigor, and critical thinking. Thanks to Scott Standley for his assistance gathering data and information, particularly for Chapters 4 and 8. All errors of fact or judgment are, of course, solely my own.

Special thanks to Lynne Rienner and Lisa Tulchin for their support.

My connection to Africa, and in many ways this book, owes much to the warmth and hospitality of Ashari and the late Violet Mutongwizo and their children. *Ndatenda Baba naAmai.*

Most important, my deepest love and gratitude to my family for their patience, especially to Donna for pushing me back into the office to finish the book.

1

The Complexities and Uncertainties of Development

MARCH 2007 MARKS A HALF CENTURY SINCE GHANA BECAME independent from Great Britain, kick-starting Africa's postcolonial era. The early independence years were confident and hopeful. Africa was thought to have a glorious future ahead, a land of young vibrant nations that would not only set their people free from foreign oppression but quickly end the blight of poverty and deprivation. An international "development industry" emerged to assist the continent on this quest. Early euphoria, however, was soon followed by instability, frustration, and disappointment. By the end of the millennium, few countries had much to celebrate. Botswana impressively built a stable democracy and raised its national income twelve times over since 1960, but it was largely alone. Much of the rest of the continent has made little progress. Many have grown poorer.

Yet hope springs eternal. The international community has continually responded to Africa's distress with renewed fervor to save the continent from poverty—and sometimes from itself. In 2005, declared the "Year of Africa," a modern-day crusade was launched with new pledges to do much more: more aid, freer trade, new technologies, and greater engagement. The development business—of which I (usually) proudly consider myself a part—has grown immense and, in many ways, never had better times, with new resources, tools, ideas, and energies. Despite this renewed (and mostly welcome) attention, Africa still faces a bewildering array of challenges if it is to have a more prosperous future. Nowhere on the planet is the concentration of poverty greater, or the problems so complex and seemingly intractable. This is why so much of the development community is focused on Africa—and evidently where its efforts are mostly going to be judged in the future.

The Purpose of This Book
Given the growing interest globally, more and more universities are offering, and students are taking, courses on the economics or politics of

1

Africa, area studies, and development studies. This book is written to give a simple, but hopefully not simplistic, introduction to the main themes, trends, and players in contemporary African development. It is intended for students approaching these issues for the first time, budding activists, and new practitioners getting started in their careers. By no means is this text intended as a survey of the academic literature, a primer on economic development theory, or a how-to guide. Instead, it is supposed to give the reader some basic facts, information, and words of caution *before* they approach development for study or work.

When teaching at both the undergraduate and postgraduate levels, I found that a popular start to a course was to hold a no-question-is-too-dumb session where students could ask fundamental background questions, such as "What is really the difference between the World Bank and the IMF?"; "Why are Africans still so poor if they get so much aid?"; or "What does the WTO actually do?" Given the cross-cutting multidisciplinary nature of development, there are also usually great differences in baseline knowledge: some students might know about HIV/AIDS, but not about trade, or they would know about a current issue such as debt relief, but not the history of where such efforts came from and why they are shaped the way they are. This book will bring that introductory session to a wider audience, to discuss broad trends in a frank and accessible way, to encourage the reader to think critically about the complicated issues at hand, and to help students ask informed questions about Africa's development challenges. It offers no answers.

What Is Development?
There is no agreement on what exactly "development" means. The narrowest economic definition is to make poor people less poor by raising their incomes. For individuals, this entails helping them to find greater opportunities and to be more productive so that they can live better and longer lives. For an economy as a whole, this involves generating economic growth to raise average incomes and reduce the number of people living below a defined poverty line.

A focus on income measures and on economic growth rates has been criticized as too confined, so some have preferred to define development more broadly using welfare or quality-of-life measures, such as health (infant mortality, access to doctors, clean water) or education (average years of schooling, literacy rates) indicators. The United Nations, for example, combines these into its annual Human Development Index, which includes income, school enrollment, literacy, and life expectancy to rank all the world's countries. An even more expansive view (largely originating in the work of Nobel laureate Amartya Sen) considers the mark of economic development and social progress to be the freedom of people to participate in and make choices about their own future.

Different definitions of development are far from mutually exclusive, however. Although this book uses a mostly orthodox economic perspective that promoting development on the African continent is about increasing economic growth rates, it treats income as a means to a better life rather than an end in itself. This approach assumes some universal goals: more income is better than less, living longer is preferable to early death, and education is superior to ignorance. At its broadest, the development question asked here is "How can the standards of living be improved in Africa?" At the same time, it must also be recognized that such questions are not merely technical. Development is ultimately not about bricks and budget systems but about social change.

Digging Holes vs. Capital Flows

One fundamental divide worth mentioning upfront is, as was once caricatured by a colleague, the "digging holes vs. capital flows" notions of development. The former perspective thinks about development as organizing a series of activities such as digging wells, building schools, or teaching children how to read and grow new crops. For a "hole digger," development is about delivering more services, executing projects, managing logistics, and imparting knowledge. The "capital flows" viewpoint is that promoting development is about getting the environment right so that people do such things naturally. This view of the world thus scrutinizes policies, incentives, available resources, and institutions and how they interact with the global economy. By this perspective, promoting development is not so much what you do for a country as it is what you help to leave behind. The right metric for this view of development might not be "How many kids did you vaccinate yesterday?" but rather "What kind of vaccination system would be there if you left tomorrow?"

Whichever outlook one chooses—and there are pros and cons to each—the international community's role in promoting development is secondary to national efforts by Africans themselves. And where external players are active, their role encompasses much more than simply aid. This book treats the international aid system as central, but only in the context of the evolving ideas about policy, political organization at the national and international levels, and global economic issues such as trade and investment.

What Is Africa?

This book is about contemporary Africa. It focuses primarily on the postcolonial period of the past five decades with an emphasis on issues and debates most prominent in the early years of the twenty-first century. "Africa" is sometimes used to refer to all the countries on the mainland continent plus the six island nations of Cape Verde, Comoros, Madagascar, Mauritius, São Tomé and Príncipe, and Seychelles. In much of the literature, however—including this book—the term "Africa" and even "the continent" is instead used synonymously with what more accurately would be called sub-Saharan Africa to mean just the forty-eight African countries, excluding Morocco, Algeria, Tunisia, Libya, and Egypt. Such a distinction is surely arguable, but in the development world the countries of North Africa are typically placed in the Middle East (for example, by the World Bank) because they are in many ways more a part of the cultural and political life of that region. (Confusingly, Sudan and even Djibouti are sometimes also considered North African.)

African Diversity

Every book on Africa opens with a caveat about its great diversity. This one is no different and for good reason: the continent is a varied amalgamation of countries, societies, and people that make generalization difficult. There are hundreds of languages and thousands of dialects spoken on the continent. Many of Africa's cities are crowded, bustling hives of activity with high-rise buildings, the latest technology, and many of the same stresses and strains of modern life elsewhere on the planet. At the same time, vast stretches of the continent are sleepy, underdeveloped places that seem not to have changed for millennia.

Africa's political diversity is just as stark. Botswana and Senegal have been mostly stable democracies since independence, but Equatorial Guinea and Togo have been perpetual dictatorships. Ghana and Mali have gone from military rule to open and fairly free societies, while Zimbabwe has plunged in the opposite direction. Malawi and Zambia have no modern experience with war, but Angola and Sudan have seen

Table 1.1 Snapshot of Sub-Saharan Africa

Number of countries	48
Total population	719 million
Life expectancy	45.6 years
Infant mortality rate	101 deaths per 1,000
Literacy	51% of adult women, 68% of adult men
GDP	US$554 billion
Average GNI per capita	US$600

Source: World Bank; all data are for 2004, except health data are for 2003.

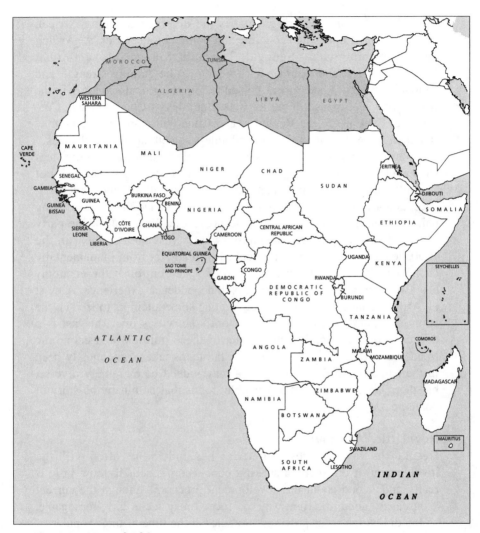

Fig. 1.1   Map of Africa

almost no peace over the past three decades. Uganda, Mozambique, and Burkina Faso have all managed to recently increase growth and reduce poverty rates, but Kenya, Niger, and Burundi have seen disappointing growth and rising poverty.

Indeed, the most glaring trend is the divergence among African countries facing opposing economic and political trajectories. A growing number of countries—Senegal, Tanzania, Ghana, Mozambique, Botswana, Mali, and South Africa—seem to be gaining strength and national confidence and appear poised to join the global economy in the twenty-first century as full participants. But others—Chad, Malawi, Côte d'Ivoire, Central African Republic, and Congo all come to mind—may find themselves falling farther behind unless something drastic changes.

While Africa's diversity is indisputable, much of the continent shares related problems and has faced similar misfortunes. Nearly all of Africa's nations are fairly young, just a few generations since independence, and are still going through what might be called the early growing pains of nation building. After widespread establishment of one-party states, a wave of political openness swept across the continent in the 1990s leaving few countries untouched (if many far from fundamentally changed). The attempt—and failure—of state control of the economy has also been a nearly universal postindependence experience. Almost all African countries have since undergone some attempts to free up the economy and reorient the government's activities over the last two decades. Yes, the details and results of these political and economic trends have varied tremendously, but the paths taken have mostly been in the same rough direction. Africa may indeed be extremely diverse, but there are essential and discernible trends that dominate the story of contemporary Africa.

How Little We Know

Despite the vast changes that Africa has undergone, often with the involvement of outsiders, a striking conclusion is actually how little is really understood about the development process. Although the current "consensus" about the right way to proceed may seem fairly reasonable, so too did all the other previous strategies at the time of their popularity. Forcing poor people at gunpoint to live in collective villages (as happened during *ujamaa* in Tanzania) is unthinkable today, but was once thought a practical way to promote development. The international donors in particular are prone to a continuously evolving mea culpa with hubris, what might be called the "yes, but *now* we have it right" syndrome.

A recurring theme in the progression of development thinking is that past strategies had mistakenly overlooked some crucial aspect, but the missing link has now been identified and everything can be fixed this time around. Africa was initially thought to just lack infrastructure and capital. When providing those things did not work, investing in basic education and health was added. When that strategy also failed to generate growth, it was thought that bad policies must be the problem. After some policies were corrected (but many were not) and the results were still disappointing, the next answer was governance and institutions— essentially where we are today. Yet there are at least three decisive areas where the development "experts" admittedly still have little clue:

- *The growth process.* Economists simply cannot say what exactly causes growth and thus are unable to come up with clear remedies to generate faster growth. There are lots of ideas and many hints, but no unambiguous answers that apply universally.
- *Institutional change.* There is a lot of talk about "institutions" and "capacity," but actually very little agreement on what these terms exactly mean, much less how to change or build such things.
- *The politics of development.* Development economists have belatedly recognized that local politics are the reason why the paths chosen so frequently appear illogical and self-destructive. Yet much of the real politics in any country happens beneath the surface, out of view and poorly grasped by external donors or analysts. But acknowledging that politics matters is not the same as understanding how it affects the economy and the incentives to promote development.

Given these sizable holes in confidence, humility seems appropriate. The continent has in many ways been a laboratory of both good and bad ideas, perhaps the unavoidable outcome of its political and economic weakness. But the generally sorry record of African development so far suggests that any ideas and fads pronouncing to have found the magic bullet to resolve an inherently complex problem, such as quickly eradicating poverty in a scantily understood foreign land, should be viewed with extreme skepticism.

What We Do Know

The case for modesty does not mean that we have learned *nothing* about development. In fact, there continues to be a massive endeavor to extract lessons from different development experiences, with an army of thousands of economists, sociologists, anthropologists, public health specialists, and other assorted experts dedicated full time to flying around the world, collecting data, interviewing people, monitoring, evaluating, consulting, and in every possible way thinking about how to make Africa less poor. The World Bank alone has 12,000 staff (a large portion of which work on Africa), while the major donor agencies each employ thousands more, plus there are hordes of contractors, university researchers, and NGO (nongovernmental organization) workers. Some have dismissed these gargantuan efforts as a total failure and a waste of time and money. But participants in the development business have undoubtedly saved millions of lives and also learned quite a lot. Even if there is no clear solution to poverty and the puzzle of slow economic growth, there have been some unmistakable lessons, especially about necessary prerequisites and things *not* to do. A few of the least-controversial examples include:

- Peace and security are preconditions for development.
- High inflation is bad for the poor and for economic growth.
- Vaccinations are an effective way to save lives.
- Governments are very inefficient at doing some things, such as owning and managing factories and farms.
- There are some things the state must do, such as protect property and deliver basic services.
- Transparency is preferable to secrecy, especially when it comes to public budgets and government contracting.

Misconceptions and Misinformation

While there is still much uncertainty and debate about development ideas, there is perhaps just as much misinformation about what international agencies actually do in the development arena. Street protestors have found the World Bank, the International Monetary Fund (IMF), and the World Trade Organization (WTO) easy targets, painting them as puppets of a global conspiracy to keep developing countries poor and in their place. These institutions do have major faults and there are plenty of reasons to critique them and what they do. But much of the criticism heard on the streets, on the Internet (and, sadly, in many classrooms) is simply propaganda. The World Bank may be a behemoth and is occasionally bumbling, but it rarely "imposes" anything on any unwilling government. (In fact, Chapter 7 will argue that it is the governments that usually have power over the Bank.) Similarly, the IMF can be inexplicably narrow-minded in its mission and often heavy-handed, but it does not, as is frequently claimed, set caps on health spending in poor countries. And on the flip side, the saintly reputation in some circles of nongovernmental organizations is often undeserved. Some NGOs loudly demand to be heard and claim to speak for "the people" but are themselves accountable to no one.

Behind much of the debate about development and the appropriate role of the state, international organizations, NGOs, corporations, and other players are often deep ideological convictions, especially over whether market capitalism is a force for good or evil. Despite what is commonly asserted, there is no secret nefarious plot against the poor being hatched in a smoke-filled room in the basement of the World Bank. The methods and results of the international agencies may not always be pretty or successful, but their intentions are indeed to build a better world.

The Various "Languages" of Development

The discourse on development also operates in different circles using different—and often unintelligible—languages. The advocacy community is typically looking for simple emotional messages and short-term answers as part of its efforts to boost public awareness, lobby politicians, and (of course) to raise money. An example is the recent call to

---

Political Elites: Champions or Charlatans?

Based on the caricatures common in much of the debate about development, African governments and leaders seem to have split personalities. In many parts of the literature, the role of the state is thought to be fairly benign, with poverty reduction and promoting the public good assumed to be the goals of government leaders. By this view, taken by some antipoverty activists, the main barriers to development are technical problems or the outside world, which is placing impossible demands upon well-meaning but beleaguered African officials. The other caricature, more common in the political-science literature and among salty development skeptics, is that the problems are mostly political and that African elites are mainly out to help themselves and keep their grip on power. By this view, the state is little more than a tool for theft while the development agenda is mostly a facade masking a series of rackets being perpetrated upon the donors and the African people. To take one example, is the Republic of Congo's president Denis Sassou-Nguesso, the esteemed chairman of the African Union, the leader of a poverty-stricken country coming back from years of debilitating war, and therefore deserving of debt relief so he can use the savings to better help his people? Or is he a thug that came to power at the head of a vicious gang called the Cobras who could care less about his own people and when attending UN meetings on poverty thinks nothing of blowing $300,000 of his country's money living it up for a week at a swanky New York hotel?

"double aid to halve poverty," a catchy phrase that may help to boost aid budgets but, as history suggests, will probably turn out to be incorrect. Academics think largely about long-term theoretical relationships and statistical models that can find associations, for instance, between the prevalence of conflict and an economy's growth rate. Aid workers, researchers, and policymakers working in the development business are a third set. This crowd is often process-obsessed and driven by internal bureaucratic dynamics, such as trying to figure out which kind of loans are best used under which kind of circumstances. But the development business is also infused with cynics who have been working in the field for a long time and have been chastened by past experiences. All three groups talk about similar things (like the efficiency of aid, the importance of local politics, and the need to do better in the future), but they all use completely different words and often have their own indecipherable lingo. Here is one (strictly hypothetical yet hopefully illustrative) example, all talking about basically the same thing:

> *Advocate*: "The donors must cooperate better if we are going to lift more people out of poverty."
> *Academic*: "The real per capita GNI growth rate and the log of ODA/GDP (lagged t-2) are robustly and positively correlated once the indices of donor proliferation and aid fragmentation developed by Acharya, de Lima, and Moore (2006) are added as independent variables."
> *Practitioner*: "Donor coordination is being implemented in the context of the international consensus reached at Monterrey on the actions needed to promote a global partnership for development and accelerate progress toward the MDGs through the OECD's High Level Forum on Joint Progress Toward Enhanced Aid Effectiveness (Harmonization, Alignment, and Results) with monitoring by the Joint Venture on Monitoring the Paris Declaration." [I am embarrassed that I understand this one!]

Ten Tips for Sensibly Studying African Development

With all these caveats in mind, here are some tips to avoid disillusionment and despair as you plunge into the dilemmas of African development.

1. *There are no panaceas and few quick fixes.* Development is about the complex and usually messy evolution of societies and economies. Single solutions are tempting—more aid, more democracy, eradicate corruption, get prices right, find better leadership—but inevitably leave the true believers disheartened. Africa is the graveyard of silver bullets; be wary of those peddling the latest version.

2. *Don't believe the (good and bad) hype.* Africa has been the object

of extreme optimism and pessimism, at times simultaneously. Those seeking to get attention or raise money will invariably invoke emotional appeals to crisis, usually with pictures of underfed children ("flies on the eyes" is a perennial favorite and an immediate red flag). While the continent certainly has its share of real crises and people in need, the imperative for attention and fund-raising by some groups encourages continual publicity of "emergencies." At the same time, there are salesmen for Africa who seem blindly optimistic. There is always someone claiming that the continent's real problem is media misrepresentation and that it has finally "turned the corner."

3. *Resist the temptation to exoticize.* Perhaps it is the accumulation of wildlife documentaries or news reports of famine and war, but many Westerners seem to think of Africa as if it were another planet. My first visit to Africa (to Zimbabwe's capital Harare in 1990) was a shock not because it was so strange but rather because it seemed so normal. Yes, the people were poorer than in the United States, but the lives of Zimbabweans mostly revolved around issues similar to those of people back home: family, jobs, schools, healthcare, traffic, the cost of gasoline, and the local sports teams. For many Africans, daily life is indeed a tenuous struggle and the continent undoubtedly faces some especially tough problems. But Africa is still just a place on earth like any other.

4. *Development is always political.* As much as outside donors and activists sometimes like to think of development as a technical exercise about delivering better seeds or fixing a mechanical problem, it is always a deeply political act to get involved in a country's development trajectory. The World Bank, for instance, likes to dress up its governance agenda in apolitical terms such as "transparency" and "accountability," but changing the way government works intimately affects the distribution of power within a country. Indeed, all interventions—even the most seemingly benign act such as child nutrition programs—have implications for the allocation of influence and resources within a village or a family.

5. *Development is more than money.* A huge—and probably excessive—amount of attention is paid to the bottom line of how much money is spent, as if that were a good measure of development efforts. (Economist Bill Easterly once said that judging success by the size of aid flows is like reviewing films based on their budgets.) It is of course true that money is required to do developmental things, such as build schools and roads or pay civil servants. But development is about much more than aid flows—and often it is not about money at all. There is little relationship, for example, between spending on healthcare and actual health. In fact, money may frequently be secondary to bigger issues such as markets, opportunities, and incentives. If there is little reason for

children to attend school (maybe because they are needed on the family farm or there are no jobs after graduation) and teacher expectations are low (perhaps their wages are paid six months late and there is no oversight, so they never bother to show up), then all the money in the world will not create a functional education system.

6. *Be careful with "facts."* Development is rife with myths that get repeated often enough that they eventually are accepted as facts. One example is the urban legend that Tanzania writes 2,400 reports for donors every year. This has been cited by numerous reports and even the president of the World Bank once used it in a speech calling for less red tape. But the source of this fact is a hypothetical story from a 1996 book on aid that suggested *if* a country had to write quarterly reports for every project and had 600 different donor projects (a not unusual figure), then it would result in 2,400 reports. Although Tanzania undoubtedly prepares many reports for its many donors, there is no evidence whatsoever that 2,400 is the right (or even close) figure. There are similar stories, such as a "fact" peddled by some campaigners that debt "kills 19,000 children per day," a figure arrived at through a convoluted series of errors and dubious assumptions.

7. *Be skeptical of data.* Much of the development agenda is driven by quantitative analysis as part of the push to make the process more rigorous and "scientific." While this may be well intentioned, the problem for Africa is that the data is almost always unreliable. Even basic information such as gross domestic product (GDP), exports, the number of children in school, or how much a country spends on hospitals is often little more than an educated guess. Sometimes formal surveys are done through a census or by an external agency, but these are fairly infrequent. Instead, models are typically used to make estimations, but usually with very large margins of error. This makes comparison, especially across countries or where differences are small, extremely difficult to do with much confidence. For example, is a country with an average income per capita of $240 really 20 percent better off than its neighbor at $200? If a country's reported primary school enrollment rate jumps from 38 percent to 42 percent the next year, do we really believe that more children are in school? If aid agencies are setting their budgets based on showing such "results," then the incentive for both donors and recipients is to overestimate gains. At the same time, there are often reasons people would rather not disclose information to a government agency or an enumerator. Next time you read about changes in access to clean water in Niger, remember the old saying about drawing conclusions from bad data: "garbage in, garbage out."

8. *Keep perspective on Africa's size.* Africa may loom large in certain development circles, but it is a tiny player on the global stage.

Twenty African countries each have a total population of less than 5 million people, about the size of metropolitan Washington, DC. Botswana features prominently in the development literature (including this book), but it is a small country of mostly desert and swamps with only 1.7 million people. African economies are even more minuscule relative to the global marketplace. The economies of all forty-eight African countries combined are about the same size as Chicago's. The county in which I live (Montgomery County, Maryland, next to Washington, DC) has a larger GDP than forty-six different African countries (South Africa and Nigeria are bigger). Even my town (Bethesda, population about 55,000) has an annual income greater than twenty-four individual African economies. These comparisons are worth recalling the next time you hear that a multinational corporation just cannot wait to pry open some untapped African market.

9. *Get to know some specific countries.* Cross-country comparisons and understanding regional trends can be useful, but it is essential to complement this with some in-depth country cases. Learning about the history and cultures of a country can help give context to current development efforts and make sense of what can seem at first glance irrational. Consider picking some lesser-known countries too. There are more than 12,000 books in print about South Africa and more than 900 on Ghana, but less than 100 on Burundi, Guinea-Bissau, or Burkina Faso. Why not try Cape Verde or Mali?

10. *Go!* Reading and learning about Africa is fine, but nothing beats going there in person. If you have the opportunity, travel around as much as possible, talk to people, see how they live, and you will probably find that much of what you expect is wrong. And you can trust your own eyes. On a recent trip to Tanzania, I had been reading reports on the plane about robust economic growth, but when I went to the main port in the capital, Dar es Salaam, I noticed almost no activity. Nothing was being loaded or unloaded, even though it was a Tuesday afternoon at the only port for a huge swath of the hinterland. To me, this was a hint that Tanzania's economic success story was probably less widespread than advertised. But more important than checking out the facts, going to Africa is an enriching and often inspirational experience. You may even catch the "Africa bug," a compulsive attraction to the continent that infects many of its visitors and keeps them coming back. Zimbabwe certainly did that to me.

Structure of the Book
The book is organized into three sections—looking at the domestic context, a set of core development questions, and finally at regional and international linkages. In each chapter, the intention is to provide some

basic background information, analysis of the trends, and an explanation of the contemporary issues, actors, and institutions that students may encounter as they delve deeper into the subject. I have intentionally avoided using footnotes to keep the text as readable as possible. At the end of each chapter are suggested readings to learn more about the topics covered, but the recommendations here are far from exhaustive. Full citations are listed in the bibliography.

The next section provides context for Africa's development, starting with its history and the effects of colonialism in Chapter 2. Chapter 3 examines the nature of authority and gives basic background on some of the most influential leaders, including ten "Big Men" that readers probably know of and another ten that they probably do not (but should). Violent conflict is dealt with in Chapter 4, including a brief description of some of Africa's recent conflicts, plus some ideas on the causes and effects of civil wars, as well as efforts to prevent and end conflict. Political trends, including the unsteady rise of democracy in recent years, are the focus of Chapter 5.

Chapters 6 through 10 cover some of the most central development issues, beginning with the puzzle of Africa's slow growth. Chapter 7 follows with a look at the politics behind economic reform, including why some of the problems identified in Chapter 6 appear so resilient. Chapter 8 outlines the major ideas, institutions, and current controversies in the aid industry. Debt relief, a leading issue for antipoverty activists for much of the past two decades, is the subject of Chapter 9. Chapter 10 explains the various definitions of poverty, including income and other measures. The second half of Chapter 10 also briefly addresses the role of public services in reducing poverty and the special case of HIV/AIDS in development.

The final section looks at Africa's regional connections and its relationship with the rest of the world. The New Partnership for Africa's Development and the plethora of regional institutions are laid out in Chapter 11. Chapters 12 and 13 explore the main issues and debates around the movement of goods and capital, respectively, across borders. Chapter 14 concludes with a very brief summary of some of the broad themes of the book.

It is also worth noting here that emergency relief, gender, the environment, technology, migration, demographics, and culture are all important development-related topics that are not specifically covered. This book also only briefly touches on public health and education issues, which are often the primary focus of many students approaching Africa for the first time. This is deliberate; public health and schooling are admirable fields and are of course central to the development story, but the purpose of this book is partly to help students with that perspective to also understand some of the political, economic, and financial issues that unavoidably intrude on a more technical approach to development.

For Further Reading

Some of the best books for understanding African development include Nicolas van de Walle's *African Economies and the Politics of Permanent Crisis, 1979–1999* (2001), William Easterly's *The Elusive Quest for Growth* (2001), and *Africa's Stalled Development: International Causes and Cures* by David Leonard and Scott Straus (2003). Two classics that all students should see are Goran Hyden's *No Shortcuts to Progress: African Development Management in Perspective* (1983) and Robert Bates's *Markets and States in Tropical Africa* (1981). For an overview of the history of dominant ideas about development, see Colin Leys's *The Rise and Fall of Development Economics* (1996) and Deepak Lal's *The Poverty of Development Economics* (2000). To read Amartya Sen's ideas about development, see, among many, his *Development As Freedom* (1999). For another take on the divide between development approaches, in this case between the "finance ministry" and "civil society" tendencies, see Ravi Kanbur's "Economic Policy, Distribution, and Poverty: The Nature of Disagreements" (2001). For students looking for standard development economics textbooks, see Michael Todaro's *Economic Development* (2005) or *Economics of Development* (2006) by Dwight Perkins, Steven Radelet, and David Lindhauer. For a highly readable history of economic thought, look no further than Robert Heilbroner's *The Worldly Philosophers: The Lives, Times and Ideas of the Great Economic Thinkers* (1953).

The best Africanist journals are *Journal of Modern African Studies* and *African Affairs*. The leading journals for development economics that are accessible to nonspecialists include *World Development, Economic Development and Cultural Change, Development Policy Review*, and the *Journal of Development Studies*. The *Journal of Economic Perspectives* also often covers development economics in a nontechnical format, as does the *World Bank Research Observer*. *Finance & Development* is a free quarterly magazine that summarizes some of the best research coming out of the international institutions.

For general information about Africa, see *Africa South of the Sahara,* an annual yearbook that contains histories of each country, along with some basic data. The Economist Intelligence Unit provides quarterly *Country Reports* on every country in Africa, plus annual *Country Profiles. Africa Confidential* is a wonderful, and usually reliable, source for the inside buzz on African politicians. There are now multiple websites for gathering

African news, including many in Africa itself. *AllAfrica.com* aggregates news articles from more than 100 news organizations in Africa.

The best source for economic data is the World Bank, especially its *World Development Indicators*. Also useful are IMF country reports, especially the statistical annexes that are produced regularly on each country. A growing number of central banks in Africa are also producing regular information and posting it on the Web.

When looking for information about African development, a lot can also be learned from novels, and there are a huge number from which to choose. Some classics are Chinua Achebe's *Things Fall Apart* (1958) and his *Anthills of the Savannah* (1988), Graham Greene's *The Heart of the Matter* (1948), V. S. Naipaul's *A Bend in the River* (1979), and the writings of Wole Soyinka (who won the Nobel prize for literature in 1986). A few more recent novels worth considering are Tsitsi Dangarembga's *Nervous Conditions* (1988), *The House of Hunger* (1993) by Dambudzo Marechera, and Norman Rush's *Mating* (1991). One of the most amusing and insightful books on the World Bank's relations with Africa is Michael Holman's witty *Last Orders at Harrods* (2005). There are many novels about South Africa and the apartheid era, including Alan Paton's classic *Cry the Beloved Country* (1948) and the huge bodies of work by Nobel literature prize winners J. M. Coetzee and Nadine Gordimer. For a sarcastic essay on stereotypes used in writing on Africa, see "How to Write About Africa" by Binyavanga Wainaina in *Granta* (2006).

PART 1

The Domestic Context

2

History and
the Legacy of Colonialism

SUB-SAHARAN AFRICA HAS UNDOUBTEDLY HAD AN UNLUCKY history that severely affects its development progress today. Most obviously, the boundaries of African states were set by European powers over a century ago and nearly all of these national borders, no matter how illogical, remain in place today. The process of colonization by Europe of most of Africa also had a major impact on the local authorities, altering the evolution of political institutions and putting Africa on a trajectory that almost certainly contributed to the disappointing development outcomes seen since independence. At the same time, however, colonialism is often used as a scapegoat for the failings of current leaders. This chapter presents a brief review of African political and economic history and some of the issues from the colonial period that may be affecting the contemporary development context. It is by no means intended as a comprehensive account of Africa's long precolonial and complex colonial history, but merely to highlight some of the key facts and trends that are still deeply relevant today.

Precolonial Political Organization

Much of Africa's precolonial history remains unknown because few African societies were literate or formally recorded their history. What is known is that Africa's early history was far from static. Indeed, it was marked by large waves of migration and long-distance trading. Politically, many Africans lived in smaller clan- or family-based units, which were sometimes loosely organized into larger groups with various degrees of central authority. At the same time, Africa also had a number of significant kingdoms or empires that were highly complex, centralized, and in some cases spanned more than a thousand miles. A few examples include:

- The Monomotapa Empire, which is thought to have reached its peak around the middle of the fifteenth century, stretched across southern Africa and had its capital at Great Zimbabwe.
- The Buganda Kingdom, which rose in the eighteenth century, ruled over present-day central Uganda.
- The west African Ashanti Kingdom, which centered in what is today central Ghana, rose in the late sixteenth century, and had a vast trading empire of gold, ivory, and slaves. The Ashanti became relatively urbanized and developed commercial agriculture. Politically, it was centralized, had a standing military force, and included some aspects of early consultative democracy.
- The Songhai Kingdom spread across the Sahel, peaking in power in the sixteenth century, and at one point stretched from modern-day Nigeria all the way across Mali to the Atlantic coast. Its political capital was at Gao in Mali, but one of its major cities was Timbuktu, a center of early Islamic scholarship and an important trans-Saharan trading hub that goes back perhaps as early as the tenth century.
- The Axum Kingdom in modern Ethiopia rose in the first century and stretched, with several breaks, into modern times.
- Shaka Zulu used new military techniques and weapons to build a powerful Zulu Kingdom around modern-day KwaZulu-Natal in South Africa in the early nineteenth century.

Early European Arrivals

The Portuguese were likely the first Europeans to arrive in sub-Saharan Africa in their quest for an eastward sea route to India. It is thought that Bartolomeu Dias rounded the Cape of Good Hope around 1487. The Portuguese subsequently set up small military posts along the coasts for restocking their ships. Although some former Portuguese colonies claim "500 years of colonial rule," the Portuguese rarely ventured inland from these early posts in Angola and Mozambique. The French also began expanding along the West African coast, establishing a post in 1624 in Senegal. In 1652 Jan van Riebeeck, working for the Dutch East India Company, landed in Cape Town and started the Cape Colony, the first real European attempt to settle in Africa.

Toward the end of the eighteenth century, Europeans began to systematically explore and map Africa, setting the stage for greater political involvement and commercial activity. Explorer penetration can be easily viewed through the evolution of maps. Those up until the mid-nineteenth century are largely blank in the middle of the continent. (One from 1839 on the wall of my office even has several wrong guesses about the location and sources of major rivers.) Among the most famous explorers was the Scottish missionary David Livingstone, who explored central Africa in the 1850s and was the first European to reach Victoria Falls. Alexandre Serpa Pinto also crossed southern and central Africa and went even farther up the Zambezi River in 1869. That same year, Welsh journalist Henry Morton Stanley was sent by the *New York Herald* newspaper to find Livingstone. Stanley returned to Africa several times, including as an agent for the Belgian king, Leopold II. Stanley helped Leopold establish the Congo Free State around 1882, a vast area of central Africa exploited by Belgium for rubber and other commodities. Savorgnan de Brazza traveled into the western Congo basin and raised the French flag over the newly founded Brazzaville in 1881.

By the end of the nineteenth century, European explorers had found the sources of the great rivers—the Nile, the Niger, the Congo, and the Zambezi. The adventures of Stanley and his contemporaries captured the European imagination and the recognition of the continent's economic potential. Growing economic and military competition among European powers, combined with technological advancements in transportation, communication, and weaponry, helped to spark the subsequent "scramble for Africa."

The Scramble for Africa

Up until the 1880s, little of the continent was actually under European control—but that was to change quickly. In 1884 German chancellor Otto von Bismarck convened a conference in Berlin for the major powers to divide up the continent. Although the conference was couched in humanitarian terms, the purpose was to establish rules for conquest and to avoid intra-European conflict over territory in Africa. The final agreement was that any territory could be claimed as long as it was nominally occupied and the other countries were notified. Another major decision at Berlin was the agreement that the Congo Free State belonged to the Congo Society, an organization controlled by King Leopold II. In effect, this made 2 million square kilometers in the heart of Africa the private property of a European monarch who would never set foot in Africa. Conquest of Africa accelerated after the Berlin conference, and by the end of the century, every part of sub-Saharan Africa was part of a European claim, except for Liberia and Ethiopia.

Britain pushed into Africa from two points, the Cape Colony in the far south and Egypt in the north. Cecil Rhodes's dream was to link British colonies right across the continent "from the Cape to Cairo." At the same time, France was seeking to build an east-west empire to connect its holdings in Senegal across the Sahara to the Niger River and on to the Nile and as far as Djibouti on the Red Sea. Indeed, these two imperial axes cross at Fashoda in southern Sudan, where the French and British came to the verge of war in 1898. But, as at Berlin, in the end they backed down and agreed to separate spheres of influence.

The British Empire

The British Empire, which at its height covered nearly a quarter of the earth, included large swaths of Africa. The main areas under their control included Nigeria, Sierra Leone, and Ghana in the west; Sudan, Kenya, and Uganda in the east; and large parts of southern Africa. In general the British Empire in Africa used two models of colonization. In most places it implemented indirect rule, placing a British administrator on top of local chiefs or other existing political structures. In these colonies, Britain sought to extract resources where possible and to assert its imperial power, but not to create wholly new societies or to establish large European populations. Kenya and Rhodesia (later Zimbabwe) were fundamentally different. In these settler states, British citizens were encouraged to emigrate and settle, especially after World War II when African land was sometimes given to veterans. In these places, where the British presence was thought, at least initially, to be more permanent, British policy was more guided as serving the minority settler population. In practical terms, this meant that Kenya and Zimbabwe each saw much greater investment in infrastructure, better-quality schooling, and at independence each had much more advanced and diversified economies. Two important legacies from British colonial rule are the English language and the prevalence of English law. Lastly, Britain (if not necessarily its settlers) appeared among the earliest in recognizing that colonialism in Africa was a doomed venture and that Africans would soon take over the reins. In general, the British handover of power to local nationalists was orderly and the disengagement was more complete, at least relative to that of the French.

French Colonialism

In French Africa, there was a much closer relationship between the colonies and Paris. The French used a more direct style of colonial rule than the British and were more aggressive in trying to remake African societies in their image, including a policy of encouraging and accepting small numbers of *evolues*, or educated black African elites who were considered (almost) French. Despite this closeness, France also realized that independence was coming and quickly arranged independence for its colonies. In a single year, 1960, no less than fourteen former French colonies gained independence. Unlike the British, however, the French have maintained much closer ties. Most former French colonies, for example, use the CFA franc as a national currency, which was pegged to the French franc (since 1999 it has, of course, been pegged to the euro, but the French retain control over the exchange rate). The French also in general remain intimately involved in national policymaking and security matters in West Africa.

Portugal in Africa

The Portuguese colonies fared the worst, at least partly because Portugal itself was poor and run by fascist dictators António de Oliveira Salazar (1932–1968) and Marcelo Caetano (1968–1974). The Portuguese rulers were the least interested in developing the countryside and made the fewest investments in schools or health for the African population. Importantly, because Portugal never expected to cede control and then left in a hurry, there were no preparations for the transfer of power. Thus, at independence, each of Portugal's former colonies had only a handful of college graduates and inherited few skilled workers to manage the transition to a new country.

Other European Colonists

Britain, France, and Portugal were the main colonial powers in Africa, yet other countries were also involved. Germany had hosted the Berlin conference and was an enthusiastic colonizer, taking control in the late nineteenth century of Southwest Africa (later Namibia), Tanganyika (later mainland Tanzania), Togo, Cameroon, Rwanda, and Burundi. Its colonization was considered among the harshest, including revelations of attempted genocide against the Herero and Nama peoples in Namibia. But after World War I, Germany lost its overseas colonies and the League of Nations gave control to other nations. Belgium (which had

Table 2.1   Africa's Main Colonial-Linguistic Divisions

Linguistic Group	Official Language	Examples
Francophone	French	Côte d'Ivoire Senegal Cameroon
Anglophone	English	Nigeria Kenya Zambia
Lusophone	Portuguese	Guinea-Bissau Angola Mozambique

assumed sovereign control of the Congo from the king in 1908 after revelations of atrocities) was granted Rwanda and Burundi. Southwest Africa was ceded to South Africa, while the French took Togo and Cameroon, and Britain controlled Tanganyika. Spain had a single colony in Africa, Equatorial Guinea, which gained independence in 1968. Italy had its own grand imperial hopes, but its foray into Africa was relatively minor. Italy controlled Eritrea and a small part of what is now Somalia from 1885 to 1941. It also briefly occupied Ethiopia during World War II, but was never a colonizer in the same way as its European counterparts. (But you can still see the inscription "Mussolini" with a red star over a tunnel on the road north of Addis Ababa.)

Africa's Noncolonies: Ethiopia and Liberia

Ethiopia, once called Abyssinia, has a long history of centralized political empire going back to the first-century rulers based in Axum. During the European scramble for Africa, Italy attempted to take the country, but lost militarily to the Ethiopians in the Battle of Adowa in 1896. The Amhara elite sought to consolidate their rule and modernize the country to resist further European aggression. Haile Selassie became emperor in 1930 and accelerated this process. The Italians tried again during World War II to rule Ethiopia and did occupy the country from 1936 to 1941. British-led African forces retook the country, and in early 1942 Britain and the United States negotiated a treaty recognizing Ethiopian sovereignty. Selassie was returned to power and ruled the country until a coup in 1974.

Liberia was a colony of freed American slaves beginning in 1822 and was supported largely by private religious and philanthropic groups. In 1847 the "Americo-Liberians" declared independence and the Republic of Liberia was born. But rather than reintegrate into local African societies, the settlers regarded themselves as "Americans" and sought to model their new government on the United States. Like some of the European settler states in Africa, Americo-Liberians mostly sought to keep themselves separate from the indigenous African populations. Liberians with roots among the settlers maintained control over the country until 1980, when President William Tolbert was deposed and killed by Samuel Doe, setting off a series of internal conflicts (see Chapter 4).

South Africa's "Independence"

European entry into South Africa began in 1652 with the arrival of Jan van Riebeeck, who set up the Cape Colony on behalf of the Dutch East India Company. Dutch settlers slowly expanded their territory throughout the eighteenth century, occasionally clashing with the indigenous Xhosa. Britain seized the Cape of Good Hope area in 1797 during the Fourth Anglo-Dutch War and formally annexed the Cape Colony in 1805. The descendants of the Dutch and other early European settlers known as Afrikaners (or Boers) grew increasingly resentful of new British rule, including attempts to expand rights for Africans in the Cape. In the 1830s thousands of Afrikaners embarked on the "Great Trek," migrating deeper into the hinterland. The Afrikaners set up their own states, the "Boer Republics" of the Transvaal and the Orange Free State. But the discovery of diamonds and gold encouraged the British to take a new interest in the Boer Republics. The Afrikaners held the British off during the First Boer War of 1880–1881 using guerrilla tactics. But they could not do it again in the Second Boer War of 1899–1902 when the British sent much larger forces and employed brutal tactics against civilians, including what is recognized as the world's first concentration camps. The Union of South Africa, incorporating the Cape and Natal Colonies and the two Boer Republics, was established in 1910. The agreement explicitly left out the Bechuanaland Protectorate (now Botswana), Basutoland (Lesotho), and Swaziland, allowing those three countries to remain independent and eventually become sovereign states.

The right-wing National Party won power in 1948 and quickly began to implement a policy of segregating the races, known as "apartheid." Agitation for greater rights by Africans grew throughout the second half of the twentieth century, most notably by the African National Congress (ANC). Two key events were when sixty-nine people were killed in Sharpeville by police in 1960 during a protest against requirements that all Africans carry passes, and riots in Soweto in 1976, sparked by rules forcing Africans to learn Afrikaans instead of English. Antiapartheid protests grew in the mid-1980s, as did international isolation through sanctions. In 1990 a ban on the ANC was lifted, and its leader, Nelson Mandela, was released from prison after twenty-seven years. In South Africa's first free elections in April 1994, the ANC won by an overwhelming majority, and Mandela was elected president.

Independence Arrives

A confluence of events and trends triggered the end of Europe's domination of sub-Saharan Africa. Although the pressures for independence were a long time coming, independence came in a relatively quick wave. Sudan was first in 1956. Ghana was next in 1957, an event typically considered the beginning of Africa's independence movement. The French followed by shedding Guinea in 1958, and fourteen more colonies followed suit in 1960. In rapid succession over the next few years, almost all the remaining African colonies gained freedom from their colonial powers. Portugal was the main holdout and tried to maintain its African territories. But after a revolution at home in 1974, it abandoned its colonies the following year. White settlers in Rhodesia had declared their own independence in 1965, but after a long and bloody civil war with nationalist guerrillas, it too was transformed into an independent Zimbabwe in 1980. Africa's last colony was Namibia (formerly Southwest Africa), which had been administered by South Africa since World War I. In 1990, it finally became independent, closing the door on five centuries of European colonization on the continent. For many, however, the decolonization process was not truly complete until 1994, when South Africa held its first free elections and white minority rule ended.

Social Legacy of Colonialism

Colonialism and the arrival of European ideas, technology, and systems had colossal effects on Africa—the influences of which are still deeply felt today. As real and in many ways catastrophic as this was, there are also many reasons for people today to either exaggerate the legacy or to use it as a convenient scapegoat for other failings or mistakes. This is mentioned not to minimize the devastating effects of colonialism and the economic exploitation that accompanied political domination, but rather to keep in mind that interpreting the colonial legacy remains deeply political and vulnerable to cynical manipulation.

A few aspects of the social impact of colonialism that certainly are felt today include:

• *Culture.* Much of Africa today retains outward aspects of European culture, including language, dress, and cuisine. In many cases, the continuation of some cultural imports is clearly pragmatic, such as countries with multiple local languages keeping the colonial language as a neutral option. But there are also concerns that the colonial experience undermined Africans' confidence in their own culture and that many have come to accept the European racist notion that African cultures are inferior. Even if this is not explicit today, it may underlie the tendency of many to underappreciate African ingenuity or to seek foreign solutions to African problems.

• *Ethnicity.* Identities based on blood linkages—be they ethnic, familial, or clan—are very real in most of Africa because, as in Europe, traditional political organization was based on such relationships. Although ethnic identity is a fluid and often arbitrary concept, it seems to nevertheless have extraordinary power to influence how people treat each other. There is some evidence that colonial ideas of race and ethnicity may have delineated, and in some cases evidently exacerbated, ethnic

Table 2.2   Africa's Decolonization

Year	Country	Colonial power (formerly)
1956	Sudan	UK/Egypt
1957	Ghana	UK
1958	Guinea	France
1960	Nigeria	UK
	Somalia	UK
	Cameroon	France (Germany)
	Benin (Dahomey)	France
	Burkina Faso (Upper Volta)	France
	Chad	France
	Congo-Brazzaville	France
	Côte d'Ivoire	France
	Gabon	France
	Mali	France
	Senegal	France
	Mauritania	France
	Niger	France
	Togo	France
	Central African Republic	France
	Madagascar	France
	Democratic Republic of Congo (Zaire, Congo)	Belgium
1961	Tanganyika (merged with Zanibar to form Tanzania in 1962)	UK (Germany)
	Sierra Leone	UK
	British Cameroon (split to Cameroon and Nigeria)	UK
1962	Zambia (Northern Rhodesia)	UK
	Malawi (Nyasaland)	UK
	Uganda	UK
	Rwanda	Belgium (Germany)
	Burundi	Belgium (Germany)
1963	Kenya	UK
1965	The Gambia	UK
1966	Botswana (Bechuanaland)	UK
	Lesotho	UK
1968	Swaziland	UK
	Mauritius	UK (France)
	Equatorial Guinea	Spain
1974	Guinea-Bissau	Portugal
1975	Comoros	France
	Angola	Portugal
	Mozambique	Portugal
	São Tomé and Príncipe	Portugal
	Cape Verde	Portugal
1976	Seychelles	UK
1977	Djibouti (French Somaliland)	France
1980	Zimbabwe (Rhodesia)	UK (declared by settlers in 1965)
1990	Namibia (Southwest Africa)	South Africa (Germany)

differences. In Rwanda, for example, it is not at all clear that Hutus and Tutsis saw themselves as distinctly different until the Belgian authorities classified people as one or the other and then implemented policies of deliberate discrimination. (Pointing this out does not mean that the Hutu-Tutsi clashes or the 1994 genocide is the fault of the Belgians, but it does suggest that colonial influences contributed to ethnic division.)

   • *Racism.* One version of ethnic discrimination that is explicitly tied to European colonial rule is racism. Beliefs in African racial inferiority were clearly part of the justification for colonialism in the first place, and such sentiments continue in many ways, if less obviously. In the countries that experienced race-based violence, such as Zimbabwe, South Africa, or even Kenya, the black-white tensions can still be felt. Racism is also a lingering issue for many of the Asian minorities and the growing numbers of mixed-race people, most obviously for "Cape coloreds," the term still used in South Africa today to describe the large population of people concentrated in the western Cape who have some combination of African, European, and Asian ancestry.

   • *Religion.* Colonialism and geography are major determinants of African religious patterns. Islam came to Africa along trading routes, reflected in the dominance of that religion across the Sahel and along the coast of East Africa. The first Christians in sub-Saharan Africa were probably in Ethiopia, which has had orthodox Christian churches perhaps as far back as the fourth century. However, for most of the rest of the continent, Christianity arrived through missionaries, especially during the nineteenth century. Because many of the European powers actively encouraged missionaries, they were often the vanguard of eventual colonial domination. At the same time, mission schools were often the only formal educational opportunities for African children, and many of the continent's most prominent nationalist leaders were first taught at mission schools.

Slavery

The most devastating historical impact on Africa is probably the export of an estimated 11 million of its inhabitants. Prior to the nineteenth century, slavery was commonplace in much of the world, and many African societies accepted it as a feudal-style labor arrangement or the rightful winnings from military conquest. African slaves were not only common within the continent, but exports to the Middle East and parts of North Africa appear to have occurred centuries before Europeans began exploring the African heartland. But the growth of the transatlantic slave trade, which began in the sixteenth century and was mainly between West Africa and the Americas, turned slavery into a major business for both European and African slave traders. Ghana's Ashanti Kingdom, for example, actively traded gold, ivory, and slaves, first to Portuguese merchants and later to the Dutch and British. The slave trade peaked in the late eighteenth century as demand for labor in the Americas grew, especially from sugar plantations where an estimated 90 percent of all slaves in the Americas worked.

The abolition of slavery is sometimes described as the first human rights campaign, and grew primarily out of religious societies in Great Britain. Faced with growing pressure from the public and the clergy, the British Parliament abolished its slave trade in 1808, outlawed slavery in 1833, and then later used the Royal Navy to try to stop the trade. Despite British steps, other European nations, such as Spain, Portugal, and France, continued to traffic in human cargo. In the interim period between Britain's criminalization of slavery and the final suppression of the transatlantic trade in 1867, more than 3 million Africans were forcibly transported to the Americas.

Ironically, the antislavery movement in Europe was one of the critical motivations and justifications for European conquest of the African continent. As the Europeans divided up the continent politically, one of the early tasks for the colonial regimes was to curb slavery and the slave trade. British general Charles Gordon, for example, was sent up the Nile to expand British influence, and one of his orders was to try to suppress the slave trade in Sudan. Belgium's King Leopold justified his expanding control over Congo in part on the supposed humanitarian mission to root out slavery (even as he directly profited from the trade). The eventual abolition of the slave trade in the Americas led to the decline of the practice of slavery, a step not formalized in North America until the 1860s. Unfortunately, some forms of slavery continue today, especially in places such as Sudan and Mauritania, although more in the form of a contemporary version of feudalism than the explicit business trade of the past.

African Nationalism

The experience of colonialism and the process of decolonization also had a major impact on the political and ideological landscape in Africa. Since African "nations" for the most part did not exist prior to colonialism, one of the major challenges for the emerging leadership was to build a sense of national identity. The fight against colonial authorities provided the initial impetus for such a movement, which developed primarily from the growing number of educated Africans that agitated for greater indigenous political autonomy. African nationalism was not only a political movement, but also a cultural reassertion of Africans' rights not to be dominated or controlled by outsiders and a rejection of the colonial ideology that suppressed African freedoms and self-worth.

A key turning point was the important role played by Africans in the battle against fascism during World War II. Many Africans who served with the Allies were distraught that many of the values they supposedly defended during the war—such as democracy, freedom, and self-determination—did not apply to them. The independence of India from the British Empire in 1948, largely based on the emergence of Indian nationalism, encouraged African leaders to pursue similar goals. The victory of Vietnamese nationalists against the French at Dien Bien Phu in 1954, the first major defeat of a colonial army by local nationalists, was also a spark that catalyzed nationalist guerrilla movements to seek independence through military means in Africa. After the eventual end of colonialism and the disappearance of an obvious imperial enemy to unite opposition, African nationalism—the process of redefining political units and loyalties—has been much more difficult and continues today (see Chapter 5).

Socialism

Another important ideological hangover from the colonial period is socialism. Leftist ideas—such as collective ownership and heavy state control of the economy—took root in many African countries for three main reasons. First, the Soviet Union was a critical supporter in terms of money, weapons, and training for many African guerrilla movements. Along with this support came Soviet ideas of planning and economic management that led, in some countries such as Mozambique and Angola, to explicit Marxist-Leninist parties after independence pursuing Soviet-like economic models. Second, there are some aspects of many African cultures, such as the communal treatment of land ownership and collective decisionmaking, that appeared to be more similar to socialism than a liberal capitalist model based on individualism and private ownership. Third, state control of the important parts of the economy (what Marx called the "means of production" and Lenin called "the commanding heights") seemed to many leaders a natural economic complement to their newly won political independence. If political independence was throwing off the yoke of colonial political domination, then why not also seize the economy to end exploitation and mobilize local resources for national purposes? Although many of the socialist policies (and much of its language) have since been jettisoned (see Chapter 7), state economic intervention lives on in many forms to support patronage (see Chapter 3).

Pan-Africanism

In the early twentieth century, led by African American activist W.E.B. DuBois among others, there occurred the rise of ideas of solidarity and unity among all African peoples around the globe. Pan-Africanism, as it came to be known, was influential among African nationalists who saw common cause in fighting the colonial powers and seeking independence. At the same time, several of the African nationalists and early political leaders—especially Kwame Nkrumah of Ghana, Ahmed Sékou Touré of Guinea, and Julius Nyerere of Tanzania—became proponents of a Pan-African vision for Africa's political future (see Chapter 3). Nkrumah in particular envisioned a formal, continent-wide political union. Pan-Africanism was the intellectual rationale for the formation of the Organization of African Unity (OAU) in 1963. Although Pan-Africanism as an amorphous idea continues today, it has never coalesced into a meaningful political structure (see Chapter 11).

Traditional African Authorities

The arrival of European colonists had a major impact on the existing political leadership in Africa. Given the huge diversity of precolonial political institutions and the broad range of colonial experiences, it is impossible to generalize about the impact of colonialism on traditional African authorities. In some places where European military might was overwhelming, the traditional political structures were broken. But many others found ways for some form of the old system to survive through adaptation or cooperation. What does appear clear, nearly universally across Africa, is that while colonialism introduced the structures of the modern state to Africa, vestiges of traditional authority and organization remain today. In places such as Zimbabwe, where most of the ruling chiefs were co-opted by the Rhodesian regime and thus discredited after independence, there still remain minor local roles for chiefs. In several countries that had traditions of royalty that were forced out by either the colonial masters or by independent governments, they have recently come back, although largely in ceremonial roles. The throne of the Asantehene, king of the Ashanti in Ghana, has been revived, but mainly in a cultural capacity. The Buganda Kingdom in Uganda plays a similar social rather than overtly political role. However, there are also cases where traditional authorities still wield considerable authority. In Botswana for instance, the *kgotla*, or village council, retains important authority over many matters. The sultan of Sokoto, the traditional ruler of the Hausa in northern Nigeria, retains a huge amount of influence in that part of the country. Most starkly, Swaziland is still a formal monarchy and perhaps the most obvious example of the endurance of traditional authority (see the box below).

Weak and Conflict-Prone States

One important legacy of colonial rule is the prevalence of weak political states that are highly vulnerable to conflict. The inherited colonial borders are a large part of this problem. Lines between states were drawn based on European economic and strategic concerns rather than related to the social and political realities that existed on the ground. This resulted in many political, linguistic, and ethnic groups being both bunched together and split apart. Current African states tend to have multiple ethnic and linguistic groups that may provide little basis for a cohesive political unit. The Democratic Republic of Congo (formerly Zaire), for instance, includes more than two hundred distinct linguistic groups. At the same time, because colonial powers often used rivers as natural borders yet groups of people tended to live along both banks of a river, many ethnic groups found themselves divided among different states. For example, the Limpopo River that separates South Africa and Zimbabwe also divides the Ndebele people. Many borders continue to be the source of tension, with ongoing demarcation disputes today, including hostilities along the Nigeria-Cameroon, Ethiopia-Somalia, Chad-Libya, and Ethiopia-Eritrea borders.

Another legacy is the system of weak political institutions left behind after the colonial withdrawal. In the British colonies, where the move to independence was typically deliberate and took place over a long transition period during which formal education systems were in

---

Swaziland: Africa's Last Kingdom?

The people of the current Swazi nation migrated down from East Africa, probably about five hundred years ago, settling in their current location in the early 1800s. King Mswati II consolidated their territory and, to help fend off the expansionist Zulus, formed strategic alliances with Boer farmers in the area and the British. Ties grew to the South African and British authorities, and Swaziland came under British control as a protectorate after the Boer War ended in 1902. But even as European influence increased, the king maintained authority over the local population. Swazi law and custom, including the authority of the king, continued to play a dominant force in the lives of the local population, even while the British established a European-style legal system to administer the country. The British deliberately kept Swaziland out of the Union of South Africa in 1910, and following the introduction of apartheid, the British began planning for eventual Swazi independence. The transition was slow, but Swaziland became an independent state as a constitutional monarchy in 1968. Although the new state had an elected parliament, it was later dissolved by King Sobhuza II in 1973. Today, there is a parliament and prime minister, but they mainly play an advisory role, and ultimate authority remains in the hands of the monarch, currently Mswati III.

place, the newly independent states had fairly well-developed civil services. In the Portuguese colonies, where withdrawal was hasty and formal education extremely limited, the incoming African governments had only a handful of skilled bureaucrats and very few established institutions of the modern state (see Chapter 6).

Pawns of Larger Global Forces

Just as Africa's colonial destiny was mainly determined by foreigners sitting in a conference room in Berlin, Western engagement in much of postindependence Africa has seen the continent mainly in terms of larger global forces. Most obviously, African decolonization occurred during the height of the Cold War, the geostrategic and ideological competition between the United States and the Soviet Union. Although the struggle was considered "cold" because the United States and USSR never directly fought, it was in fact "hot" in many parts of the world, including in Africa, through proxy wars. Angola is the most obvious example, where the Soviets supported the ruling Movimento Popular de Libertação de Angola (MPLA) government and the Cubans sent thousands of troops and medical personnel in the 1980s. The United States directly backed the União Nacional pela Independência Total de Angola (UNITA) rebels and indirectly supported the South African military invasion of Angola.

More broadly, the major global powers viewed Africa mostly though a Cold War lens. Allies were chosen and backed based on their allegiance. US support for Joseph Mobutu in Zaire was almost entirely owing to his utility in containing communism and Soviet influence in the continent. At the same time, however, African leaders were able to manipulate Cold War fears to extract resources, favors, or protection from both sides. Indeed, there is little evidence that African leaders embraced either communism or capitalism with much enthusiasm, preferring to pursue their own agenda but wrapping it in the language of their preferred patron—thus allowing the occasional changing of sides without much impact on the ground. Siad Barre, dictator of Somalia from 1969 until 1991, for instance, switched from Soviet to Western allegiance in the late 1970s.

With the end of the Cold War and the collapse of the Soviet Union, there was a lot of concern in Africa in the early 1990s that it would be forgotten. Although this does not appear to have materialized—indeed, attention to Africa has probably never been greater than it is today—it may still be the case that major powers engage in Africa mainly as part of a broader agenda, such as global security or the expansion of democracy.

Economic Legacy

The economic impact of colonialism on Africa is a tough question. On the one hand, colonial rule was both justified and supported by explicit economic exploitation. Africa's natural resources, such as gold, rubber, copper, and timber were extracted without much benefit to Africa itself. The labor of African workers was often for the benefit of foreigners. (In one of the most blatant such cases, in the early part of the twentieth century African workers from Mozambique were sent to work in the gold mines of South Africa and payment for their labor was made in the form of gold sent directly to Lisbon.) The introduction of colonial taxes forced many Africans into wage labor or pushed them to produce surpluses. Slavery, of course, also exacted an economic toll. In many ways the form of crude capitalism that colonialism introduced was highly imperfect, skewed heavily against Africa, and was, by today's standards, deeply unfair.

On the other hand, colonial rule brought some of the aspects and institutions of a modern economy. Europeans constructed roads, railways, and ports. Admittedly, these were built to serve the colonial economy. Railways, for example, typically connected mines to ports in order to facilitate the extraction and export of resources. But for many African countries, these basic infrastructure investments are still crucial to the current economy. Colonial administrations also brought formal schooling and healthcare to many parts of Africa for the first time (although it was often inferior and targeted mainly to help serve colonial interests). Literacy in Africa may have been only around one-quarter of the population around the time of independence, but this is from a base of near zero just a few generations earlier. However imperfect and unfairly the colonial economic impact was, it did in some small measure help to prepare Africa for engaging with the modern world and participating in the global economy.

Ties That Still Bind

One of the remarkable features of contemporary Africa is the enduring connection to European powers. French-speaking Africa is perhaps the starkest example of this, where the links between France and its former colonies are strongest. In most of francophone Africa, French is still the official language, large numbers of French citizens continue to work in Africa, and France maintains security through active troop presence. Economically, trade and business is dominated by French firms, the West and Central African currencies are tied to the French franc (technically, to the euro since 1999, but the relationship remains controlled by Paris), and even the budgets of many countries are drawn up by French bureaucrats. Britain maintains a much less intimate relationship with its former colonies, but nonetheless the economic, political, and cultural connections remain strong. In fact it is possible in parts of Africa today to find children in British-style school uniforms, learning a British curriculum, and having their exams graded in Cambridge.

For Further Reading

Here are only a few suggestions out of the huge literature on African history. Thomas Pakenham gives an account of the critical period of colonization in *The Scramble for Africa, 1876–1912* (1991). Paul Nugent's *Africa Since Independence: A Comparative History* (2004) is perhaps the best recent history book accounting for the legacies of different colonial experiences. Another solid choice is Crawford Young's *The African Colonial State in Comparative Perspective* (1994). A very long-term perspective on African history and the importance of endowments is contained in *Guns, Germs, and Steel: The Fates of Human Societies* (1999) by Jared Diamond (this popular book is discussed in more detail in Chapter 6).

One of the early anticolonial revolutionary texts was Franz Fanon's *The Wretched of the Earth* (1963). Other important inspirational anticolonial works are those by Kwame Nkrumah, Julius Nyerere, and Jomo Kenyatta (see "For Further Reading" for Chapter 3). Two assessments of the impact of colonialism on political and economic development are Mahmood Mamdani's *Citizen and Subject: Contemporary Africa and the Legacy of Late Colonialism* (1996) and Pierre Englebert's "Pre-Colonial Institutions, Post-Colonial States, and Economic Development in Tropical Africa" (2000). One author that argues some of the favorable benefits of colonialism (and from a Marxist perspective) is Bill Warren in his *Imperialism: Pioneer of Capitalism* (1981). Two books that seek to dispel the myths of "tribalism" are Crawford Young's *The Politics of Cultural Pluralism* (1976) and Leroy Vail's *The Creation of Tribalism in Southern Africa* (1989).

Adam Hochschild provides a detailed account of Congo's brutal colonial experience in *King Leopold's Ghost* (1998). On the violence in Rwanda, see *We Wish to Inform You That Tomorrow We Will Be Killed with Our Families: Stories from Rwanda* by Philip Gourevitch (1998) and Gerard Prunier's *The Rwanda Crisis: History of a Genocide, 1959–1994* (1995). Of the many books on South African history, perhaps the most comprehensive is Leonard Thompson's *A History of South Africa* (2001).

3

Big Men, Personal Rule, and Patronage Politics

ACROSS AFRICA THERE IS A GREAT DIVERSITY OF POLITICAL SYS-
tems, and each country has its own complexities linked to its history, geography, and evolution of its social groups. At the same time, many African
countries have followed a similar pattern in the postindependence era and
share similar characteristics in the way governance has progressed. In particular, the politics and developmental trajectory of many African countries
appear to have been dominated by a handful of powerful men or, in many
cases, by a single man who often stays in power for an extended period.
This has often been called the "Big Man" syndrome.

The Big Man is a cliché, but it also aptly describes a particular political system dominated by individuals and personal relationships, with the
peace kept through the distribution of money, jobs, and favors. In many
African societies there is also a cultural attitude of respectful deference
(and sometimes fear) toward the wealthy or powerful, with expectations
that the Big Man—be it a local chief, a warlord, or a president—will take
care of those under his wing and punish those who oppose him. The
biggest of the Big Men is the president, who is thought of not only as a
political leader but also often as the "father of the nation," an all-powerful and perhaps superhuman person whose authority is unquestioned. His
presence is everywhere, his portrait on the national currency and in every
shop. In the end it is about an unusual concentration of control and influence in the hands of a few. This chapter will explain a few of the concepts behind the Big Man idea, present descriptions of their rule, and
then detail some of the continent's most important Big Men, with whom
students of African development should be familiar.

Power Concentration

It may appear strange to talk about heavy concentration of power in
states that are considered very weak (see Chapter 6). But, even if many
African states appear unable to perform some fundamental functions of

37

the state (such as providing security or basic services such as garbage collection), there is nonetheless considerable decisionmaking and influence in the presidency, both formally and informally. The legal powers of the president in some African nations tend to be vast and may include easy provision to dismiss parliament or to introduce new laws. In a few cases "emergency" powers can last decades and provide a veneer of legality for crackdowns on potential opponents. But the concentration of power at the top is also reinforced by informal ways of operating, such as disregarding inconvenient laws or subverting the chains of authority or regulations that may exist only on paper.

In many cases, there may be little of a real "state" operating below the surface. That is why a small group can often successfully mount a coup and seize control of a country merely by taking the presidential palace, the airport, and the radio station. This is, of course, changing in many African countries through the growing delegation of power to local authorities, external auditing and oversight, or the introduction of checks and balances via increasing the role of parliaments and the judiciary (see Chapter 5). But for the most part, political systems remain dominated by the leader at the top, both de jure and de facto.

Personal Rule

African political systems are also often described by political scientists as being characterized by "personal rule." This is where informal personal relationships matter the most and decisions are made by individuals rather than bureaucracies. Personal rule can indicate that the laws of the country are applied very selectively and that rules are subverted by the powerful and do not apply to those connected to political leaders. The route to power is restricted and depends on who you know, where you were born, and perhaps what language you speak. Critically, personal rule also often means that there is little distinction made between public resources and private wealth. The resources of the state are also those of the president and those around him.

Patronage Politics

A related aspect of personal rule is the politics of patronage. This is a political system that operates based on the distribution of goods, money, and favors in exchange for support. (In the academic literature, this is sometimes called clientalism, prebendalism, or neopatrimonialism, but they all more or less describe a similar pattern.) Patronage politics means that leaders use the institutions of the state, which might include civil service jobs and access to credit, licenses, regulatory decisions, government contracts, and even cash, to keep selected groups satisfied.

In return, these groups provide political support to the leaders, blocs of votes, and sometimes recruits for enforcing leaders' power. For the political leadership, the state structures are used to extract resources and provide favors and privileges for clients. In turn, the state affords opportunities for personal gain, such as padding state contracts or using regulatory authority to extract bribes.

Predatory Regimes

The prevalence of patronage and other kinds of abuse of public power can lead to a "predatory regime," or government that acts like a parasite on the country, draining resources for itself. This goes beyond normal tax collection, where the state gets itself involved in any activity where it can get a cut or where officials can siphon something off. Once governments become predatory, they are not interested in anything like promoting the private sector or providing schools for the poor, but rather become focused on manipulating the arms of the state for their own gain. Unfortunately, this all too aptly describes the motives of many of Africa's current regimes. An extreme version of this phenomenon is a "kleptocracy," where the government seems to exist only in order to steal, with Mobutu's Zaire perhaps the most famous example.

Characteristics of Big Man Rule

The convergence of these phenomena—power concentration, personal rule, and pervasive patronage—are the essence of the Big Man syndrome. In many ways this kind of political system seems to have emerged from the weakness of inherited colonial institutions combined with underlying political authorities and expectations of governance. Regardless, the Big Man syndrome has resulted in some similar patterns of politics across the continent. First, most African countries became one-party states, where political opposition was either banned outright or harshly repressed. Second, political leaders in Africa have tended to remain in power a long time, with the same leader reigning for two or even three decades. Many of the early political leaders even declared themselves "president for life." Third, many of these regimes headed by a Big Man, even those that started with idealistic goals, frequently descended into predatory patterns or tyranny. Fourth, policies and rules tend to be arbitrary and unpredictable, making it easy for the state to prey on farmers and businesses. This has often resulted in massive declines in economic activity and, all too often, led to outright crisis. In many cases, the Big Man and the patronage system have proved ultimately unsustainable, leading to ongoing economic crises. Lastly, despite frequent rhetoric, politics in Africa is frequently much less about policy or ideology, and much more about factional loyalty. This is one reason why, regardless of whether African leaders chose the West or East during the Cold War, they usually pursued similar types of economic policies that were neither communist nor capitalist, but rather embraced a level of state control that sustained the patronage system and reinforced their own wealth and power.

Limits on the Big Man Idea

The notion of the Big Man may explain some African leaders and their political systems, but it is not without its limitations. Some leaders have been archetypal Big Men, at times to the point of caricature, but many others are slowly moving their countries toward models that more closely resemble a state based on a social contract between the rulers and the ruled. It is also true that this is not an exclusively African syndrome; many of the aspects of the Big Man are present in all societies. Patronage, corruption, and even mass megalomania exist in all regions of the globe. Some of these characteristics do, however, appear to be particularly severe in Africa.

The other limitation of the Big Man concept is its circularity. In some ways the Big Man is simply descriptive of the way leaders are treated and politics work in some places. But as a causal factor, it is far from clear that Big Men are responsible for Africa's problems, or whether the continent's political and economic troubles have simply given rise to Big Men. It is extremely common to hear in the press and on the street that bad leadership is the cause of African poverty and political instability. But Africa has also had plenty of capable and gifted leaders who also seem to have fallen into similar patterns. In the end, the concept of the Big Man is useful when thinking about certain politi-

---

Is Patronage Corruption?

Patronage politics is not exactly the same as corruption, but the two are closely related and may feed off each other. Political leaders who must continue to dole out resources may resort to "grand corruption," such as raiding public coffers, creating false government contracts, or seizing private assets, in order to maintain stability and their position in power. At the same time, public jobs are often considered avenues to engage in "petty corruption" for extra income, such as small payments demanded by police officers or border guards. This can, of course, result in entrenched corruption, where the system itself is sustained by graft and under-the-table favors on all sides.

cal systems and histories. But it does not really suggest an answer to Africa's governance problems.

Africa's Big Men: Who Are They?

Africa has lots of Big Men, prominent leaders who have changed African history and whose legacies—both good and bad—have had a major impact on the continent. In this section are listed ten Big Men that all students of Africa probably know already, and a further ten that are less well known, but should become familiar. One caveat, however: the label of Big Man used here is somewhat looser than the ruinous syndrome described above. Some of the men listed below have been great leaders and did not fall into destructive or maniacal patterns of rule. Others, however, are caricatures of the Big Man and culpable in mass murder. But each has put an indelible personal stamp on Africa's political and economic development.

Ten Big Men You Probably Know

1. *Nelson Mandela* is probably the most famous African of all time and both a moral and political leader for the continent, if not the world as a whole. Mandela, a lawyer by training, advocated in the early 1960s for the African National Congress to take a more aggressive military stand against the apartheid regime. He was arrested for his part in a bombing campaign and spent the next twenty-seven years in prison, much of which was spent on the notorious Robben Island. From jail, Mandela grew to become the single most important figure in the anti-apartheid movement, and the "free Mandela" campaign was a focal point for international efforts. His negotiated release occurred February 18, 1990, and was a critical watershed in the end of apartheid. Mandela won the Nobel Peace Prize in 1993 and was elected president of South Africa in April 1994. Setting himself apart from many of the vaunted freedom fighters before him, Mandela retired after one term. Nevertheless, he has remained heavily engaged in a range of African political causes, including the battle against HIV/AIDS and peace in Burundi.

2. *Kwame Nkrumah* was the first head of state of Ghana, which in 1957 became the first African colony to gain independence from a European power. Nkrumah was one of the fathers of African independence, arguing not only for self-determination for the then-Gold Coast colony, but also for a more radical Pan-African ideal, including his proposed "United States of Africa." He helped to start the Pan-African Congress in 1945 and was one of the founders of the Organization of African Unity in 1963. His most famous mantra was that Africans should "Seek ye first the political kingdom and all other things shall

come" (perhaps presaging the trend of using political authority for economic gain). Although Nkrumah is still revered in Ghana and much of Africa today for his ideas and achievements, his presidency was disastrous. His rule quickly degenerated into a dictatorship, with the declaration of a one-party state in 1964 and a growing personality cult. His economic policies, which included nationalizing the gold mines, state control of prices, and large prestige projects, led to a collapse in living standards and eventually a full-blown crisis. Nkrumah was overthrown by his own military in 1966 and died in 1972 while in exile in Romania.

3. *Julius Nyerere* led the former British protectorate of Tanganyika to independence in 1961, and later became president of Tanzania following the mainland's union with Zanzibar. Nyerere, like nearly all of his contemporaries, instituted a one-party state that at times became highly oppressive. Although considered a moderate, Nyerere increasingly sought ties with China and embraced Maoist ideas for economic development. He attempted to achieve his goal of a socialist and self-sufficient state through a policy of *ujamaa*, a Swahili word that means "unity" or "family" but in practice meant mandatory collective farming. After forcibly relocating farmers, in many cases at gunpoint, the results were (perhaps not surprisingly) calamitous. Poverty and hunger increased sharply. Although Nyerere's economic ideas failed miserably, he also played an important political role in the region, taking a lead in supporting nationalist movements in Mozambique and Zimbabwe (then Rhodesia). In 1979, Nyerere invaded Uganda to oust the homicidal regime of Idi Amin (see below). He voluntarily retired in 1985, but remained active politically. Nyerere died in 1999 and is probably still most remembered as an idealist who remained humble and untouched by the corruption that infected many of his peers.

4. *Jomo Kenyatta* was another of Africa's leading nationalists. His early campaign for African political rights took him to England where he collaborated with Kwame Nkrumah among others to agitate for greater African rights. Kenyatta was jailed and then exiled for a supposed role in the Mau-Mau uprising against the colonial authorities. After his release, he negotiated with the British for a new constitution and independence for Kenya, which arrived in 1963. His Kenya African National Union (KANU) party dominated the first election and he became president the following year. Kenyatta was initially known for his conciliatory stance toward white settlers and colonial officials, encouraging them to remain and allowing many to keep their jobs. As a result, Kenya did not suffer some of the early economic trauma and outflow of investment experienced by many other newly independent countries. However, Kenyatta's rule was also marked by an increase in ethnic

rivalry and growing political authoritarianism, including the declaration of a one-party state in 1974. He died in 1978, leaving a legacy of tension between his Kikuyu and other ethnic groups, as well as repressive state machinery in place for his successor, Daniel arap Moi.

5. *Mobutu Sésé Seko* may be the archetypal African Big Man. Joseph Mobutu was in the colonial army of the Belgian Congo in the early 1950s when he switched sides to join an emerging nationalist movement. Following Congo's independence in 1960 he returned as a high-ranking military officer and within three months (and with the apparent support of the US Central Intelligence Agency) led a coup that ousted and killed Prime Minister Patrice Lumumba. Five years later Mobutu declared himself president and quickly centralized power. His rule, which eventually lasted thirty-two years, set new standards for kleptocracy and megalomania. Mobutu renamed the country "Zaire" and himself Mobutu Sésé Seko Nkuku Wa Za Banga (which translates as "The all-powerful warrior who, because of his endurance and inflexible will to win, will go from conquest to conquest, leaving fire in his wake"). Economically, he was a disaster, nationalizing firms and expelling businessmen, but this allowed him to control the copper mines and other national assets. He built lavish palaces across the country and amassed a personal fortune worth billions of dollars. Much of it came from pocketing aid and loans that were stashed in Swiss banks or in European property. Mobutu was able to maintain close relations with the West because he was considered a bulwark against communism, for example by channeling support to Angolan rebels. After the end of the Cold War, external support for Mobutu waned and his position, as well as his health, deteriorated. Congolese rebels, supported by the Rwandan and Ugandan armies, overthrew him in May 1997 and he died in exile in Morocco four months later.

6. *Idi Amin Dada* of Uganda is probably Africa's most notorious Big Man, known for his eccentricities and pathological behavior. Amin joined the King's African Rifles of the British colonial army and was a champion boxer and swimmer. After independence, he rose through the army ranks and developed a reputation for brutality. Initially an ally of Milton Obote, the country's first prime minister, the two schemed to smuggle gold and ivory out of neighboring Congo, and Amin eventually became army chief of staff. Amin packed the military with fellow Muslims and his kinsmen from northwestern Uganda. Relations with Obote cooled, and upon learning Obote planned to arrest him, Amin launched a coup in January 1971 and declared himself president. He quickly sought to suppress any countercoup by torturing and executing Obote supporters, other military leaders, and much of the country's edu-

cated elite. Ethnic violence exploded, while Amin himself grew increasingly paranoid (and probably insane). In 1972 he expelled the country's 70,000 Asians, claiming that God had ordered him to do so. In all, between 300,000 and half a million Ugandans were murdered during Amin's reign. Two critical events led to his downfall. In 1976 an Air France flight hijacked by the Palestinian Liberation Organization flew to the country's main airport at Entebbe at Amin's invitation. The rescue operation by Israeli paratroopers left Amin's air force in tatters and his position increasingly isolated. His erratic behavior increased and, after attempting to annex part of his neighbor, Tanzanian troops, aided by Ugandan exiles, invaded and deposed him in April 1979. He fled to Libya and then into exile in Saudi Arabia until his death in 2003.

7. *Yoweri Museveni* is credited with bringing Uganda back from the abyss, after the disastrous and murderous regimes of Idi Amin and Milton Obote. Museveni started his political career with education in Tanzania and military training in Mozambique, then returned home but quickly fled again in 1971 after Amin seized power. Museveni took part in the 1979 Tanzanian invasion to unseat Amin, and then led his own National Resistance Movement forces to overthrow Obote, taking the capital Kampala in January 1986. Museveni was determined to break the cycle of sectarian bloodshed, so he instituted a nonparty political system to prevent ethnically based party competition from sparking a new round of violence. He created a nationalist "Movement" system and a series of locally elected "Resistance Councils" to manage local affairs. Just as importantly, he enacted far-reaching economic reforms that allowed the economy to recover strongly. Museveni invited the Asian community, which Amin had expelled, back and built a very close relationship with the major international donors, especially the World Bank and the British government. By the early 1990s, Uganda had become one of the donor favorites and Museveni was hailed as a one of a new generation of progressive African leaders. Some of the shine has recently come off his star, however, as Uganda has become embroiled in regional conflicts, corruption seems to be worsening, and Museveni seems unwilling to relinquish power. Under growing external pressure, Museveni has allowed multiparty politics again, but he changed the constitution to allow him to run for a third term, which he won in early 2006. Whether he clings to power and undermines his legacy of saving Uganda remains to be seen.

8. *Robert Mugabe* and his rule over Zimbabwe is a tragic tale of a once-respected founding father descending into tyranny and economic ruin. Mugabe was one of the early nationalist leaders in then-Rhodesia as a founder of the Zimbabwe African National Union (ZANU), one of

the two main parties fighting against Ian Smith's white-supremacist regime. Mugabe's faction fought out of Mozambique with Chinese arms and support and gradually gained popularity among the population, especially among the majority Shona. Following British-mediated talks at Lancaster House, Mugabe and ZANU surprised the world by winning in a landslide election held in 1980. Mugabe's early rule was marked by racial reconciliation and large improvements in social services for the African population. But the mid-1980s was also marred by a vicious crackdown against potential guerrillas in Matabeleland in the southwest of the country, killing perhaps 20,000 people. Mugabe sought to ensure that his party (ZANU-Patriotic Front, after the 1987 merger with its main rival) was unchallenged, but also tried to maintain relations with the United States and Europe. A crucial turning point was 2000, when Mugabe lost a constitutional referendum that would have further consolidated his power. He appeared shocked at the result and responded by unleashing his security forces and party militias against both commercial farmers and the labor-based opposition party. As repression and corruption increased and the economy crashed, relations also soured with the donors. Increasingly isolated, Mugabe blamed his country's problems on external conspiracies involving the British government, the IMF, and homosexuals, among many others. The plunge from admired leader to despot and pariah means that Mugabe will probably be most remembered for turning what had been one of Africa's great hopes into another failed state.

9. *Charles Taylor* of Liberia is one of Africa's most notorious warlords. He went to college and drove a taxicab in Boston before joining Samuel Doe's regime. Taylor was arrested in the United States in 1984 for embezzlement, but while awaiting extradition back to Liberia, he escaped from prison and fled to Libya to plot his return. Taylor built a guerrilla army in Côte d'Ivoire and launched an insurgency against Doe in 1989, quickly seizing control of much of the country. Within a year, one of Taylor's then-allies had penetrated the capital, Monrovia, and killed Doe. But the rebels fractured and the country plunged into a civil war that killed hundreds of thousands of people. Taylor developed a reputation for brutality and inhumane tactics, and was accused of widespread use of child soldiers. Following a fragile peace deal, national elections were held in 1997 and Taylor won by a wide margin, possibly because the population feared that the war might resume if he lost. (One of his infamous campaign slogans was "He killed my ma, he killed my pa, I'll vote for him.") As president, Taylor expanded his influence in the region, most notably through active support for rebels in Sierra Leone and growing involvement in illegal diamond trading. By 2003

Taylor's rule was under severe threat by two separate rebellions, war crimes charges against him from a UN tribunal, and US pressure because of his possible links with Al-Qaeda. In August 2003, he resigned and went into exile in Nigeria, but in March 2006 was arrested attempting to flee the country in order to evade a special UN court that has charged him with war crimes.

10. *Olusegun Obasanjo* has made the remarkable transition from Nigerian military leader to democratically elected president and one of the continent's most prominent and influential figures. Obasanjo was a career soldier, rising to chief of staff under Murtala Mohammed, who had seized power in a coup in 1975. Murtala was assassinated the following year in another coup attempt and Obasanjo became the new head of state. But rather than follow the usual path of military dictators, Obasanjo oversaw a transition back to civilian rule and handed power over to Shehu Shagari, who won election in October 1979. This was the first time in Nigerian history that a leader had voluntarily retired. The military returned to power in another coup in 1983 and Obasanjo became increasingly vocal against the regime, and he was jailed in 1995 by then-dictator Sani Abacha. Obasanjo was released after Abacha's death and went on to win election as president in 1999, and reelection four years later. A Yoruba from the southwest and a born-again Christian, Obasanjo's political success has depended on his unique balance among the country's many ethnic, religious, and regional factions. Obasanjo's international reputation is based on his active leadership and advocacy for the continent in areas such as peacekeeping and debt relief. He is also highly regarded for promoting better governance, including as one of the founders of corruption watchdog Transparency International. A crucial test of Obasanjo's legacy will be whether his steps to break the entrenched patronage and corruption that plague Nigeria will outlast his own presidency.

Ten Big Men You Probably Don't Know But Should

1. *Félix Houphouët-Boigny* was Côte d'Ivoire's first president and ruled for thirty-three years until his death in 1993. He was ideologically conservative and maintained extremely close relations with the French. Under his patriarchal leadership, Côte d'Ivoire was one of Africa's most stable and prosperous countries (and the world's leading cocoa producer), while Abidjan became the cultural and commercial center of francophone West Africa. Despite these successes, Houphouët-Boigny was autocratic, banning any political opposition, until grudgingly forced by France to liberalize in 1990. One of his famous quotes was, "There is no number two, three, or four. . . . There is only a number one: that's me and I do not share my decisions." At the same time, he was prone to

grand wasteful projects, including moving the country's capital to his hometown of Yamoussoukro, where he also built the world's largest church at huge public expense. His reputation as a source of stability has been highlighted by the chaos that has enveloped the country since his death.

2. *Kenneth Kaunda* is the father of Zambian independence and was a key figure in the antiapartheid movement. He was a teacher and active in civil disobedience against the colonial authorities of then-Northern Rhodesia before becoming president at independence in 1964. But Kaunda's economic management was a disaster. He put massive bureaucratic controls in place and nationalized the copper mines, leading to precipitous declines in living standards. Politically, he was also intolerant of opposition and declared a one-party state in 1972. However, he was extremely active in the region and allowed other nationalist movements, including the African National Congress, to base operations in Zambia. As corruption worsened and the country became increasingly dependent on external aid, Kaunda was forced to allow multiparty elections. In 1991, Kaunda lost to Frederick Chiluba and, to his great credit, stepped down amicably. Despite a ruinous economic legacy, the effects of which are still felt today, Kaunda is still highly regarded for his work in the anticolonial and antiapartheid struggles.

3. *Léopold Senghor* was far from a typical African Big Man, but rather was an intellectual who rose to become Senegal's founding president. Senghor won a scholarship to study at the Sorbonne in the 1930s and was one of the leading African thinkers and writers in Europe, credited with developing the concept of "negritude," which was an anticolonial ideology and one of the foundations for Pan-Africanism. Despite his philosophical leanings, Senghor served in a French military unit in World War II, was interned in a Nazi prison camp, and after the war became a representative for Senegal in the French parliament. Senghor became president of Senegal at independence in 1960 and tried to institute his own form of indigenous socialism. He was never able to create his ideal society, but his country also never suffered from many of the political and economic problems of many of its neighbors. Senghor ruled for twenty years before retiring in a smooth transition in 1980. Although Senghor is still considered the father of Senegal and an important political leader, he will probably be best remembered as one of Africa's greatest poets. Before he died in 2001 he became the first African member of the Académie Française.

4. *Gnassingbé Eyadéma* was head of Togo, a sliver of land between Ghana and Benin, for thirty-eight years until his death in February 2005, at the time Africa's longest-serving president. He led a coup in 1963 and

claimed to have personally shot then-president Sylvanus Olympio. A second coup in 1967 allowed Eyadéma to seize control and become president, ushering in his long despotic and repressive rule, where he was reported to have fed his opponents to crocodiles. He was "reelected" three times in uncontested votes, until pressure in the early 1990s forced him to allow more open elections. But Eyadéma was able to manipulate elections and suppress potential challengers enough to win again in 1993 and 1998. He was then able to change the constitution to remove term limits and allow him to run and win for the sixth time in 2003. After he died in February 2005, his son Faure Gnassingbé followed his father's pattern. An attempt to immediately take over was thwarted by regional intervention, but Gnassingbé won an election two months later using his father's old tactics: the old patronage networks combined with electoral rules that barred his main challenger (Gilchrist Olympio, the son of his father's old opponent) from running.

5. *Omar Bongo.* After Eyadéma's death, the title of longest-serving African ruler now belongs to Omar Bongo of Gabon. Bongo's rule has been characterized by intimately close relations with France, the accumulation of vast oil wealth, and personalization of rule. The selection of Bongo as a successor to Gabon's first president, Léon M'ba, was almost certainly arranged by French officials, and Bongo has kept his ties ever since. Bongo is probably one of the wealthiest heads of state in the world as a result of Gabon's considerable oil wealth and a fuzzy line between public and private money. Bongo's one-party rule gave way to ostensible multiparty elections in the 1990s. After a close election in 1993, he has consolidated his power through patronage, corruption, and manipulation. Term limits were removed in 2003, allowing him to remain de facto president for life. Bongo has used his French links, oil wealth, and family connections (he is married to the daughter of Denis Sassou-Nguesso, president of neighboring Congo) to expand his influence well beyond Gabon's borders. Bongo's reputation for corruption and drama includes links to an embezzlement case at French oil company Elf in 2003 and repeated association with international sex scandals involving, among others, an Italian fashion designer and a former Miss Peru.

6. *Jerry Rawlings* is one of Africa's most charismatic and enigmatic characters. A flight lieutenant in the Ghanaian air force—a title he used even after becoming head of state—his rise to president was unlikely and in some ways accidental. During the political chaos in Ghana in the late 1970s he was among a group of disgruntled petty officers imprisoned for mutiny. He was sprung by allies within the military and wound up as leader of a coup in June 1979. His junta executed three former military leaders, but then quickly organized elections and handed power

over to a new civilian administration. But things did not improve, so Rawlings dramatically seized power again eighteen months after the first coup, this time on New Year's Eve. After months of debate and internal maneuvering, Rawlings took the surprising step of embracing economic liberalization and turned to the IMF for help. Over the next decade, Rawlings pushed through one of the most thorough economic reform programs on the continent and oversaw the recovery of the economy after years of steep decline. In the early 1990s Rawlings allowed multiparty elections and was reelected in 1992 and 1996, before retiring in 2000. Although he was accused of involvement in human rights violations early in his reign, Rawlings is probably best known as a quirky reformer prone to passionate, if sometimes undiplomatic, outbursts.

7. *Paul Kagame* is best known as a military strategist who managed Rwanda's recovery back from the 1994 genocide and whose skills enabled his small country to become a major regional player. Like many Tutsis, Kagame fled the country as a child and was raised mainly in Uganda. Kagame became close to and then fought alongside Yoweri Museveni, participating in the ousters of both Idi Amin and Milton Obote. Kagame and other Tutsi exiles created the Rwandan Patriotic Front (RPF) and, after Museveni successfully took power in Kampala, turned their attention back to their homeland. After two failed invasions in the early 1990s, Kagame and the RPF began talks on power sharing with the Hutu-dominated government in Kigali. But once the genocide erupted against Tutsis in April 1994, the RPF invaded again to stop the massacres and drive out the Hutu "Interahamwe" militias responsible. Under Kagame's command, the RPF efficiently swept through the country and seized power within a few months. Pasteur Bizimungu was named president, but Kagame (officially the vice president and minister of defense) was clearly in charge. Kagame continued to pursue the Interahamwe, driving Rwandan forces deeper into Zaire. When it became clear that his neighbor was harboring the militias, he supported Congolese rebels that marched to Kinshasa and overthrew Mobutu. Then, after Kagame became disenchanted with newly installed Congolese president Laurent Kabila, he launched a second war in 1998, and probably would have taken Kinshasa again had Zimbabwean forces not intervened. Kagame's reputation has suffered internationally, however, since he also fell out with Museveni and has been accused of suppressing political opposition at home. Kagame formally became president in 2000 and won reelection in 2003. Although his military adventurism and authoritarian tendencies may have tarnished his image, he remains one of Africa's most influential power brokers.

8. *Meles Zenawi* has been head of state of Ethiopia since 1991 and

has emerged as one of Africa's most prominent leaders. Meles comes from the Tigray region in the far north of Ethiopia and left medical school to join a rebellion in the mid-1970s against the communist regime also known as the "Derg." He rose to become head of the Tigrayan People's Liberation Front (TPLF), one of the main guerrilla groups that eventually overthrew the Derg and its leader, Mengistu Haile Mariam, in May 1991. Meles became the leader of the umbrella ruling party, the Ethiopian People's Revolutionary Democratic Front (EPRDF), and the country's president (and later prime minister). He quickly built a positive international reputation as one of Africa's most intelligent and eloquent leaders. He also took steps to help Ethiopia recover from a difficult economic and political period by building close ties with international donors. Meles, who had worked closely with Eritrean rebels during the insurrection, also allowed Eritrea to formally secede. A 1998 border war with Eritrea, in addition to growing concerns about stalled reforms and growing political repression, however, have damaged his image in the West.

9. *Ibrahim Babangida,* often known by his initials IBB, was the military ruler of Nigeria from 1985 to 1993 but remains one of the most powerful men in Africa. A career military officer from the Muslim north, Babangida overthrew General Muhammadu Buhari in August 1985, promising to halt human rights abuses and to hand power back to civilians soon. IBB proved particularly adept at manipulating Nigeria's political factions and public opinion in his favor—and also at acquiring immense wealth. Babangida sought to stage-manage the transition back to civilian rule, even going so far as to create the two parties to contest elections (which he named "Republicans" and "Democrats") and to even write their platforms. That process (unsurprisingly) failed, and then in relatively free elections held in 1993, Babangida annulled the result, canceling a victory for Mashood Abiola. But under heavy pressure from strikes and protests, IBB stepped down and gave power to a weak interim administration, which was quickly overthrown by Sani Abacha. Babangida has remained a kingmaker in Nigeria, playing a key role in Obasanjo's return to power and clearly still harboring presidential ambitions.

10. *Teodoro Obiang Nguema Mbasogo* is a leader of a small, once barely noticed country that has suddenly been thrust into view by the discovery of oil. Obiang was a military officer under Francisco Macías Nguema, his uncle and Equatorial Guinea's first president. Obiang led a violent coup and killed Macías in 1979 and has been the country's head of state ever since. Obiang heads a regime that is one of the world's most insular, corrupt, and oppressive, but few outsiders took note since the country—a former Spanish colony consisting of the island of Bioko

and the onshore province of Rio Muni wedged between Gabon and Cameroon—was so small and seemingly unimportant. All that changed in the late 1990s with the discovery of large offshore oil reserves. Obiang suddenly found himself in charge of Africa's fastest-growing economy and one of its leading oil producers. The sudden influx of cash has reinforced his rule and unleashed a frenzy of patronage, but also exposed the government to external scrutiny, including links to a scandal where Obiang reportedly arrived at a US bank with millions of dollars in cash. Despite some cosmetic steps to dampen criticism, Obiang's rule remains firm, with a highly restricted press and opposition. The main threat to his continued reign seems to be his own health.

A Potentially Long List

The twenty Big Men presented here merely scratch the surface of Africa's influential leaders, power brokers, and history-makers, which should also be familiar to students and practitioners of development. The list could of course be much, much longer. A cohort of current progressive leaders that are shaping Africa's future include Abdoulaye Wade of Senegal, Thabo Mbeki of South Africa, and Amadou Toumani Touré of Mali, among others. A number of former presidents have played key roles in their country's development but then stepped aside to allow smooth transitions, such as Senegal's Abdou Diof, Sam Nujoma of Namibia, Mozambique's Joaquim Chissano, Ali Hassan Mwinyi of Tanzania, and Botswana's Sir Seretse Khama and Sir Quett Ketumile Masire.

Of course, many of Africa's current Big Men have been in power for an extremely long time and remain so. José Eduardo dos Santos has ruled Angola since 1979; Paul Biya of Cameroon since 1982; Lansana Conté of Guinea since 1984; King Mswati III of Swaziland since 1986; and Blaise Compaoré of Burkina Faso since 1987, to name only a few examples. Some of Africa's Big Men who left power have even managed to return, such as Benin's Mathieu Kérékou, who ruled the country from 1972 until 1991, but came back to power in 1996. Denis Sassou-Ngueso similarly led the Republic of Congo from 1979 until 1992, and returned again in 1997.

Other former Big Men of note who individually altered the course of their own countries include Hastings Kamuzu Banda of Malawi, Sékou Touré of Guinea, Haile Selassie and Mengistu Haile Mariam of Ethiopia, Siad Barre of Somalia, Daniel arap Moi of Kenya, Samuel Doe of Liberia, and Hassan Gouled Aptidon of Djibouti. And Africa has unfortunately had no shortage of notorious Big Men, such as the homicidal Milton Obote of Uganda and the delusional (and possibly cannibalistic) Jean-Bédel Bokassa of the Central African Republic, who crowned himself emperor in a lavish ceremony.

Lastly, not all of Africa's most important leaders have been heads of state or even political. Some economic leaders have been highly influential, such as Ghana's former finance minister Kwesi Botchwey and Uganda's Emmanuel Tumusiime-Mutebile, each of whom were critical to their country's economic trajectory. A few of Africa's most recent Big Men have even gained their influence not through politics, but through business: for example, Sam Jonah, chairman of mining giant AngloGold Ashanti.

What About Big Women?

Africa's political scene has been heavily dominated by men and there are no Big Woman equivalents to Mobutu or Babangida. But this is not to say there have not been prominent women in African politics. Most obviously, Ellen Johnson Sirleaf became Africa's first woman head of state when she was elected president of Liberia in 2005. Sirleaf had been the country's finance minister in the 1980s and later held positions in the UN and World Bank. With one of the toughest jobs ahead of her in rebuilding her war-torn country, the world will be watching closely.

Even if Africa has had only one female president, the continent has no shortage of great women who have become highly influential. One of the early powerful women on record was Mbuya Nehanda, a spirit medium who inspired and led a revolt in 1896 (known as the first *chimurenga)* against European forces in what is now Zimbabwe. More recently, Winnie Mandela is perhaps the best-known African woman and was once considered a potential president of South Africa. Graca Machel, the widow of Mozambique's Samora Machel and Nelson Mandela's second wife, has also become a global leader on a range of international development and education causes.

Several women have successfully risen, if not yet to president, to top political posts, such as Mozambican prime minister Luísa Dias Diogo and former Nigerian finance minister Ngozi Okonjo-Iweala. In Zimbabwe, where many women gained prominence for their roles in the liberation struggle, Joyce Mujuru is vice president and Margaret Dongo is a leading opposition voice. Wangari Maathai, the 2004 winner of the Nobel Peace Prize, is a prominent cabinet member in Kenya. African women have made particular gains in parliaments, especially in Rwanda, Mozambique, and South Africa where they represent at least one-third of the delegates. Despite these notable accomplishments, the sad fact is that women tend not to be among the political leadership in Africa, and in many countries they are not major political forces. The reasons for so few Big Women are complex, but include cultural factors such as a predominance of patriarchal societies, economic factors such as household demands on women that limit their professional opportunities, and pervasive attitudes of sexism.

For Further Reading

There is a vast literature on the nature of politics in Africa. One of the earliest and most influential writings on personal rule in Africa was *Personal Rule in Black Africa: Prince, Autocrat, Prophet, Tyrant* by Robert Jackson and Carl Rosberg (1982). Some of the seminal writings on patrimonialism include Robin Theobald's "Patrimonialism" (1982) and Richard Joseph's *Democracy and Prebendal Politics in Nigeria: The Rise and Fall of the Second Republic* (1987). Among the more recent work that incorporates political economy analysis is *Africa Works: Disorder as Political Instrument* by Patrick Chabal and Jean-Pascal Daloz (1999), Jeffrey Herbst's *States and Power in Africa: Comparative Lessons in Authority and Control* (2000), and Jean-François Bayart's *L'Etat en Afrique: la politique du ventre* (1989), which is also available in English translation as *The State in Africa: The Politics of the Belly* (1993). An edited collection that touches on many aspects of patronage in Africa is Christopher Clapham's *Private Patronage and Public Power: Political Clientalism in the Modern State* (1982). Joel Migdal explains the paradox in his *Strong Societies and Weak States: State-Society Relations and State Capabilities in the Third World* (1988). For a book that draws heavily on the experience in Ghana, see *The Politics of Patronage in Africa: Parastatals, Privatization, and Private Enterprise in Africa* by Roger Tangri (2000). For a discussion of personal rule in Mobutu's Zaire see *The Dialectics of Oppression in Zaire* by Michael Schatzberg (1991).

There are many books and articles on each of the individual Big Men listed above, including multiple autobiographies and collected speeches. Here are listed just a few of the more notable books: Nelson Mandela has authored *Long Walk to Freedom: The Autobiography of Nelson Mandela* (1994) and *The Struggle Is My Life*, which was originally published as a tribute on his 60th birthday in 1978 but is available in more recent revised versions. Kwame Nkrumah wrote several books about revolution and African unity, and his own autobiography is *Ghana: Autobiography of Kwame Nkrumah* (1957). He is also the subject of dozens of books, a recent example of which is David Birmingham's *Kwame Nkrumah: Father of African Nationalism* (1998). Julius Nyerere also wrote multiple books on the subject of socialism and his ideas of *ujamaa*, including *Nyerere on Socialism* (1985). Jomo Kenyatta's most famous work was *Facing Mt. Kenya* (1962). A journalistic account of the final days of Mobutu's rule is Michela Wrong's *In the Footsteps of Mr. Kurtz: Living on the Brink of*

Disaster in Mobutu's Congo (2002). An amusing but also insightful novel about Idi Amin's personal doctor is *The Last King of Scotland* by Giles Foden (1999). Yoweri Museveni's autobiography is *Sowing the Mustard Seed: The Struggle for Freedom and Democracy in Uganda* (1997). Leopold Senghor's poetry and writing are widely available including *The Collected Poetry of Leopold Senghor,* translated by Melvin Dixon (1998). An excellent and highly detailed account of Jerry Rawlings's battle as a small boy against Ghana's traditional Big Men is Paul Nugent's *Big Men, Small Boys and Politics in Ghana* (1995). Another book on Rawlings's personal role in Ghana's recovery is Kevin Shillington's *Ghana and the Rawlings Factor* (1992). A vivid account of rule in imperial Ethiopia and inside the court of Haile Selassie is *Emperor* (1989) by the veteran Polish journalist Ryszard Kapuscinski. Gretchen Bauer and Hannah Britton's *Women in African Parliaments* (2006) and Aili Mari Tripp's *Women and Politics in Uganda* (2000) chart the progress and challenges of integrating women and gender issues into African political life.

4

Violent Conflict and Civil War

VIOLENT CONFLICT HAS BEEN AN UNFORTUNATE FATE FOR many African countries, and is often identified as one of the key reasons for the continent's poor development performance. Conflicts have broken out frequently in Africa, have tended to last a long time, and have often spilled over into neighboring countries. The effects of such violence have been devastating for those affected, their neighbors, and for the continent as a whole. Certain countries, such as Sudan and Angola, have been in an almost perpetual state of war since independence. Armed conflict itself also often played a role in facilitating decolonization, most starkly in Zimbabwe, Namibia, and Mozambique.

Yet painting all of Africa as consumed by war is patently false. Many African countries have no modern experience with any significant outbreak of violence, including Zambia, Botswana, and Malawi. In other countries conflict has been sporadic and contained in relatively small pockets within the country, such as in Ghana, Burkina Faso, Kenya, and Niger. Experiences of recovery are also extremely diverse. Uganda, Rwanda, and Mozambique have recovered robustly from internal war, yet Somalia, Sierra Leone, and Burundi seem to be progressing much more slowly.

Although it is difficult to generalize about conflict in Africa, violence and postconflict reconstruction are major trends shaping the continent's development. This chapter will briefly describe a number of contemporary conflicts in Africa that development students should be familiar with, as well as introduce some of the major issues related to war on the continent, including causes and costs of conflict and the emerging donor strategies for postconflict recovery.

Spectrum of Violence
Africa has experienced the full spectrum of organized violence. Classic interstate war has been relatively rare, but has occurred with Tanzania's invasion of Uganda in 1979, South Africa's incursions into Angola in

the 1930s, and the Ethiopian-Eritrean border war of 1998. Aspects of the Rwandan military's 1997 invasion of Zaire to help overthrow the government and the intermittent tensions between Nigeria and Cameroon over the Bakassi Peninsula are arguably other examples.

However, most conflict in Africa has been internal war involving nonstate actors. These have included full-scale civil wars, such as those in Angola, Côte d'Ivoire, and the Biafran secessionist war in Nigeria, but also many conflicts of lower-level, slow-boil violence, often perpetuated by an insurgency, such as Mozambique's conflict with Renamo or Uganda's current struggle against the Lord's Resistance Army. Lastly, there have also been small, largely contained outbursts of violence from simmering tensions that have not directly involved the state security forces (except to intercede), such as in northern Ghana in the 1990s or the occasional sectarian riots in Nigeria. Most African civil conflicts involve light arms, sometimes little more than AK-47s or even machetes, although the Angolan civil war featured modern fighter jets and set-piece tank battles.

Prevalence of Conflict

At the global level the number of internal conflicts has been declining over the past several decades, but Africa seems to have been moving in

---

Warlordism

Warlordism is an extreme form of alternative authority, where a strongman rules over a territory through the use of force but usually without any formal structure. Warlords are sometimes described as more like a mafia than a rebel force with a political agenda or state security forces. This can happen where the central government is too weak to enforce its will in a particular part of the country or during a civil war where a local militia maintains control. Warlords have appeared in many parts of Sierra Leone, Liberia, Democratic Republic of Congo (DRC), and others where the state has broken down in large parts of the country. Nearly all of Somalia has been controlled by warlords since the dissolution of the central state in 1991. Some warlords, Charles Taylor in Liberia is one example, can take over the whole country and make the transition to head of state. Warlords are an obvious challenge to development since their presence undermines security (why bother building a farm or setting up a business if it is likely to be seized by armed thugs?) and directly threatens the establishment of public institutions (warlords typically chase away government workers and teachers since they want to discourage any other authorities).

Table 4.1   African Countries with Civil War

In the 1960s	In the 1990s
Angola	Angola
Guinea-Bissau	Burundi
Mozambique	Congo, Republic of
Nigeria	Ethiopia
Rwanda	Liberia
Sudan	Mozambique
Uganda	Rwanda
Zaire/DRC	Sierra Leone
	Somalia
	Sudan
	Zaire/DRC

Source: Paul Collier and Anke Hoeffler, World Bank, 2001.

the opposite direction. By one definition of civil war used in the literature (at least 1,000 people killed per year), the number of African countries having a conflict rose from eight in the 1960s to eleven in the 1990s (see Table 4.1).

Contemporary Conflicts

Africa continues to have more than its fair share of conflicts, with a number raging in recent years. Although the exact definitions of such conflicts are fluid and open to debate, the three broad categories are interstate wars, regional conflicts, and internal civil wars/armed insurgencies.

The only major interstate conflict in recent times has been the border war between Ethiopia and Eritrea:

• *Ethiopia-Eritrea.* These two countries began as close allies, with the ruling parties of each having fought together to depose the Marxist regime of Mengistu Haile Mariam in 1991. Just two years later, Eritrea became independent with the blessing of Ethiopia. But tensions between the two increased gradually as political and economic rivalry simmered. The breaking point came in May 1998 when Eritrea moved troops into the border area around Badme, a desolate corner of almost no economic or strategic value. Ethiopia responded to the provocation and a full-scale war broke out, claiming an estimated 70,000 lives. Although an international commission tried to demarcate the border, both countries have continued to disagree, and UN troops have been deployed to keep the two sides apart.

There are at least three large interlocking regional struggles on the continent.

• *Central Africa/DRC.* Sometimes called "Africa's World War," the recent central African conflict has been fought mainly in the eastern parts of the Democratic Republic of Congo (DRC, formerly Zaire), but has directly involved at least seven countries and dozens of various militias. The war was initially sparked by civil war in Rwanda in 1994, when the Rwandan Patriotic Front (RPF) chased the genocidal Interahamwe militia into then Zaire. Once the RPF had regained control of Rwanda and Zaire's Mobutu was seen as protecting the Interahamwe, Rwanda launched an invasion, backed by Uganda and various Congolese factions opposed to Mobutu. The longtime Zairian leader was weak and increasingly isolated, and the Rwandan-backed rebels marched all the way to Kinshasa, deposing him in May 1997 (see Chapter 3). Rwanda then set up a buffer zone along the border and continued to pursue the Interahamwe. But Rwanda fell out with the new Congolese president, Laurent Kabila, and relaunched the war in 1998. This time, Kabila was able to get help as Angola, Namibia, and Zimbabwe sent troops and halted the Rwandan and rebel advance. A stalemate ensued with the country carved up among multiple foreign armies and factions. Meanwhile, Rwanda and Uganda began to attack each other inside DRC, presumably fighting over spoils. In 2002 a nominal peace process got under way, allowing gradual withdrawal of the foreign armies and attempting to build a sustainable political system in DRC. Estimates of the overall death toll from this war are 3–4 million, mostly Congolese civilians.

• *West Africa/Mano River Basin.* As in central Africa, a series of smaller conflicts spilled over and then became interlinked into a larger conflict as parties supported factions across borders in pursuit of an advantage at home and in retribution for another's support. Liberia broke out into civil war in 1989 after Charles Taylor and his Libyan-trained rebels invaded the country from Côte d'Ivoire (see Chapter 3). As Taylor captured territory and eventually power in an election in 1997, he expanded his influence by supporting rebels in Sierra Leone, especially Foday Sankoh's Revolutionary United Front (RUF), which gained control of Sierra Leone's diamond fields and earned a reputation for brutality. Accusing Guinea of supporting another Liberian rebel group, Taylor then helped to launch an insurgency in that country as well. Meanwhile, rebel groups based in Guinea and Liberia moved into Côte d'Ivoire in 2002, helping to plunge that country into civil war. British intervention in Sierra Leone in 2003 has stabilized that country, while Taylor's exile helped to allow a new round of elections in late 2005. But the region remains highly fragile, with insurgencies and refugee flows continuing across all four countries' borders.

• *The Horn of Africa/East Africa.* The internal conflicts across East Africa have become intertwined as countries have tended to both interfere with their neighbors and have little control over their own borders. The collapse of Somalia in 1991 is perhaps the most extreme example of spillover, with armed Somali groups making regular incursions into Kenya and eastern Ethiopia. In return, Ethiopian troops have pursued rebels across the "border" into Somalia and at various times provided arms and support to Somali factions as proxy fighters. The war in Sudan has also provided an opportunity for mutual exchange of rebel support, with Sudan aiding Ugandan and Ethiopian antigovernment groups, while Uganda and Ethiopia have given aid to Sudanese rebels. Tenuous peace processes in Somalia and Sudan have lessened the severity of the fighting and potential for wider regional conflict, but these cross-border complexities remain.

Civil wars and low-level armed insurgencies are the most prevalent type of conflict in Africa. Among the most notable ongoing or recent such conflicts are:

• *Sudan.* Africa's largest country by area, nearly as large as all of Western Europe, has been in some form of civil war since at least the 1950s. For much of the past two decades the northern Muslim elites have dominated the government, while southerners have fought for some form of autonomy. The primary rebel group, the Sudan People's Liberation Front, which had fought for southern autonomy since the early 1980s, reached a fragile peace accord with the government in 2002. Other conflicts, notably in the western region of Darfur, have continued and even accelerated since 2003.

• *Uganda.* In recent years Uganda has faced rebellions on at least two fronts. The notorious Lord's Resistance Army has fought an insurgency in the north since about 1987. This shadowy group, led by Joseph Kony and known for kidnapping children, mixes Christian fundamentalism and traditional mysticism, purportedly aiming to replace Uganda's constitution with the Ten Commandments. In the western parts of the country the government also faces guerrillas based in eastern DRC, some connected to former president Milton Obote's disbanded army.

• *Somalia.* Somalia has a nominal coalition government supported by the UN in the city of Baidoa, but it has little actual control of any territory. Although certain Islamic factions captured the capital Mogadishu in June 2006, the country remains carved up into fiefdoms controlled by various warlords. Outside of the self-declared independent zones of Somaliland and Puntland in the north, low-level conflict continues.

• *Democratic Republic of Congo.* Although much of the internal conflict in DRC involves foreign armies and militias that are still active in the country, there are also numerous armed internal factions battling against the Kinshasa government. A UN-monitored peace accord has been in place since 2002, but there are still regular skirmishes and the long-term political reconciliation process is delicate.

• *Rwanda.* The most recent trauma in Rwanda was the hundred days of organized violence over April–June 1994, in which an estimated 800,000 civilians were murdered. Although the country has mostly been pacified since the Tutsi-dominated RPF seized control after the massacres and many of the Hutu civilians who fled have since returned, it continues to pursue radical militias and the remnants of the Interahamwe inside DRC.

• *Burundi.* Similar to neighboring Rwanda, Burundi has a history of Hutu-Tutsi tension, with outbreaks of major violence in 1972, 1988, and the latest wave since 1993. A peace agreement was signed in 2000 under intense international pressure and mediation from African leaders, including Nelson Mandela, calling for ethnic balancing within politics and the military. Relatively successful elections were held in May 2005, but not all parties have joined the process and the peace remains extremely fragile.

• *Angola.* Angola's civil war began even before independence, but intensified after the Portuguese fled in 1975. The country became one of the hottest proxy sites of the Cold War, with Cuban troops and Soviet hardware aiding the government and US support and South African troops supporting rebels before a 1989 cease-fire agreement and mutual withdrawal. After the country's first-ever multiparty elections were held in 1992, the peace collapsed after the rebel leader, the União Nacional pela Independência Total de Angola's Jonas Savimbi, refused to accept electoral defeat and restarted the war. But the killing of Savimbi in 2002 (probably with the help of US intelligence) enabled a new peace agreement and most rebels came into the government.

• *Côte d'Ivoire.* Once known for its stability under the long reign of Félix Houphouët-Boigny (see Chapter 3), Côte d'Ivoire's political situation gradually deteriorated in the late 1990s. A coup on Christmas in 1999 was the immediate spark. Although elections were held in 2000, and the coupmakers lost, a leading northern candidate was excluded and the country was increasingly divided. Tensions, exacerbated by a north-south religious and ethnic split, broke out into the open in 2002 when rebels launched another coup attempt, igniting the current civil war. A stalemate emerged, with the country roughly divided in half, after French (and later UN) troops intervened in 2003.

• *Nigeria/Niger Delta.* Grievances by local groups in the oil-producing Niger Delta have intensified over a series of issues, including oil spills, disputes over sharing revenue, and local rivalry. A watershed event was the 1995 execution of delta activist Ken Saro Wiwa by then-dictator General Sani Abacha. Despite the return of democratic rule to Nigeria in 1999, rebel groups (and criminal gangs) have been waging a low-level war against the government and oil installations in the area. As a result, large parts of the delta have been militarized and threaten to explode into a wider conflict.

Other conflicts that are simmering or that have recently cooled but threaten to bubble up again include the Casamance region of Senegal, where secessionist rebels in the south have battled the government for independence for two decades. The Republic of Congo has also been a flashpoint, where rebel factions aligned with competing politicians (and with dramatic names like the Cobras and the Ninjas) have fought for control of the capital, Brazzaville. This situation has stabilized somewhat after Angolan troops helped President Denis Sassou-Nguesso pacify most areas of the country. Countries such as Chad, Central African Republic, and Mauritania have long histories of insurgencies and general instability, with the government controlling little of the countryside. Several border areas have also been almost perpetually tense, including the Chad-Sudan border and the Bakassi peninsula, which straddles the Nigerian-Cameroonian border.

Costs of Conflict

There are multiple costs to conflict, not least the terrible human toll. The true number of deaths in Africa caused directly or indirectly by war will never be known, but it is undoubtedly in the millions. The economic costs are also extremely high and can be categorized into four levels:

• *Individuals.* War has a very differential impact on individuals. Politicians and leaders of armed groups can often gain financially through war (which can be a huge incentive for them to keep fighting). The combatants themselves may also do fairly well through pay, looting, and other benefits (although many combatants are involuntarily recruited and only involved because their original livelihood has been destroyed). For the vast majority, especially civilians caught up in the fighting, the impact of war is frequently death or debilitation, with the destruction of property and the disruption of normal farming and trading. Direct battle deaths are often only a tiny fraction of the total war deaths, estimated at only 3 percent in Sudan and 6 percent in

Table 4.2   Estimated Deaths, Selected Conflicts

	Battle deaths	Total war deaths
Angola, 1975–2002	160,475	1.5 million
Nigeria, 1967–1970	75,000	Up to 2 million
Sudan, 1983–2002	55,000	2 million
Democratic Republic of Congo, 1998–2001	145,000	2.5 million

Source: Human Security Centre, *Human Security Report,* 2005.

DRC (see Table 4.2). Psychological trauma can also be substantial given the violence, rape, use of children as soldiers (see the box below), and human trafficking that often are deliberately deployed to break social cohesion.

• *National.* The effects of civil war on an economy are often obvious, with infrastructure damaged, normal activity interrupted, and the labor pool either diverted to fighting or lost from injury and death. One conservative estimate is that a civil war costs an economy as a whole more than 2 percent of GDP for each year of fighting, a figure that accumulates over time. The true economic impact is probably even greater, given the amount of resources diverted to military spending, the costs of reconstruction, and the lingering effects on human health.

• *Regional.* Even if a neighboring country is not dragged into the war, its economy will still be affected through the combined effects of reduced trade, forced migration, spread of disease, and the need to bolster one's own security. One estimate suggests that real GDP growth will be nearly 1 percentage point lower because of war in a neighboring country. This has a huge cumulative effect on Africa, with its multiple borders and hot spots.

• *Global.* Civil conflict in Africa also places a burden on the rest of the world. There are direct costs in terms of spending on peacekeeping and peacemaking, plus even greater indirect costs from lost trade and investment opportunities. In 2005 alone UN peacekeeping operations in Africa cost nearly $4 billion and required over 65,000 military and civilian personnel (see Table 4.3 on page 67). Conflict also appears to contribute to a range of transnational afflictions, such as international crime, drug trafficking, terrorism, and disease.

Causes of Conflict

There is of course no single cause of a particular conflict, or for Africa's frequency of conflicts. Among the reasons most often considered are:

Child Soldiers

One of the most tragic developments in African conflicts has been the use of child soldiers. These youths, who can be as young as eight years old, are usually forcibly recruited and then subjected to brutal treatment designed to cut them off from their previous communities, such as the killing of a family member and the use of drugs and other brainwashing techniques. Although many children serve as porters, sentries, or concubines for adult soldiers, they also are directly involved in combat, making up for their size with modern weaponry. The problem is so widespread that the majority of African conflicts include at least some child soldiers, and perhaps as many as 70 percent of the combatants in civil wars in Sierra Leone and Liberia were under eighteen years old. There are an estimated 30,000 child soldiers in DRC and several thousand more fighting against their will with the Lord's Resistance Army in northern Uganda.

• *State weakness.* In the places where conflict has arisen—such as Sierra Leone or Republic of the Congo—the state has tended to be extremely weak, with the government often controlling little territory outside of the capital (and even there sometimes only during the day). An extreme case would be Somalia, which has seen outright state collapse.

• *Strength of traditional power structures.* The flip side of state weakness is the enduring influence of nonstate authorities, including traditional leaders, warlords, or other kinds of local strongmen that offer sources of power and legitimacy alternative to the state.

• *Poverty.* Deprivation itself seems a major source of violence, with poor countries many times more likely to fall into conflict than rich ones. This may be the case because people are more desperate when they are closer to poverty or when opportunities for people are lower. For example, it may be the case that large numbers of unemployed young men is an enabling factor for war to start.

• *Political struggles over resources.* In an environment of scarce resources, squabbles may break out in the battle over spoils. Much of the fighting in eastern DRC is over control of minerals, such as copper or coltan. Some have postulated that environmental pressures, such as shortages of potable water or fertile land, can also be contributing factors to violence.

• *Non-reconciliatory political systems.* A "winner takes all" system, where those in political power and their supporters "eat" while the rest are excluded, can lead to conflict. Marginalized groups within countries may feel that the political system has no path for them to address grievances or redress injustices, giving them little choice but to turn to organized violence. This is certainly one interpretation of the uprising in the Niger Delta, where local groups feel they are not benefiting from oil production and that their attempts to resolve the dispute peacefully have gone nowhere.

   • *External meddling.* A contributor to conflict in Africa has often been outsiders. This can include other Africans, such as Liberia's Charles Taylor stoking the fire of civil wars in Sierra Leone and Côte d'Ivoire, or world powers, such as US and Soviet support for opposite sides in Angola or an influx of inexpensive light weapons from abroad.

Ethnicity and Conflict

A common explanation for conflict in Africa is ethnicity. In the popular media it is sometimes still called "tribalism," while academics use the more sterile phrase "ethnolinguistic fractionalization" (or often just ELF). Given the diversity of African societies, there are undoubtedly fissures based on culture, language, religion, or family/clan differences underlying many of the continent's outbreaks of violence. This is similarly the case where political control is significantly based on ethnicity, either the exclusive control by one group over the others or a deliberate balance of ethnic groups to maintain a peace. Ethnicity can thus be a supporting or exacerbating factor in many cases of conflict, a tool used by leaders to exploit tensions and hatreds toward other political or economic ends.

   But, like most of the other factors, ethnicity by itself does not explain very much. In fact, much of the historical work on African ethnicity suggests that many of the so-called tribal identities are constructs from colonial times or other social manipulation by politicians. (There is of course a raging debate in most African societies about "authenticity.") In addition, much of the research suggests that very diverse societies are less prone to conflict, but societies with two or three ethnic groups competing for dominance (sometimes called "polarized societies") are more at risk of war. It may also depend on the kind of political systems in a country. Ethnic tensions in a dictatorship may boil over, but in a democratic system they may have other outlets. Some have even argued that ethnic diversity helps build democratic institutions since it forces groups to bargain. Nevertheless, even if the origins and explanatory power of ethnicity are under dispute, appeals to ethnic nationalism do appear to have enormous influence to motivate groups of people, including perpetuating mass violence against others.

Conflict-Underdevelopment Linkages

There also seem to be strong linkages between conflict and underdevelopment—and in both directions. Conflict itself is thought to be a major contributor to Africa's poor economic performance and one reason the continent has fallen farther behind other regions of the globe. Security is considered a crucial prerequisite for development. This is not to say that a small number of people cannot get rich from war (every war has its profiteers), but that for a society to progress and the economy to expand, some semblance of peace is required. People need to feel safe before they invest, trade, and engage in the normal economic activity that will make them and their communities wealthier.

At the same time, underdevelopment itself can create conditions for violence to break out. One of the critical factors used to predict the risk of war is low income. Although the pathways for such a connection are far from obvious, it does make sense that poor people may face different incentives to participate in war (an unemployed youth in rural Burundi may have little to lose and much to gain from becoming a soldier). It may also be the case that poor societies tend to have weaker political institutions to resolve grievances or provide economic opportunities.

The Resource Curse

One factor that many have posited as a contributing factor to conflict in Africa is the presence of natural resources. It appears fairly clear that oil raises a country's chances of plunging into war. The link is less obvious with other commodities such as diamonds or gold, which may also play a role, if not in sparking war then in perpetuating them. Exactly why natural resources have this effect is still far from well understood, but the prevailing ideas suggest that it has something to do with the effect of such products on institutions in a country; if a government can get revenue from oil or gems, it has little reason to develop a relationship with the society, and people who feel they are not getting their fair share usually have few options for peaceful recourse. Small high-value products ("lootable" things) such as diamonds or coltan can also be used to finance civil war, partly explaining the longevity of conflicts in places such as the Mano River Basin or eastern DRC. If the "resource curse" is indeed a major factor, then one way to reduce the risk of conflict is to promote economic diversification.

The International System for Conflict Mitigation

There are a range of international efforts to prevent violent conflict from occurring, to try to end conflict once it starts, and to help rebuild once the shooting is over. Although all of these have been fairly irregular and often improvised, there has been a trend of trying to build more reliable systems—with mixed results. With growing concern among the major powers that "failed states" increasingly pose a threat to global security, such efforts are likely to accelerate.

• *Regional responses*. Individual African leaders, often working through regional organizations such as the Economic Community of West African States (ECOWAS) or the African Union (AU) (see Chapter 11) often mediate potential conflicts or use diplomatic or military means to try to end fighting. Nelson Mandela and South Africa have played an active role in mediating between competing political groups in Burundi to prevent a recurrence of war, while the AU quickly intervened in Togo after the death of longtime president Gnassingbé Eyadéma to reverse a coup and prevent the outbreak of possible civil war. ECOWAS has also been an example of regional operations, having deployed troops to make or keep peace in Liberia, Sierra Leone, Guinea-Bissau, and Côte d'Ivoire. The AU has also launched an ambitious peace and security initiative, but its future remains far from certain.

• *International responses*. The international community has also responded in various ways to African conflict, albeit in an often uneven and ad hoc manner. In 2005 the UN launched a new "Peacebuilding Commission" that is supposed to coordinate the UN's prevention activities. The UN, as well as US diplomats, have been also active in trying to discourage the resumption of the Ethiopian-Eritrean border war. French troops have frequently intervened in its former colonies (usually, but not always, to save the government), while the British played a very active role in Sierra Leone, using paratroopers to enforce a peace and defeat the main rebel group. UN peacekeeping has also been extremely active in Africa, with twenty-two different operations over the past twenty years and seven of the fifteen active UN peacekeeping operations in 2006 (see Table 4.3). A recent example is the UN Mission in Sierra Leone where 18,000 troops had kept the peace from October 1999 until December 2005 at a total cost of some $2.8 billion. The United States and others have also been providing training for African militaries with the aim of creating a standby peacekeeping force for rapid deployment. International donors are also increasingly focused on postconflict reconstruction as both a development issue and as a way to help prevent future conflict. Where necessary, the UN has been able to step in to provide a transitional authority, usually as an interim administration before national elections can be organized.

Although the costs of war are increasingly appreciated, moves toward greater international involvement in African conflicts are not without controversy. Western publics are loathe to commit resources and their own soldiers to faraway places not normally considered to be of vital national interest. At the same time, Africans have worried that some efforts encroach on national sovereignty and sometimes impose unsustainable solutions that may make matters worse. One response has

Table 4.3   Active UN Peacekeeping in Africa, 2006

	Since	Approximate Military and Civilian Personnel	Budget for Fiscal Year 2005/2006
UNMIS (Sudan)	Mar. 2005	8,000	$969m
ONUB (Burundi)	June 2004	6,000	$308m
UNOCI (Côte d'Ivoire)	Apr. 2004	9,000	$438m
UNMIL (Liberia)	Sept. 2003	18,000	$761m
UNMEE (Ethiopia/Eritrea)	July 2000	4,000	$186m
MONUC (DRC)	Nov. 1999	20,000	$1.2bn
MINURSO (Western Sahara)	Apr. 1991	400	$48m

Source: United Nations

been to propose greater external involvement in African conflicts, including some radical solutions such as bringing back UN trusteeship of certain countries that appear unable to govern themselves (effectively redefining the concept of national sovereignty). Another response has been to consider stepping back and intervening less. There is some evidence to suggest that intercession by outsiders can prolong certain conflicts, and perhaps that short-circuiting conflicts through intervention stops the normal process of state building and reconciliation. By this argument, "autonomous recovery" may be the preferable option for building a lasting peace in some African countries.

Postconflict Donor Strategies

External donors have increasingly recognized that postconflict recovery presents special development challenges. As such, the strategy for helping countries after a war is significantly different from that of other low-income countries. There is often talk of building a continuum from immediate humanitarian aid to long-term development. This has forced donors who may have traditionally avoided such situations into new areas, such as the World Bank's recent embrace of "disarmament, demobilization, and reintegration" programs and reform of the police and legal systems in addition to its traditional roles in rebuilding infrastructure and macroeconomic management. In addition, where the regular aid business is moving toward handing out aid based on performance (see Chapter 8), the tactic for postconflict countries is not to wait for things to improve but to engage immediately in the aim of both supporting the peace process and steering the country in the right direction. For example, the World Bank has a special grant window for postconflict countries (a

The Special Case of Genocide

The most extreme case of violence is genocide, which is treated as a separate phenomenon from regular conflict. The UN defines genocide as acts intended to destroy a national, ethnic, or religious group. Social scientists have tended to add that genocide is committed by the state or state elites. Some studies have found that the probability of genocide is highest when autocratic regimes advocate an extreme ideology based on the exclusion of ethnic groups. The most recent cases of genocides in Africa are Rwanda, Burundi, and Darfur in Sudan. Even in these cases the declaration of genocide has not been without controversy, because such a distinction has implications for international action by outsiders: by UN convention, the international community is supposed to intervene to halt genocide. In practice, of course, this has rarely happened.

recent list was Angola, Burundi, DRC, Eritrea, Guinea-Bissau, Republic of Congo, and Sierra Leone), allowing them much more cash than they would otherwise receive. In fact, Africa's largest recipient of World Bank money recently has been not one of its "stars," but rather DRC.

For Further Reading

A useful source for information about conflicts is the International Crisis Group and its website (www.crisisgroup.org), which keeps extensive background information and frequent updates. The *Human Security Report* (2005) is a useful resource for general trends and information tracking global conflict. There are many conflict datasets, including Paul Collier and Anke Hoeffler's dataset for the World Bank's "Economics of Conflict" project, the "Major Episodes of Political Violence" dataset run by Monty Marshall at the University of Maryland's Center for Systemic Peace, and the "Armed Conflict Dataset" produced by Uppsala University and the International Peace Research Institute, Oslo (known as "PRIO").

The essential reading on warlords is William Reno's *Warlord Politics and African States* (1998). Collier and Hoeffler have also written extensively about the various costs and causes of conflict, including "Greed and Grievance in Civil War" (2001). Other studies include "Why Are There So Many Civil Wars in Africa? Understanding and Preventing Violent Conflict" by Ibrahim Elbadawi and Nicholas Sambanis (2000), "Greed, Grievance, and Mobilization in Civil Wars" by Patrick Regan and Daniel Norton (2005), and James Fearon's "Primary Commodity Exports and Civil War" (2005).

The issue of ethnicity and war are dealt with by Fearon and David

Laitin in "Ethnicity, Insurgency, and Civil War" (2003). Two books that seek to dispel the myths of "tribalism" are Crawford Young's *The Politics of Cultural Pluralism* (1976) and Leroy Vail's *The Creation of Tribalism in Southern Africa* (1989). The issue of child soldiers is dealt with comprehensively by P. W. Singer in *Children at War* (2005). A recent novel told from the perspective of a child combatant is Uzodinma Iweala's haunting *Beasts of No Nation* (2005).

An excellent overview of the resource curse is "What Do We Know About Natural Resources and Civil War?" by Michael Ross (2004). Terry Lynn Karl's *The Paradox of Plenty: Oil Booms and Petro-States* (1997) tackles the issue of why oil-rich states may be among the worst economic performers. A related argument is made about the link between conflict and environmental scarcity in Thomas Homer-Dixon's *Environment, Scarcity, and Violence* (2001).

Two edited volumes on international efforts to help build peace are *Turbulent Peace: The Challenges of Managing International Conflict,* edited by Chester Crocker, Fen Olser Hampson, and Pamela Aall (2001), and *Ending Civil Wars: The Implementation of Peace Agreements*, edited by Stephen Stedman, Donald Rothchild, and Elizabeth Cousens (2002). A useful overview of the links between economic activities during war and prospects for the postwar environment is "The Legacies of War Economies: Challenges and Options for Peacemaking and Peacebuilding" by Heiko Nitzschke and Kaysie Studdard (2005). A critique of the international system is Steven Krasner's "Sharing Sovereignty: New Institutions for Collapsed and Failing States" (2004). The autonomous recovery argument is best outlined by Jeremy Weinstein in "Autonomous Recovery and International Intervention in Comparative Perspective" (2005).

For a look inside US diplomatic efforts at peacemaking in Africa, see the memoirs of two former assistant secretaries of state, Chester Crocker's *High Noon in Southern Africa: Making Peace in a Rough Neighborhood* (1993) and Herman Cohen's *Intervening in Africa: Superpower Peacemaking in a Troubled Continent* (2000). An examination of trends in African efforts at peacekeeping can be found in "African Capacity-Building for Peace Operations: UN Collaboration with the African Union and ECOWAS" by Victoria Holt and Moira Shanahan (2005).

On the growing trend toward taking weak and fragile states as a foreign policy issue for the West, see Stewart Patrick's "Weak States and Global Threats: Fact or Fiction?" (2006), the UK Department for International Development's "Why We Need to Work More Effectively in Fragile States" (2005), and the Commission on Weak States and U.S. National Security report, *On the Brink: Weak States and U.S. National Security* (2004).

On the evolution of international donor strategies, see "Post-Conflict Recovery in Africa: An Agenda for the Africa Region" by Sergio Michailof,

Markus Kostner, and Xavier Devictor (2002), the World Bank's "World Bank Group Work in Low-Income Countries Under Stress: A Task Force Report" (2002), and Collier and Hoeffler's *Breaking the Conflict Trap: Civil War and Development Policy* (2003).

There is abundant literature on genocide. For an investigation into the causes of genocide, see Barbara Harff's "No Lessons Learned from the Holocaust? Assessing Risks of Genocide and Political Mass Murder Since 1955" (2003). Samantha Power explores the United States' responses to genocide in *A Problem from Hell: America and the Age of Genocide* (2003). For African country cases, see René Lemarchand's *Burundi: Ethnic Conflict and Genocide* (1994), Mahmood Mamdani's *When Victims Become Killers: Colonialism, Nativism, and the Genocide in Rwanda* (2001), Michael Barnett's *Eyewitness to a Genocide: The United Nations and Rwanda* (2003), and Gerard Prunier's *Darfur: The Ambiguous Genocide* (2005).

5

Political Change and Democratization

DESPITE VAST DIVERSITY AMONG AFRICAN COUNTRIES, contemporary political trends tend to come in large waves that sweep over the continent with remarkable uniformity. Independence occurred in the majority of countries within a few years of each other. Nearly all newly sovereign African rulers then quickly moved to establish one-party states. Then, in the late 1980s and early 1990s, most African countries moved to create or reestablish some form of multiparty democracy, or at least the appearance of such a change. Given the concomitant rise of ideas about governance, the links between political change and economic progress have also gained prominence in the development literature. This chapter sets out some of the broad trends, concepts, and players related to African democracy.

One-Party States
The transition to independence was in almost every case accompanied by an election to establish an indigenous African government to replace the colonial authorities. But in many cases—Côte d'Ivoire, Malawi, Kenya, and Zambia, to name but a few—the eventual winner banned or severely hampered any legal opposition and sought to entrench the ruling party as the sole political player. In other countries, such as Ghana and Nigeria, repeated military coups followed the establishment of the one-party state, bringing bouts with military dictatorships and often heavy constraints on political parties. A few countries, such as Angola and Mozambique, had never had elections and the dominant guerrilla movement simply moved into the capital as colonial authorities left. Regardless of how they started, the results were starkly similar. With few exceptions, African states put strict legal limits on political organization and on the rights of assembly and speech throughout the 1970s and 1980s. In many countries, the only legal newspapers or television were state-owned and often controlled explicitly by the ruling party for

71

propaganda purposes. By the mid-1980s, there were few real multiparty democracies on the continent, with Botswana and Mauritius being the most prominent exceptions.

Wave of the 1990s

Within a decade, nearly all African countries had held new elections with at least two competing parties. The major transitions resulting from elections in this period, of course, were the first multiracial elections held in Namibia in 1989 and in South Africa in 1994. For the most part in the rest of Africa, however, these early elections did not result in changes in leadership. A few exceptions to this include Zambia, where Frederick Chiluba and his union-based opposition party beat Kenneth Kaunda; Malawi's Bakili Muluzi, who defeated longtime dictator Hasting Banda; and Nicephore Soglo's (one-term) victory over Mathieu Kerekou in Benin. Perhaps more important than the results of these elections were changes in the political environment. Many of the most egregious laws restricting freedom of association or banning public criticism of the president were rescinded. Political parties were generally allowed to organize and campaign. Leaders were no longer considered presidents for life, and in most cases some constitutional term limits were introduced. Freeing of the media allowed an explosion of independent newspapers, private radio stations, and an avenue for citizens to vent against the government through popular talk radio. (Some of the absurd laws, such as Malawi's bans on long hair for men or on women showing their ankles in public, were also lifted.) In many countries, the lid of authoritarianism was blown off and people were allowed to form new groups to openly compete for power and influence.

Adaptable Autocrats and Hybrid Regimes

Despite the nearly universal, if incomplete, liberalization of the political scene, most of the ruling parties and political leaders did not lose power. Instead, they adapted to the new environment and learned how to survive, even when facing a potentially hostile electorate. In some cases, the ruling party did appear to maintain credibility in the eyes of the majority and were able to legitimately win reelection. Examples of this might include the ruling Chama cha Mapinduzi in Tanzania or Frelimo in Mozambique. But for many others, political elites simply found ways to win elections through expanded patronage, co-option, or even theft. This could occur through vote buying, deal making with potential opponents, unofficial harassment or disruption of the opposition, manipulation of voter rolls, and, when necessary, outright electoral fraud. In effect, many African countries introduced regular elections every four or five years, but political systems often continued to operate more like authoritarian regimes, what political scientists have called "hybrid regimes."

In some ways these trends might be dismissed as normal growing pains of young nations and new political systems, or as the lingering habits of elites who are understandably resisting their loss of power and privilege. There has even been some backsliding, such as constitutional changes to repeal term limits in Togo, Gabon, Guinea, and Uganda, allowing presidents to extend their rule. (Similar repeals were considered in Malawi, Namibia, and elsewhere.) But at the same time, the erratic nature of political trends in Africa is also a sign that new ideas of citizen participation and the institutions that support democratic governance simply will take time to emerge. In fact, there is some evidence that, even where the first or second multiparty election allows the ruling party to remain in place, the pressure for more open politics eventually results in change. After twice reelecting Jerry Rawlings in Ghana, voters rejected his handpicked successor and elected the opposition in 2000. That same year Senegal elected Abdoulaye Wade as president, the first time in the country's forty-year history that the leader was not from the Socialist Party. Kenya, after twice reelecting Daniel arap Moi in disputed national elections, voted Mwai Kibaki and his umbrella opposition movement into power in 2002. But in many cases (including both Kenya and Ghana), the "new" political leaders from the opposition are actually recycled old politicians who were at one point in the past part of the former ruling party. The result has often been disappointment with opposition movements that have generally failed to live up to expectations after taking power.

External Factors

The transition to more open politics and competitive multiparty elections has its roots in changes both internal to Africa and in the global context. The fact that so many elections occurred within a short time and that so many countries followed similar paths suggests that external conditions were critically important. The timing so close to the fall of the Berlin Wall in 1989 hints that the end of the Cold War was likely a significant factor. Both the Soviet Union and the West had supported many authoritarian regimes to gain allies and prevent the other from gaining further influence. But once Angola and Ethiopia could no longer count on the USSR for military and economic help, or similarly Kenya or Zaire on the West, the external support for their rule weakened significantly. In fact without the Cold War concerns, other agendas within Europe or North America, such as promotion of human rights or democracy, rose up the chain of priorities, giving further impetus to a prodemocracy push from the outside. Not only were Mobutu and Moi no longer protected, but left without any real geostrategic value they instead became targets. Donor funds, once given with the tacit knowledge they were little more than bribes to keep leaders' allegiance, increasingly came with explicit political conditions.

Internal Pressures for Change

Pressure for political change also was—and still is—brewing from within. Most African states were facing deep economic crises and a waning ability to manage political stability in the old style. Political movements, including parties, labor unions, and civic groups, also began to more directly challenge the authorities and agitate for greater freedoms. Ordinary Africans were becoming increasingly educated and urbanized, encouraging more organized opposition, growing demands from a citizenry fed up with corruption, and burgeoning popular expectations. The political changes under way in Eastern Europe—combined with modern communication that allowed Africans to witness such changes for themselves on television—created a demonstration effect and added to hopes that similar changes could happen in their countries. As time wore on, the memories of the anticolonial struggle, which tended to bring credibility and stature to the leadership, have also waned. Demographic trends are a critical factor; as populations grow and become younger on average, fewer and fewer citizens have any direct memory of the independence movements, while more and more of those born after independence gain the vote. This combination of global geostrategic trends and internal upheaval and pressure for change are materially transforming the model of African governance, but this is a process that will remain ongoing and unpredictable. (Democratization has been messy everywhere else, so why should Africa be any different?)

Democracy and Liberalism

Political liberalization and democratization are not exactly the same thing. Liberalization is removal of restrictions on political participation, whereas democracy refers to a specific form of government where people have the ultimate say in who runs the state and how it operates. Liberalization may, in practice, lead to democratization but not necessarily. Most often when activists in the West speak of democracy or democracy building, they are referring to liberal democracy, a form of government based on individual rights and private property. In such a system, the purpose of the state is to protect and enforce these rights. Central to the concept of liberal democracy are other ideas, such as equality under the law, due process, checks and balances, protection of minorities, and freedom of expression. These ideas tend to be represented in particular institutions, such as an executive constrained by a written constitution, a legislature, an independent judiciary, and regular elections to select leaders. Outside of the state, it is also thought necessary to have an open and free media, alongside an active and engaged civil society.

In most African countries both the concepts of liberal democracy and its typical institutions may be unfamiliar or at least fairly new. This suggests several lines of criticism of those who promote liberal democracy on the continent. Some ideas behind liberalism, especially conceptions of the individual, are alien in many African cultures. Liberal democracy is thought by many to be an imported concept that might not apply well in African societies, and politicians have often used this in the past to justify one-party states, claiming that ethnic rivalries will turn violent in a multiparty system. Ideas of tolerance and protection of minorities also sometimes clash with African views of authority, which may be based on deference, patronage, and the raw exercise of power. Despite the sometimes large gap between the language of liberalism and the actual attitudes and modes of governance across much of Africa, the march of democracy does appear to be moving toward a more liberal order, if in fits and starts.

Elections vs. Democracy

One common critique of democratization efforts in Africa is the overemphasis on elections. Elections themselves are the most visible event in a democracy, are normally the means to select political leaders, and are one of the main ways in which an electorate can make a judgment on a politician's performance. Thus, elections can be high-profile milestones in a political transition and a way to get rid of unpopular elites. For all these reasons, many donors have focused their efforts on the electoral process. This has resulted in vast improvements in the management of elections, such as voting procedures, compilation of voter rolls, counting, and oversight. But encouraging the mechanics of an election is much different from promoting ideas and values of liberalism. In many ways the idea of a liberal democracy operating in sub-Saharan Africa requires not a mere change in formal arrangements, but a wholesale social transformation—a change that undoubtedly also brings upheaval and conflict with the preexisting order. Political evolution in the West was no different; the process of state formation and the rise of liberalism in Europe were neither easy nor smooth, but rather violent and erratic. This also means, in the short term, that democratization in Africa will be highly imperfect, will certainly move backwards in places, and can increase instability.

Alternative Legitimacy

One possible reason democracy has not taken hold more firmly across Africa is because the continent is far from a *tabula rasa*. All African societies have structures of authority, nearly all of which gain legitimacy through means other than elections. Whereas the liberal model views each individual as autonomous acting in their own interest (in theory, if not in practice), alternative forms of authority still dominate most of Africa, especially those based on ethnicity, patronage, or violence. For every Big Man that rules a whole country, there are thousands of "little Big Men" who run the villages and neighborhoods. Such alternative authorities run the gamut from warlord to chief to mere gang leader. They gain their legitimacy and loyalty from the population for a range of reasons, such as hereditary chiefdom, money, or often fear. One common feature of these "strongmen" is that they offer an alternative to the central state and have no need for elections. In many cases, strongmen co-opt state structures or even take formal positions within the state (e.g., local governor or local party head). But their means of governance nevertheless differ dramatically from the liberal model based on individual rights and the selection by the people of their leaders. Indeed, even when elections are free and fair, many people will take cues from the local strongman, resulting in the common pattern of extremely high voting concentration.

Ethnic or Religious Cleavages and Democracy

There are multiple cultural, physical, and social cleavages among African societies, and their divisions heavily influence political organization, and hence the trajectory of political change. Ethnicity is perhaps the most obvious form of alternative social organization that many view as a threat to the establishment of democracy. ("Tribalism" is a similar concept, but it is a loaded word that is generally avoided in the academic and development literature.) This is because ethnic identity often determines political identity and, at times, has been a contributor to violent conflict (see Chapter 4). Indeed, the tendency for political parties to organize along ethnic lines and the history of ethnic-based fighting in many countries were prime reasons given by leaders for instituting one-party states under a banner of "national unity." Although such reasoning was convenient for leaders keen to tighten their grip on power, it was not without basis. Most of the past and current conflicts in Africa have had some ethnic or linguistic component. Many of the alternative authorities also use ethnic chauvinism as a means to bind the group, such as the ethnic-based youth gangs of Brazzaville (with intimidating names like the Cobras and Ninjas) or the multiple militias operating throughout the eastern regions of the Democratic Republic of Congo.

The impact of ethnicity on democratic transitions has tended to fall along a continuum. At one end is the denial of ethnicity. In countries where one ethnic group clearly dominates, either demographically or by control of the military and arms of the state, there has been a tendency not to formally recognize ethnicity in state structures. In countries such as Angola or Mozambique, ethnicity was officially denigrated as backward, while in Zimbabwe the ruling party has tried to co-opt minority group leaders (with some success). In the middle are countries with multiple smaller ethnicities where politics is often about bargaining among the various ethnic groups to ensure a balance. In Ghana and Kenya, for example, there are ethnic biases in the political parties, but stability is maintained by building coalitions across ethnic lines or apportioning positions of authority across influential groups. At the other end of the spectrum are countries that openly embrace the realties of ethnicity within the country and try to adapt to the state. This might include allowing local autonomy for chiefs or, in the cases of Ethiopia and Nigeria, formal federalism, where much of the power lies in regional states. (Although the definitions of the "regions" are geographical, the ethnic undercurrents are undeniable.) South Africa has probably gone the farthest along the route of embracing ethnic diversity, delegating large amounts of authority to the provinces and recognizing eleven official languages.

Another social division that seems particularly politically salient is religion. There has been a clear rise of Islamic parties along the East African coast and in the Sahel. Many of the countries along the West Africa coast—especially Côte'd'Ivoire and Nigeria—have regional political dynamics that appear north-south, but also have a strong Muslim-Christian element. The Islamic Party of Kenya and the Civic United Front in Tanzania have both gained popularity among Muslim populations and increased the potential for religious tension in those countries. In Nigeria, where Islamic fundamentalism is on the rise in the north, there have been bouts of violence that were openly about religion, such as the 2000 riots in Kaduna that killed perhaps two thousand people. This is not to say that religious diversity cannot coexist peaceably with emerging democracy, and in fact religious conflict is probably more the exception than the rule in Africa. Ethiopia has had substantial Christian and Muslim populations for centuries and very little religion-based strife. Malawi's president from 1994 to 2004 was Bakili Muluzi, a

Key Participants in Democratization

- *Political elites.* The most influential actors in democratization remain the incumbent political leaders and their allies, including presidents, cabinet members, and the many power brokers that gain their influence via their connection to the leadership.
- *Political parties.* Both ruling and opposition parties are increasingly significant as formal political bodies challenging each other in elections. Opposition parties or umbrella movements that aggregate multiple opposition groups under one banner are frequently the focal point for organized political change.
- *Civil society.* This is a broad term that includes any organized group of citizens outside the state. Typically, the kinds of groups under this heading are labor unions, professional organizations, and any kind of NGO. Although such groups are frequently romanticized and their impact often exaggerated, they do appear to be increasingly influential in terms of setting the agenda and holding government officials accountable for their actions. In the African context, the most powerful elements in "civil society" (although the term is rarely applied to them) are often ethnic, clan, or familial groups, whereby people identify more strongly along these lines than with groups formed around an issue or professional affiliation.
- *External donors.* Most of the major international donors are involved in one way or another in democracy promotion. The United States is perhaps the least subtle about its efforts and the most willing to use overt language. The United States Agency for International Development (USAID) has a "democracy and governance" unit and the National Endowment for Democracy (NED) is publicly funded and directly involved in democracy promotion. NED also finances the International Republican Institute and the National Democratic Institute, which are linked to the major US parties and train political parties in developing countries.
- *International organizations.* A range of regional and international organizations are involved in election assistance and monitoring. The UN can help to organize elections in a postconflict situation, while most of the regional groupings in Africa and Europe (e.g., the Southern African Development Community [SADC], the AU, the EU, and the Commonwealth) send election monitoring teams. The SADC has also established certain regional standards for elections, although there are no enforcement mechanisms and early indicators suggest that they are having little effect (see Chapter 11).
- *International NGOs.* Several NGOs act as watchdogs for various aspects of governance, such as Transparency International, which ranks countries every year based on corruption perception surveys, or the Committee to Protect Journalists, which reports on press freedom. There are also hundreds of NGOs involved in all aspects of democracy promotion, including voter education, party organization, polling, election technical assistance, and election monitoring. To name just two examples: the Carter Center at Emory University is often considered a critical international stamp of approval that an election process has been "free and fair," and the International Foundation for Electoral Systems is a leading provider of poll-worker training and election infrastructure (ballot boxes, voter roll software systems, etc.).

Muslim who remained popular in a Christian-majority country that was able, for the most part, to avoid religious-based division.

Capitalism and Democracy

There are vast and long-standing debates about the links between political and economic change, much of which considers the relationship between liberal versions of each: market capitalism and liberal democracy. Descriptively, much of Africa, both during and after the colonial period, has had distinctly illiberal forms of both systems. The economic sphere has been highly state-centered and the political space has also been dominated by a handful of elites employing authoritarian means of control. But analysts are still unclear about the direction of causality, e.g., under what circumstances might the achievement of one encourage movement toward the other, and—from a policy proscription perspective—how to promote both in tandem.

The Western historical experience appears to show that democracy grew out of internal demands, especially the emergence of an increasingly prosperous middle class that wanted to expand their own political freedoms as well. However, in Africa it seems that, at least recently, the demands from internal groups for political openness are largely rooted in frustration over economic failure and resentment over corruption. Indeed, there are few cases on the continent of a middle class as a meaningful and politically influential force. Instead, the process of political liberalization seems driven primarily by elites, either incumbent politicians, who obviously have a stake in engineering democratization to their advantage, or opposition leaders (also elites) who use democratization primarily as a means to power. This may partly explain why so many former dictators have survived the wave of elections in the 1990s (e.g., Omar Bongo, Robert Mugabe, Denis Sassou-Nguesso) and, where there has been a turnover in leadership (e.g., Malawi, Zambia, Nigeria), the modes of governance have not been fundamentally altered.

Although activists have typically viewed democracy and capitalism as mutually reinforcing, this is far from the case in many African countries where both transitions are fraught with incentive problems for those involved. Indeed, in some cases, democracy and capitalism can appear to be in contradiction. The new demands to win elections can lead to populist decisionmaking that puts off the long-term structural changes that might be required for capitalist development to flourish, such as lifting price controls or restructuring a bloated civil service. At the same time, the idea that economic change requires a soft authoritarian touch has increasingly lost credibility, especially since many of the "reforming dictators" seem to lose momentum and fall back into old antidevelopment patterns.

Regime Type and Economic Performance

The debates over democracy and economic reform have also spurred research into whether democracies perform better in economic terms than autocracies. The anecdotal evidence, especially the experiences from fast-growing East Asia, suggested that authoritarian regimes were more likely to be able to manage high levels of economic growth. This ran counter to the thrust of liberal theory and the emerging governance agenda, which tended to suggest that feedback from the population was required to keep countries on course. A series of cross-country statistical analyses were conducted to compare the performance of democratic and authoritarian regimes. The results were mostly mixed and, despite methodological and measurement problems in all the studies, the conclusion drawn has been that economic performance does not seem to be affected by regime type alone. Nevertheless, these debates have had a major impact on Africa, with donors sometimes allowing extra latitude to authoritarian rulers who seem to be performing well (e.g., Ghana's Jerry Rawlings or Uganda's Yoweri Museveni) or using economic stagnation as a reason to encourage political change (e.g., Kenya under Daniel arap Moi).

Governance and the Language of Democratization

Despite sometimes unclear evidence about the link to economic growth, most of the donors—and the major ones are all solid democracies themselves—do favor democratic governments. The national bilateral aid agencies and NGOs are more explicit in their language when they promote democratic principles and institutions in Africa. The World Bank, however, is bound by its charter to deal only with economic or technical issues and not to get involved in politics directly. In practice, of course, this distinction is pure semantics. On the one hand, all of the Bank's work is deeply political since the economic reform agenda fundamentally affects the political balance and, especially in patrimonial political systems, access to resources. In this sense, the Bank has always been intimately involved in politics, even if it denies doing so.

On the other hand, the economics and development field has increasingly recognized that political institutions are critical factors in economic success and that bad politics is a major reason why reform plans so often fail to be implemented as expected. Therefore, the Bank and other donors have concluded that they must get more directly involved in political systems and reform of public administration if their economic strategies have any hope of achieving some positive developmental results. To get around its restricted mandate, the Bank uses technocratic language to describe aspects of democracy without ever refer-

---

Basic Governance Terms

Good governance: the exercise of power in the management of economic and social resources that leads to improved developmental outcomes

Transparency: access to timely, reliable, and relevant information about public activities and finances

Accountability: the ability of civil society to hold public officials responsible for their actions and performance

Participation: the inclusion of wide segments of society in decision-making

---

ring to it explicitly. Thus, the emphasis is not on government, democracy, and elections but rather on governance, accountability, transparency, and participation.

Measures of Democracy

There are many ways to measure political trends, but all are imperfect. The number of elections is one indicator of democracy and one frequently used to show that Africa seems to be moving toward more open political systems. But since democracy is much more than merely a poll every four or five years, analysts have also tried to measure aspects of democratic freedoms, such as protection of human rights or freedom of speech. One notable attempt at this is the "Freedom in the World" index produced annually by Freedom House. Their index scores each country in terms of "political rights" and "civil liberties" on a scale of 1–7, then averages the two. (Using their scale, "free" is 2.5 or less, "not free" is 5.5 or more.) The recent results for Africa are summarized in Table 5.1.

Governance Peer Review

Another recent attempt by Africa to rate itself on governance is the African Peer Review Mechanism. This is a voluntary program sponsored by the New Partnership for Africa's Development (NEPAD) (see Chapter 11), where countries submit to be judged by a group of eminent Africans on their progress toward meeting agreed governance standards. The idea is to make assessments in four areas: (1) democracy and political governance, (2) economic governance and management, (3) corporate governance, and (4) socioeconomic development. Although this is a work in progress and there is rightful skepticism that the process will lead to meaningful changes, it is nonetheless an important step forward that governments have agreed to be evaluated by their peers rather than hide behind national sovereignty as an excuse for tyranny and mismanagement.

Table 5.1   Freedom House Status, 2004

Free	Partly Free	Not Free
Benin	Burkina Faso	Angola
Botswana	Burundi	Cameroon
Cape Verde	Comoros	Central African Republic
Ghana	Congo, Republic of	Chad
Lesotho	Djibouti	Congo, Dem. Republic
Mali	Ethiopia	Côte d'Ivoire
Mauritius	Gabon	Equatorial Guinea
Namibia	Gambia, The	Eritrea
São Tomé & Príncipe	Guinea-Bissau	Guinea
Senegal	Kenya	Mauritania
South Africa	Liberia	Rwanda
	Madagascar	Somalia
	Malawi	Sudan
	Mozambique	Swaziland
	Niger	Togo
	Nigeria	Zimbabwe
	Seychelles	
	Sierra Leone	
	Tanzania	
	Uganda	
	Zambia	

Source: "Freedom in the World," Freedom House, 2004.

For Further Reading

There are a huge number of books and articles on democratization and political liberalization in Africa. The *Journal of Democracy*, published by the National Endowment for Democracy, is a quarterly dedicated to the theory and practice of democratization and includes many articles on sub-Saharan Africa, including "Africa's Range of Regimes" by Nicolas van de Walle (2002) and special editions on Africa (1998) and Francophone Africa (2001). The *Journal of Democracy* also published *Democratization in Africa* (1999) by Larry Diamond and Marc Plattner, which gives both an overview of trends in the 1990s and several country case studies. *Democratic Experiments in Africa: Regime Transitions in Comparative Perspective* by Michael Bratton and Nicolas van de Walle (1997) explains political trends in Africa and explores the determinants of success or failure of democratization. An excellent edited volume is Richard Joseph's *State, Conflict, and Democracy in Africa* (1999), which contains chapters by many of the most prominent Africanist academics, including Crawford Young, Richard Sklar, and Goren Hyden. Also of note is Pierre Englebert's *State Legitimacy and Development in Africa* (2000). Of the hundreds of

articles on political change, three good examples of the state of the litera-
ture include Michael Schatzberg's "Power, Legitimacy, and
Democratisation in Africa" (1993), Jeffrey Herbst's "The Structural
Adjustment of Politics in Africa" (1990), and "Democracy in Africa" by
Joel Barkan and David Gordon (1998).

The classic text on the middle class and the rise of democracy in the
West is Barrington Moore's *Social Origins of Dictatorship and Democracy:
Lord and Peasant in the Making of the Modern World* (1966). The major
survey of studies on the relationship between regime type and economic
performance is "Political Regimes and Economic Growth" by Adam
Przeworski and Fernando Limongi (1993). A much more comprehensive
book by the same authors (and two others) that covers the democracy-devel-
opment nexus in more breadth is *Democracy and Development: Political
Institutions and Well-Being in the World, 1950–1990* (2000).

The watershed World Bank publication marking its embrace of governance is *Sub-Saharan Africa: From Crisis to Sustainable Growth: A Long-
Term Perspective Study* (1989). The World Bank's *World Development
Report 1997: The State in a Changing World* is another example of the evolution of donor thinking on governance. For an analysis of some of the contradictions in the donors' good-governance agenda, see "The State,
Structural Adjustment, and Good Government" by Richard Jeffries (1993)
and Pierre Landell-Mills' "Governance, Cultural Change, and
Empowerment" (1992).

PART 2

Core
Development Questions

6

Africa's Slow-Growth Puzzle

AT THE DAWN OF INDEPENDENCE, AFRICA'S ECONOMIC PROSPECTS
were considered bright. For the most part, Africa's economies had built
a modest foundation, usually in mining or farming, that was thought
could be expanded and leveraged toward more rapid industrialization.
Instead, most African economies faltered, with only a few making real
progress and with many falling backwards. Economic growth was barely able to keep up with population growth; on nearly half of the continent the average person was poorer in 2000 than they were in 1970.
African industrialization was essentially a complete failure, and few
countries have successfully made the transition beyond a skeleton of the
inherited colonial economy. More recently, there are hopeful signs that
much of the continent is perhaps again on a more positive growth path.
But there are no clear answers as to why Africa has performed so poorly
in the past—and little agreement on what exactly needs to be done for
Africa to grow more rapidly in the future. This is not to say that there
are not a lot of possible answers to Africa's "growth tragedy," in fact the
list of potential suspects is long. This chapter lays out some of the main
explanations for Africa's disappointing growth performance over the
past half century and the parallel evolution of the proposed remedies.
The main conclusion is less a search for solutions than an illumination
of how little is yet understood.

Real GDP Growth

"Economic growth" is an increase in the value of production and income
for a given geographical space. It is used to indicate levels of economic
activity and is typically measured as the yearly change in gross domestic
product (GDP) for a country. "Nominal GDP" uses current prices and
does not account for inflation, while "real GDP" uses constant prices
and does adjust for inflation. To measure economic growth, you must
use the latter over time to get a sense of the "real" changes in the econo-

my. Therefore, saying that Chad's real GDP growth in 1992 was 6.1 percent (it was) means that the total economic production of the country rose by that amount over the previous year. Another common way to measure economic activity is to look at changes per person by dividing real GDP by the total population, giving you real GDP per capita (usually converted into US dollars to allow comparability, and often adjusted again to reflect local purchasing power). This can also be compared year to year, giving a "real GDP per capita growth rate." If Kenya's real GDP grows by 2.5 percent in a given year, for example, but the population also grows by 2.5 percent, then real GDP per capita growth is 0 percent. Even though the economy has expanded, so too has the population and, on average, no one is better off.

A related, slightly different measure of GDP also commonly used is gross national income (GNI), which also captures income earned abroad. GDP and GNI are often used interchangeably, which is technically wrong but in practice usually makes little difference. (To add to the confusion, GNI is identical to gross national product or GNP, but the latter is no longer commonly used.) Even though none of these measures are very precise in Africa (especially since much of the "real" economic activity is informal and not covered by formal GDP), they do give a fairly good indication of whether things are getting better or worse, and roughly by how much.

Why Growth Matters

Economic growth is, of course, not the same as development, but they are very closely related concepts. Real GDP or GNI per capita is the most basic measure of an economy's level of advancement: "developed countries" are those with high production or income per capita and "least-developed" are those with the lowest. For example, in 2004 Niger's GNI per capita was $230, while Canada's was $28,390. Countries with fast-growing GDPs are improving and getting wealthier more quickly than those with slower rates of growth. Countries with negative growth rates are seeing their economies erode rather than expand and, on average, people must be getting poorer. Unfortunately, about half of Africa's countries experienced negative per capita growth rates between 1970 and 2000. That is, in those countries people were on average poorer in 2000 than they were thirty years earlier.

There are, of course, many other ways to measure and define development, and there has been frequent criticism that economists and policymakers overemphasize growth at the expense of other indicators, such as quality of life (see Chapter 10). But economic growth is still an extremely useful concept, both as a marker and as a goal.

• *Useful indicator*. Change in GDP is almost certainly the best single measure we have, no matter what definition of development is preferred. This is not true because money is more important than other things, but because income can actually tell us a lot about how well people live.

• *Wealthier is better*. Income is closely related to other outcomes that everybody thinks are important, such as health. When one rises, the other usually does too, and the same goes for declines (not always, of course, but on average). Such a relationship appears to be true at the individual level (e.g., richer people have more access to resources needed to achieve a better life), and also seems the case for societies as a whole (e.g., wealthier societies have more resources and opportunities to provide for people).

• *Growth creates opportunities*. Higher growth rates can also help to create incentives for a better life. If growth is creating more jobs, kids are more likely to go to school to get training. If slow growth creates high unemployment, then fewer kids are likely to bother going to school.

• *Growth reduces poverty*. As growth accelerates and economies expand, people get pulled out of poverty. Historically, countries with high rates of economic growth have reduced poverty much faster than economies with slow growth. This relationship (or "elasticity") is of course not the same everywhere or even the same in one place over time. This is because not all growth is the same. An increase in GDP from new offshore oil production is probably not going to have the same impact on poverty as the same increase in GDP from labor-intensive manufacturing. A debate rages about how to make growth more efficient at reducing poverty (see the discussion on "pro-poor growth" in Chapter 10).

• *Africa needs a bigger pie*. Regardless of the precise poverty-growth elasticity, Africa still needs growth. Because average incomes are so low in Africa, redistribution is not really an option if the aim is to reduce the numbers of people living in poverty. In other words, it is not just about sharing the pie more fairly, it is about growing a bigger pie. In fact, in the twenty-seven African countries with average income below $1 per day, absolute equality would make everyone poor—pushing the poverty rate to 100 percent.

Africa's Growth Performance

Africa's growth in the immediate postindependence period was fairly positive, with income per capita rising about 2.4 percent per year during the 1960s. But this slowed to just 0.9 percent per year in the 1970s and became dismal afterward. The 1980s—often called the "lost decade" for Africa—saw average incomes *decline* by 1.1 percent per year. The 1990s were still a time of moving backwards, albeit slightly less quickly, with income per capita losing only 0.4 percent per year. Underneath these broad trends for the continent as a whole, there is great variance for individual countries. But for the thirty-three countries for which data are available, sixteen of them were poorer in 2000 than they were in 1970 (see Table 6.1).

Asia vs. Africa

Africa's poor growth performance is particularly stark when compared to other developing regions that have made much more progress. Between 1970 and 2000, Africa's average GDP per capita fell 0.2 percent per year, but it rose 2.4 percent in South Asia and by a whopping 5.7 percent in East Asia over the same period. Figure 6.1 shows the difference between Ghana and South Korea, two countries that started at very similar levels of income, but which have diverged sharply ever since. Figure 6.2 shows two oil-exporting countries, Indonesia and Nigeria, and their steady divergence as well.

Sources of Africa's Sluggish Growth

Why has Africa grown so slowly? The short answer is: we don't really know. The reasons for Africa's disappointing growth performance are complex and, frankly, not very well understood. There are lots of things that have been identified that are certainly bad for growth—war, for instance, or hyperinflation. But there remain a lot of unanswered questions and many (mostly unsatisfactory) theories. Part of the problem is that there is of course no universal explanation. Each economy in Africa has a variety of different starting points and faces a range of diverse constraints. Perhaps more importantly, the growth process itself—in Latin America, Europe, or anywhere—is still far from fully appreciated. This makes the lack of clear reasons for Africa's particular "growth tragedy" far from surprising. Among the many reasons thought to be part of the story are structural factors, endowments, policies, and institutions—the most important of which are discussed below. However, one of the biggest debates is whether or not there is something unique about Africa. Is there some reason that Africa grows so slowly that cannot be explained by the usual suspects? (Answer, again: we don't know.)

The answer to the mystery of African growth is more than academic. The ideas explaining the lack of growth feed directly into the prescriptions for how to help Africa grow more quickly. Over time, the popular notions have changed dramatically and are one reason for the

Table 6.1　GDP per Capita (in constant 2000 US$)

	1960	1970	1980	1990	2000	1990s avg. growth
Angola			928	878	715	−2.0%
Benin	278	308	314	300	362	1.9%
Botswana	254	436	1,247	2,487	3,135	2.3%
Burkina Faso	148	162	181	197	231	1.6%
Burundi	92	118	126	148	100	−3.8%
Cameroon	458	448	638	665	587	−1.2%
Cape Verde				886	1,222	3.3%
Central African Republic	346	348	316	275	256	−0.7%
Chad	251	233	152	195	177	−1.0%
Comoros			420	435	366	−1.7%
Congo, Dem. Rep.	324	327	252	205	89	−8.0%
Congo, Rep.	617	702	957	1,109	934	−1.7%
Côte d'Ivoire	532	840	945	705	670	−0.5%
Djibouti				1,246	830	−4.0%
Equatorial Guinea				705	2,928	15.3%
Eritrea					155	na
Ethiopia				95	102	0.7%
Gabon	1,658	3,105	4,698	4,097	3,920	−0.4%
Gambia, The		285	333	328	321	−0.2%
Ghana	281	296	239	214	254	1.7%
Guinea				367	420	1.4%
Guinea-Bissau		178	144	183	158	−1.5%
Kenya	213	239	357	379	347	−0.9%
Lesotho	111	151	312	391	493	2.3%
Liberia	698	844	747	179	173	−0.3%
Madagascar	389	409	349	281	250	−1.2%
Malawi	97	119	158	143	166	1.5%
Mali		195	233	193	223	1.5%
Mauritania	203	353	326	304	355	1.6%
Mauritius			1,564	2,522	3,727	4.0%
Mozambique			175	151	208	3.3%
Namibia			1,967	1,606	1,802	1.2%
Niger	321	325	273	197	167	−1.6%
Nigeria	291	344	409	337	332	−0.1%
Rwanda	243	231	282	257	235	−0.9%
São Tomé and Príncipe				336	314	−0.7%
Senegal	507	469	417	428	459	0.7%
Seychelles	2,379	2,646	4,531	5,644	7,619	3.0%
Sierra Leone	220	281	289	256	126	−6.8%
South Africa	2,105	3,049	3,436	3,058	2,910	−0.5%
Sudan	288	267	283	281	388	3.3%
Swaziland		727	986	1,336	1,336	0.0%
Tanzania				267	269	0.1%
Togo	188	316	383	310	291	−0.6%
Uganda				177	253	3.6%
Zambia	528	569	476	389	328	−1.7%
Zimbabwe	430	570	562	602	570	−0.5%

Source: World Bank
Note: Blank cells indicate no data available. No data available for Somalia.

Figure 6.1   GDP per Capita in Ghana and South Korea, 1960–2000

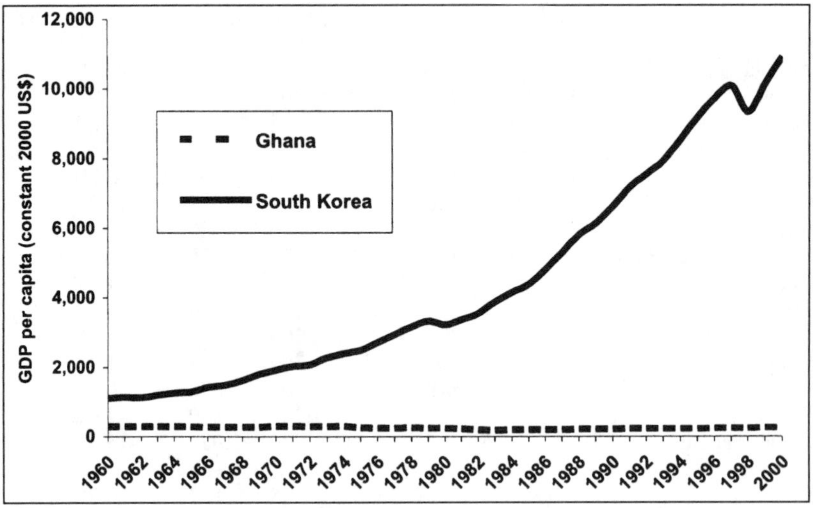

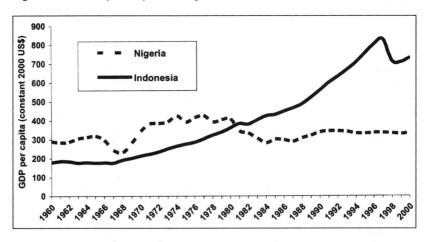

Figure 6.2   GDP per Capita in Nigeria and Indonesia, 1960–2000

roller-coaster changes in orthodox development policy over the past half century (see Chapters 7 and 8).

Structural Fatalists

One of the early, and still somewhat popular, notions is that Africa's destiny has been largely out of its own hands. By this thinking, Africa's weak economic performance is not unexpected, but rather has been cast in stone by its history and a deliberately unfair global economic system. It is fairly clear that the colonial period has had negative effects, most obviously in the loss of human and natural resources and the legacy of multiple small states and nonsensical borders. It is true that many of Africa's economies have not successfully diversified away from primary commodities and colonial-era industries. It is also the case that global trading rules, especially tariff escalation on manufactured goods, do tend to discourage moving up the value chain (see Chapter 12). What is doubtful, however, is that the global marketplace is somehow fixed to keep countries intentionally dependent. Africa's history is undoubtedly unfortunate in many ways, but by no means is the past an unavoidable destiny. The experience of many poor countries growing out of poverty (twenty-three countries have successfully graduated from the World Bank's soft-loan window because they became too rich) and the great differentiation among African countries since independence suggest that slow growth and developmental failure are far from predetermined.

Endowments

Africa does appear to have several structural characteristics that impinge on growth and that governments can do little to change.

• *Geography*. Africa's coastline is remarkably straight with very few bays, inlets, or natural ports, making trade and commerce difficult and discouraging people from living along the coasts. Few of the rivers are navigable very far inland, leaving vast stretches of the continent inaccessible. This is especially costly for the fifteen landlocked countries.

• *Climate*. Africa's climate is generally inhospitable for both human health and agriculture. The tropical climate in many parts of the continent is linked to a greater disease burden, poorer overall health, and reduced life expectancy. Malaria, which can only thrive in certain environments where mosquito carriers live, in particular imposes a huge burden on African economies. Agriculture is typically the starting point for economic development, and the main source of income and employment across Africa. But the common rainfall patterns, with long dry seasons followed by heavy rainy ones, are not conducive for many kinds of productive agriculture. This is compounded by generally poor soil quality, vast stretches of desert or semiarid land, and frequent droughts (which may even be getting worse). All of these climatic conditions contribute to poor economic outcomes.

• *Demography*. There have been ideas in the past that Africa's high fertility rates may be a drag on growth, but the thinking on this has mostly evolved to where high birth rates are considered symptoms of poverty and underdevelopment rather than causes. This is not to suggest that all women have reproductive rights, but that "desired fertility" appears more affected by social and economic factors than the other way around. In fact, for some countries it may be that low population density is an economic problem, making transportation and public services much more costly.

• *Ethnicity*. Ethnic diversity is also thought to have economic effects, although the precise pathways for such effects are far from clear. In theory, multiple linguistic and cultural groups can make organization more difficult and can fragment markets, preventing economies of scale. At the same time, ethnic diversity can be an economic asset, encouraging people to work and trade across boundaries, which can have positive effects on international linkages.

Internal Policies

Another basket of ideas about the source of Africa's slow growth is the prevalence of "bad" policies. In general these include ways in which the state created problems by getting overly involved in the economy, including failed central planning and public ownership of industry. The list of policies thought wrong-headed is long, but a few of the key ones were especially popular. Price controls or state monopolies on certain products discouraged production and led to the rise of black markets. Credit controls deterred savings. Currency overvaluation favored luxury imports over exports. Unclear private-property laws scared off investment. Public jobs were used to reward allies, creating hugely inefficient and bloated civil services. Large budget deficits led to runaway inflation and mounting debts, and crowded out private investment. In a few countries, forced "villagization" was another disastrous scheme (in Tanzania, for example, peasants were literally loaded onto trucks at gunpoint and then dumped on new collective farms) that was not only economically devastating but also a violation of basic human rights.

African governments have also been prone to excessive regulation that can cross into the absurd. Uganda once had a law that coffee could only be transported by railway (that has since been scrapped), while labor laws are so onerous in Sierra Leone that firing a worker costs nearly four years' worth of wages. To open a business in Angola it still takes fourteen steps and an average of 146 days (versus two steps and three days in Canada).

In general, by the early 1980s, it was believed that the cumulative effect of state intervention and unnecessary regulation was a major cause of African economic malaise. Thus donors insisted on policy changes as a condition for continued aid (see Chapter 7). Even if the policy reform and "structural adjustment" promises that followed were rarely implemented, the results were nonetheless deeply disappointing.

Guns, Germs, and Steel

Jared Diamond's best-selling book *Guns, Germs, and Steel: The Fates of Human Societies* (1999) has provided a detailed argument about the evolution of human progress. He opens his book with a question posed by a Papua New Guinean about why Westerners seem to have so much more "cargo" than his people. This might just as aptly apply to Africa: Why did Europeans manage to colonize Africa and not the other way around? Diamond's main contention is that geography is destiny. The physical environment leads to certain demographic trends (such as urbanization) and agricultural organization (such as domesticated livestock) that have very long-term effects on technological and developmental paths. He argues that Africa's underdevelopment is linked to the continent's geography and climate, which never encouraged the establishment of large, complex urban societies, as occurred in Europe. Diamond's arguments are not only popular—they also provide a plausible explanation for the very long-term divergence between African and European societies, which began probably sometime around the sixteenth century. But Diamond's analysis gives very little insight into short-run trends, such as why Ghana and Liberia, which have very similar structural features, have followed such very different trends over the past two decades. It also cannot really help to explain why a country such as Mozambique was able to recover so quickly from a long civil war, but Congo has not. In short, *Guns, Germs, and Steel* is a useful guide to ultra-long-term trends and provides important clues as to why some societies now face certain difficulties, but it gives little guidance for us today. If geography is the whole story, then why worry about inflation or how to buy books for school kids?

Institutions and Governance

The inability to realize policy reform or to produce higher growth forced a new examination of the possible causes. The next popular answer was that Africa's poor performance and counterproductive policies were no accident but the result of underlying bad "governance "or "institutions." Even if structural adjustment was essentially correct in substance, it failed to account for the political reasons that distorting policies were there in the first place. To look beyond policies, it was thus necessary to look at the state itself.

Many of the public institutions in Africa look like inherited Western institutions on paper, but often do not act like them. The civil service, for example, was mostly about creating jobs and controlling access to state favors, not delivering basic public services. Similarly, private property may be protected in law, but in practice enforcement was unpredictable and discouraged investment. (In some places, such as Ethiopia, there still is no private property outside the major cities.) The political systems seemed to focus on personal gain or short-term concerns over longer, public ones such as a persistent pattern of favoring consumption and redistribution of resources over investment and accumulation.

Weak States

In short, the state in Africa was all too frequently not acting like a state is supposed to. This is undoubtedly partly because the idea of the "state" itself is a European construct and African states are mostly inherited colonial holdovers. The result has been the irony of African states being both too weak and too intrusive at the same time. Political scientists have thus described them as "quasi-states," "suspended states," "collapsed states," "imported states," "shadow states," or even "disconnected states." This gloomy assessment is based on the idea that African governments are rarely able to act on their own in anything resembling a "public interest." Instead, they are thoroughly penetrated by elites and special interests that come to dominate policy decisions—leading to things such as onerous regulations and special protections for the politically connected. What looks like economic chaos usually has a political logic underneath. Even though many have been ruled by strong authoritarians, their ability to get "developmental" things done is often extremely limited and there is little incentive for them to try to do so. The question for those seeking to promote development was then how to reorient the African state to make it more effective, i.e., how to shift a political system from one based on patronage to one based on promoting the public interest.

Limits of the Governance Agenda

The main response from the donors was the rise of the "governance" agenda, seeking to promote accountability, transparency, and other concepts that were hoped would create incentives for the state to change the way it operates (see Chapter 5). Although the mantra "institutions matter" has become accepted wisdom, the next steps to fix Africa's institutions have been far from clear. First, reform of the state is supposed to be carried out by the same political elites that caused economic crisis in the first place (and are now often benefiting from its continuation). In other regions where the state has managed to organically mature and become developmental, there has often been a local middle class or independent business sector that began to demand changes. In Africa, most of the business class is connected to the political elite (or they are one and the same). A second concern is that, if donors had a difficult time getting governments to change their policies, what kind of leverage could they expect to get them to change the way government actually works, including steps that may have a personal cost for those involved?

The ideas so far are to encourage better public management and, more recently, to work on "capacity building," but there is little confidence that donors will be much more successful than before. Lastly, and perhaps most worrisome, the direction of causality between economic progress and institutional development is still not at all clear. It could be that strong, capable institutions help make societies grow more quickly, or it could be that wealthier societies demand better institutional arrangements. None of this is to say the governance agenda and institutional emphasis is wrong per se, but only that it is extremely ambitious and faces some of the same incentive dilemmas as structural adjustment.

Other Ideas Behind Africa's Poor Growth Performance

In addition to the mainstream donor agenda to promote economic growth in Africa, there are several other ideas that have influenced economic thinking, many of which overlap with those suggested above:

• *Lack of democracy.* One variant of the governance agenda is a more blatant promotion of liberal democracy. Although the international financial institutions (IFIs) avoid such openly political concepts, the bilateral donors are less constrained. Despite the various reasons donors might favor democracy other than to promote development, the link with economic growth is tenuous (see Chapter 5).

• *Neighborhood effect.* Because economies interact with each other, it is possible that African economies grow more slowly because many of their neighbors do as well. If a neighbor is in economic trouble, it can provide fewer natural trading partners, lead to smuggling or a black market along the border, and give rise to perceptions of regional risk (especially since there is some evidence that investors do not differentiate very well among different African countries). If these are true, then just being on the continent can possibly reduce growth.

• *Prevalence of conflict.* The outbreak of conflict also has a negative effect on growth, especially through the disruption of farming, trade, and other normal economic activity (see Chapter 4). Since Africa has more than its fair share of violence, this also has a suppressing effect on the economy and, combined with neighborhood spillovers, may help to explain regional stagnation.

• *Shock vulnerability.* Because African economies remain fairly undiversified and concentrated in a small number of products, they are vulnerable to shocks, such as a sharp drop in the price of a key commodity such as coffee, or weather volatility. Such risks can undermine long-term economic growth by creating uncertainty and complicating economic management (see Chapter 12).

• *Too little (or too much) aid.* The relationship between aid and economic growth is a long, unresolved, and fairly arcane debate. Aid is sometimes given in the hopes of boosting growth, so some activists have claimed that more aid is thus necessary. At the same time, there is a strong tradition of skepticism about the potential dampening effect of aid on growth in the long-term by creating dependencies and possibly undermining institutions (see Chapter 8). Thus one reason for Africa's sluggish growth could be the "wrong" amount of external aid. Whether it is too little or too much for too long, however, is disputable.

• *Poverty trap.* Another theory about Africa's slow growth is that it is simply too poor to grow fast, that it is stuck in a "poverty trap" (see Chapter 10). This idea suggests that economies are so short of resources that they are unable to generate savings to invest enough to make the transition to the next economic level. The notion of a poverty trap was partly behind the 1950s "big push" to provide foreign aid to help countries over the hump and onto a self-sustaining growth path. Unfortunately, it did not work out that way, but the idea of a poverty trap still lives on. Nevertheless, there is no empirical evidence that there exists a minimum income level needed to get growth going—if it did, then no country would have ever become rich.

Combinations and Interactions

The (rather unsatisfactory) answer to Africa's growth misfortune is some mishmash of the ideas cited above. Yet it remains far from clear how one aspect influences another, or which combinations are most relevant in which cases. Clearly, endowments (such as history and geography) influence institutions, societies, and policies—and each of these affect each other. Nor would we expect to find a combination that applied across multiple countries. History led to the creation of the franc zone, for example, which means that monetary policy has not been a problem for those countries, but the franc zone has still had disappointing growth. Kenya has a better climate than most and fairly good ports, but also faces economic stagnation.

But knowing little does not mean we have learned nothing or not begun to better understand some of these linkages. As the "institutions" literature began to dominate economic theory, for example, it was applied to some of the earlier ideas about endowments. Ethnic fragmentation, for instance, is now thought to encourage patronage-style political systems. Another example might be mapping how disease patterns affected the locations of colonial settlement, which had implications for land rights. Overall, the quest for the answer to Africa's growth puzzle is unlikely to find a universal answer, but the search itself adds tremendously to our understanding.

For Further Reading

The IMF and the World Bank provide historical data on the economic growth of individual countries. Individual IMF country reports include much more detail on national data, including sectoral growth rates. Further information on national economies can be found through some African finance ministries or statistical agencies, but coverage is uneven and format and definitions can vary.

To get a good sense of the state of thinking on economic growth in development economics, see David Lindauer and Lant Pritchett's "What's the Big Idea? The Third Generation of Policies for Economic Growth" (2002). Another excellent article with a healthy dose of professional humility is "What Do We Know About Economic Growth? Or, Why Don't We Know Very Much?" by Charles Kenny and David Williams (2001). For a more in-depth review of the various debates on economic growth theory, see the many contributions in *Handbook of Economic Growth*, edited by Philippe Aghion and Stephen Durlauf (2005). A classic text worth a look by all students is David Landes's *The Wealth and Poverty of Nations: Why Some Are Rich and Some Poor* (1998).

There are a cluster of articles looking at Africa's particular growth performance, trying to sort out the various explanations. Paul Collier and Jan Willem Gunning's "Why Has Africa Grown Slowly?" (1999) lays out both the destiny and policy factors. David Bloom and Jeffrey Sachs argue that geography and demography are the most important in "Geography, Demography, and Economic Growth in Africa" (1998). "Why Not Africa?" by Richard Freeman and David Lindauer (1999) challenges these findings that endowments are the most critical. William Easterly and Ross Levine find that ethnic divisions are a key factor in inducing policies that slow growth in "Africa's Growth Tragedy: Policies and Ethnic Divisions" (1997). Pierre Englebert suggests arbitrary borders of postcolonial states are a decisive explanation in "Solving the Mystery of the AFRICA Dummy" (2000).

A useful overview of the literature on institutions is Dani Rodrik's "Getting Institutions Right" (2004). Some of the most prominent literature includes Douglass North's *Institutions, Institutional Change, and Economic Performance* (1990) and "Institutions as the Fundamental Cause of Long-Run Growth" by Daron Acemoglu, Simon Johnson, and James Robinson (2005). Among the dissidents who question the direction of causality between institutions and growth are Edward Glaeser et al. in their "Do Institutions Cause Growth?" (2004). Hernando de Soto, a leading proponent of property rights, has several important books, including his classic *The Other Path* (1989) as well as his more recent *The Mystery of Capital* (2000).

A useful review of the "weak states" literature on Africa is Pierre

Engelbert's "The Contemporary African State: Neither African nor State" (1997). Some of the major works include Robert Jackson's *Quasi-States, Sovereignty, International Relations, and the Third World* (1990) and William Zartman's edited volume *Collapsed States* (1995).

Some of the governance-growth linkages are addressed in Daniel Kaufmann and Aart Kraay's "Growth Without Governance" (2002), Paul Collier's "The Role of the State in Economic Development: Cross-Regional Experiences" (1998), and Benno Ndulu and Stephen O'Connell's "Governance and Growth in Sub-Saharan Africa" (1999).

7

Economic Reform and the Politics of Adjustment

ALL COUNTRIES ARE UNDERGOING SOME MEASURE OF "REFORM," meaning changing laws, regulations, and policies—that is what politicians do. Across nearly all of Africa, reform has been one of the most prominent strategies for trying to increase economic growth and reduce poverty. The international community encourages reform as part of its assistance, and in many cases uses financial and diplomatic means to induce certain kinds of reforms over others, especially trying to find ways to extract the state from the economy where possible and to encourage private actors to play a greater role. But the precise agenda, the means to achieve reform, and the relative influence of various actors have all been highly controversial. At the same time, attributing reform to developmental success or failure is difficult, especially since the terms and basic facts are often hotly contested. On the one hand, it does appear that some of Africa's most aggressive reformers in recent years—Ghana, Uganda, Mozambique—have also had the strongest economic recoveries. On the other hand, there seem to be severe limits to how far these countries have changed, and plenty of room to do even better. Perhaps more importantly, it is still not well understood why some countries get on the road to reform in the first place, while others veer so badly off track. This chapter will outline the major aspects of recent economic reforms and introduce some of the dynamics thought to be at play.

State Intervention

Just as the African political story is one of state seizure of control followed by eventual, if often tentative, steps toward liberalization and democracy (Chapter 5), there is a somewhat parallel economic story. The colonial administrators tended to direct many aspects of the economy, but this was deepened further after independence when nearly all African states—regardless of ideology—seized even more control of the economy. In general, governments spent more than they raised, leading to large budget deficits and eventually high inflation and debt. There was often little transparency in the way governments conducted business, spending at the whim of the president or in murky schemes where many of the funds disappeared along the way. In many cases, there was scant regard for private property (especially that of foreigners or minorities) and little distinction made between the public purse and the private wealth of political leaders. But one of the lasting legacies of the early postindependence period was heavy government intervention, including state ownership of factories, intrusive regulations, and mountains of (usually intentional) red tape.

Nationalization

A very common policy after independence was the nationalization of major industries, whereby the owners of a company or a mine were expelled and the state seized control and management. For instance, in Zambia the government took over the copper mines that had been owned by the South African–based multinational Anglo-American, in Ghana the government nationalized the main Ashanti gold mines, and in Tanzania the same was done to the local cigarette company (all three have since been reprivatized). The state also sometimes got involved in expropriating property not only from foreigners but also from minorities within the country, such as in Uganda under Idi Amin when most of the local Asian population were expelled and their property seized.

State-Owned Enterprises

Other typical aspects of state intervention involved the establishment of state-owned companies that included not only utilities such as water and electricity, but in other cases shoe factories, farms, and breweries. In supposedly market-friendly Kenya, for example, the government owned about 150 different companies (and large shares in another 200 or so) by the early 1980s. Where enterprises were allowed to remain in private hands, there tended to be very heavy regulations covering what the companies could do, whom they could hire or fire, and how they managed their finances. In some sectors thought especially important to the economy, such as a key export crop or food source, a government might set up its own company or agency with a monopoly on sales and distribution (although many were inherited from colonial authorities). For example, in Ghana farmers were only allowed to sell cocoa to the state-run cocoa board, which until very recently had a total monopoly on exporting. "Marketing boards," which retain a state monopoly over a particular crop, continue in some countries such as Tanzania and Zimbabwe today.

To support these companies and state agencies, often called state-owned enterprises (SOEs) or parastatals, the government typically had to spend lots of money setting them up and keeping them going. In almost all cases, the government, which had limited capacity to even provide basic social services, was very ill equipped to run large commercial enterprises. Because these firms were protected from competition, they also had no overriding discipline from the market to encourage efficiency. Unsurprisingly, SOEs were rarely profitable and became increasingly reliant on support from the state itself to keep running, through increased protection and subsidies. Thus, the major parts of the economy that should have been providing resources to the state (via taxes) instead usually became a drain. Loss-making SOEs and other agencies began to gobble up ever greater parts of the budget, forcing government to cut back in other areas and to borrow ever more to cover the losses. In the case of the marketing boards, they either were subsidizing farmers (and another bleed on scarce resources) or became a way to heavily tax farmers by paying them well below market rates, thereby discouraging production (or encouraging smuggling). In Ghana in the 1960s and 1970s, for instance, the government used the profits from cocoa to subsidize large industrial projects. But as the prices paid to farmers continued to fall, reaching as low as one-quarter of international prices with the government keeping the difference, output plummeted by two-thirds. Since the industrial projects financed by cocoa taxes also mostly failed, it was a double whammy for Ghana's fledgling economy.

Rationale for State Involvement

There were several reasons why the state got so heavily involved in the economy in the first place, and this helps to understand why it has proved so difficult to change. There were at least five basic justifications for taking such steps:

- *African nationalism.* In the wake of a wrenching colonial period, there was a surge of African pride and nationalism that sought to reassert local control and rebuild the confidence of societies that had been under foreign domination for generations. Although political authority was foremost in the minds of the new African leaders (think of Kwame Nkrumah's "Seek ye first the political kingdom and all else shall come"), they also wanted to throw off the yoke of economic colonialism. At the time, using the state to "Africanize" the economy was thought a logical—and, to many, a necessary—next step to control Africa's destiny.

- *Socialist influence.* There was undoubtedly an important ideological element in many places. Countries such as Mozambique and Angola were initially led by openly Marxist-Leninist parties that were explicitly trying to emulate the Soviet model. A softer version was tried in places such as Tanzania and Ghana, where leaders such as Nkrumah and Julius Nyerere sought to use the state to create an "African socialism" where the government would manage the important parts of the economy for the greater good. Some of these leanings were because it was argued at the time that socialism was closer to the communal economic system familiar in many rural African societies. It was also no doubt a direct outcome of the Cold War, since the Soviet Union and the Chinese were supporters, with money and guns, for many of the anticolonial guerrilla movements. Many of the leaders of the armed struggles who would go on to lead their countries after independence were also schooled in Moscow or Eastern Europe. Yet even in states that were supposedly capitalist and aligned with the West, such as Kenya and Malawi, the state moved to control most economic activity, which suggests that other forces were also at play.

• *Dependency theory.* Related to the left-wing leanings of many postindependence African governments, there was also a strong ideological influence from "dependency theory." This was a powerful idea that extended colonial economic relationships into the postindependence era. While colonialism was a system for exploiting poor colonies in the periphery for the benefit of the rich countries at the center, dependency theory argued that this system continued through international capitalism. Even though countries might have gained political independence, they were still thought to be economically dependent. The obvious solution to this problem, then, was to break these bonds. If the international capitalist system was a source of dependency, and these new states wanted to be truly independent, then they would have to intervene to withdraw from the system. This meant cutting ties to the global economy, seizing control of economic activity, and perhaps expelling European business interests.

• *Development economics theory.* Another justification for state intervention was not to break the bonds of global capitalism, but rather to help jump-start economies. A new field of economics—dedicated to the special problems of poor countries and how to make them rich—called "development economics" emerged. The dominant strand of development economics argued that certain steps were necessary for the state to take in order to nurse poor economies along until they were large and mature enough to compete with the already rich. This suggested that the state should help small companies to get started, assist them to grow, and protect them from outside markets until they were large enough to stand on their own. Thus trade barriers, cheap loans from the government, and state ownership could all be justified as temporary steps to help bring African industry to the point of "takeoff."

• *Elite capture*. Although never explicitly stated, there was undoubtedly also some pursuit of control of resources by political elites. Favored firms owned by the state or with close ties to politicians sought to use the state to protect their positions or to merely steal from the public purse. Thus what may have begun as a well-meaning policy to help the economy quickly degenerated into a racket for theft and patronage. As the ideological rationales receded from changes in the global political environment, elite capture emerged as probably the greatest barrier to reform (even if it is still often couched in nationalist or developmental terms).

Backlash of Failure

As became apparent over time, there were major problems with each of these justifications. The early hopes of African nationalism leading to a resurgence were quickly dashed in the wake of growing political instability and steep economic decline. With the end of the Cold War and collapse of the Soviet Union, help from the Warsaw Pact dried up. More broadly, the idea of communism was undermined by global changes and some of the limitations of socialism became apparent. Dependency theory similarly lost legitimacy as those countries that tried to isolate themselves did much worse than countries that tried to actively engage with the global economy. Development economics also fell out of favor as it became clear that "temporary" interventions quickly became permanent and that the infant industries were rarely growing up. Instead of fostering productive industries that would add to national welfare, these firms became parasites. It also became increasingly obvious that elite capture was getting worse and that state intervention in the economy was helping a narrow few at the expense of the many. Since the beneficiaries were closely aligned with the politicians, this made fixing the problem all the more difficult.

But more important than the ideological or political changes that made intervention less defensible were the results. In Africa the record of state intervention in the economy has been simply dismal. State-owned firms not only tended to require large amounts of public funds, but they often produced low-quality products and services for the public, or sometimes none at all. Quite simply, if the state-led economic strategy had worked, African governments would never have needed to turn to international donors to bail them out.

Turning to the IFIs

The economic strategies pursued by most African countries eventually became unsustainable. Economies failed to grow fast enough, debts mounted, and capital left the continent in a huge wave. By the 1980s, many countries had hit bottom and turned to the international financial institutions (IFIs) and Western donors for assistance. The donors often agreed to provide help, but only if the African governments promised to fix the problems that were thought to have gotten them into trouble in the first place. Although there was a diversity of problems across countries, there was a general agreement that many of the policies pursued by African governments were failing and that the state was not facilitating economic progress but rather strangling it.

Structural Adjustment

The major donors decided that any future support for Africa would require "liberalization"—reducing the state's role in the economy. States would have to curb mismanagement, get out of loss-making ventures, stop overregulating the economy, and sell off SOEs that would be better managed in private hands. In 1979 Senegal reached agreement with the International Monetary Fund (IMF) to borrow money in exchange for a set of policy changes the IMF thought the country should make. In 1980 Kenya reached a similar agreement, as did Ghana in 1983. Over the next decade nearly every other African government entered into negotiations with the IMF for a similar deal, comprising some combination of aid and policy change to restructure the economy and the role of the state. For the IMF and its sister organization, the World Bank, this marked a shift toward "policy-based lending," or using loans to try to encourage policy changes. Thus began the era of "structural adjustment," which (despite changes to the name and evolution in the precise agenda) continues to this day (see Chapter 8).

Conditionality

A crucial aspect of the donor strategy was the promise of policy changes by recipients in exchange for aid—what came to be called "conditionality." The idea was not far from bribery or blackmail in many cases, whereby large loans were dangled in front of cash-strapped politicians. A prerequisite for getting the money, however, was agreeing with the lender on what they would do differently (or, in the case of the IMF, writing a "letter of intent" outlining what they planned to do over the coming years). It seemed a reasonable request, given the horrendous economic performance of those asking for the money. For the governments, making a long series of promises seemed a fair price to pay for cheap money. In practice, of course, conditionality was a near total failure. Even if the policies asked for by the donors seemed reasonable on paper, governments had little reason to actually make changes and donors found few reasons to enforce their previous demands.

Liberalization and the "Washington Consensus"

If the mechanism of trying to encourage reform through conditionality was flawed, the substance of policy recommendations was fairly orthodox and based on classic liberal economics. The policy agenda was usually a series of steps to improve macroeconomic management and free up markets to operate. In Latin America these conditions were called the "Washington Consensus" but they applied just as aptly to Africa (see the box on page 108). The terms Washington Consensus, structural adjustment, and liberalization are often misused or misinterpreted. None of these, for example, mean forcing the state to abdicate any regulatory role or to gut social or environmental protections. What they do suggest are a set of policies thought necessary to help countries emerge out of their economic doldrums based on the conclusion that state policies themselves were one critical source of the problem (see Chapter 6).

What About the Example of Asia's Tigers?

Asia's success at rapid industrialization seems at odds with parts of the Washington Consensus, where the governments actively pursued industrial policy including trade protection and cheap credit allocated by the state. Indeed, the experiences of Japan, South Korea, Malaysia, and China are often suggested as reasons why Africa should pursue liberalization. Yet there are some fairly clear reasons why such strategies have not worked in Africa in the past, suggesting that Africa should use the East Asian model with caution.

First, Asian firms getting special treatment from the government, such as subsidized credit, had to meet export targets in order to continue to receive privileges. The link to exports meant that firms still had to be internationally competitive and not merely serve a captive local market, which can breed complacency and inefficiency. By contrast, African firms tended to serve domestic markets and there were rarely specific targets required for access to benefits. Second, Asian bureaucrats were able to enforce such deals with firms and, crucially, were able to cut off nonperforming ones. In Africa there are few examples of a privileged firm having its benefits withdrawn. Instead, when times got tough, firms tended to turn back to the state for ever more protection and state assistance, making them increasingly reliant on state largesse for survival. In some cases such as Zimbabwe, where state loans to private businesses saw default rates above 90 percent, industrial policy became little more than a racket for stealing public money.

Exactly why one approach seemed to work so well in one region but not another is hotly debated. One possible difference between Asian and African industrial policy is the differential degrees of freedom from political interference for policymakers. In general, in East Asia political

The "Washington Consensus"

In 1990 economist John Williamson coined the phrase the "Washington Consensus" to describe a list of the policies most commonly given as advice to Latin American countries in the late 1980s. The list is:

1. *Fiscal discipline.* This means shrinking the large budget deficits that led to balance-of-payments crises and high inflation.
2. *Reorder public expenditure priorities.* This suggested switching spending toward things such as basic health, education, and infrastructure and away from unproductive subsidies and overbloated civil services.
3. *Tax reform.* Build a fair and effective tax system.
4. *Liberalize interest rates.* Stop the state from artificially forcing interest rates below market value, which discourages savings.
5. *Allow competitive exchange rate.* This meant not allowing manipulation of the exchange rate to encourage imports at the expense of export competitiveness.
6. *Trade liberalization.* Although how and how fast to lower trade barriers were under debate, it was accepted that moving toward more open trade was desirable.
7. *Liberalization of inward investment.* The state should not try to keep out foreign investors.
8. *Privatization.* States should sell industries they own where they are losing money or where private ownership might be more appropriate.
9. *Deregulation.* Barriers to private business operations should be reduced.
10. *Property rights.* Inspired by the work of Peruvian economist Hernando de Soto, this suggested that property rights needed to be protected and that the poor should be allowed to own land.

leaders gave the policymakers and bureaucracy the space to make technocratic decisions. In Africa, the bureaucracy was highly politicized and the firms themselves were highly politically connected (frequently owned by politicians or their family members), making any cutoffs or sanctions impossible.

There is also a strong debate about the source of the "Asian miracle" itself. One interpretation of the miracle was that state intervention was in fact critical and that industrial policy was necessary to allow firms to grow. Another interpretation is that some aspects of the model may have been helpful, but that most firms would have succeeded anyway and perhaps without the added cost to the state. Even if this can be resolved, exactly how the Asian bureaucratic model developed and how it can be better replicated in Africa remain areas of contention.

Privatization and Its Critics

Privatization has been both a centerpiece of economic reform and a locus of sometimes virulent criticism. The concept of privatization is the transfer or sale of ownership of a firm from public to private hands. The purpose of privatization is larger than just changing ownership, however. The point is usually to raise money from the sale, halt any public subsidies to the SOE, and help to improve the contribution of the company to the economy through new management, investment, and technology. Many African state-owned telephone companies, for example, were sold in the 1990s with the hope that the new owners would upgrade service. Many times privatization also coincides with liberalization of a sector. For instance, state-owned banks were sold in Tanzania at the same time that foreign banks were also allowed to enter the market. Such sales can also be partial, with the government retaining a stake, or shares can be listed on local stock markets, allowing a wide range of people to own part of the company. Kenya Airways, for example, was privatized in the 1990s, with a controlling stake sold to the Dutch airline KLM and shares also listed on the local Nairobi stock exchange, where over 100,000 Kenyans participated. But privatization has also come under fire from many directions.

• *Nationalist resistance.* The most common criticism heard inside Africa is the flip side of nationalization: privatization allows foreigners to buy the country's assets. During the privatization of Ghana's Ashanti goldfields in 1994, nationalists had taken the government to court claiming that the sale was "selling the family silver" (their effort ultimately failed, although the government retained a large stake).

• *Corruption.* Another common complaint is that public assets are sold to cronies or other politically connected people at discounted prices. This undoubtedly occurs in some cases where the sale is behind closed doors, but it is a criticism of the process rather than the policy of privatization. Such problems can usually be avoided if the bidding process is transparent.

• *Timing.* Some critics have worried about timing, claiming that selling an SOE before the regulatory environment is ready can replace a lousy state-owned monopoly with a privately owned monopoly that is just as bad. Telephone privatization in some countries, for instance, has sometimes fallen into this trap with no postprivatization improvement in service.

• *Labor.* Almost without exception, SOEs are overmanned. Thus privatization often means that jobs are lost in the short term as the company reorganizes to try to turn it around. This unsurprisingly generates opposition from labor unions and employees seeking to keep their jobs.

• *Ideological.* There are also ideological challenges based on the idea that the public sector should own certain kinds of businesses and use that ownership to target services to the poor. The best example here is water, where activists have campaigned hard to keep water delivery in public hands, sometimes using the argument that water is a basic right and should not be subjected to market forces.

Reform Implementation

Even if it could be agreed on which array of policies was most desirable, that left open the question of how to implement them. Some early advocates of reform—bolstered by success in curbing Bolivian hyperinflation—suggested "shock treatment" for economies, where they would try to do everything at once. Such an approach was thought to enable the most changes to occur most quickly and before political resistance from special interests could be organized. But such a strategy placed a huge burden on policymakers that might not have the political backing at home to implement such a wide-ranging agenda. In fact, if it were the politicians themselves who were benefiting from the status quo, it was hardly surprising that the political backing was absent.

If doing everything at once was impossible, then figuring out what to do first became a key debate. Experiences in other regions also suggested that carefully ordering reforms—called "sequencing"—was not only desirable but perhaps necessary. For example, interest rate liberalization makes sense, but if it is done quickly and without adequate banking regulation and oversight, the change can precipitate a banking crisis. (This is precisely what happened in Latin America in the late 1980s.) Although there were some broad lessons to be learned from other experiences, the "right" sequencing would be different in each case, leaving much to be negotiated.

Politics of Reform

Another major issue was managing the politics of adjustment. For the most part, in Africa reforms were promised but never implemented. Countries often suffered from "partial reform syndrome." In many cases, some of the easier reforms (such as lifting controls on the currency or lowering certain trade taxes) were undertaken, but any steps that might threaten politically connected firms were either ignored or circumvented. The donors, however, mostly played along with the charade, and governments would often make the same promises over and over again.

One of the more infamous cases is Kenya Railways. The state-owned railroad was notoriously inefficient, increasingly cost the government lots of money, and provided lousy and unreliable service. As far back as 1972, the railway was identified as a major problem and a financial drain on the treasury. The donors, for mostly the right reasons, thus kept insisting that Kenya do something about the railway both to improve service and to stop losing money that could be better spent in other areas. The government apparently had different ideas, but rather than challenge the donors directly the government adopted a passive-aggressive resistance strategy. Despite accepting donor money on the condition that they fix Kenya Railways, it continually delayed or found excuses to wriggle out of its commitment. In all, Kenya made similar promises to reform Kenya Railways dozens of times (including nearly twenty times just to the World Bank and IMF) since 1979 as part of loan conditions. Yet millions of dollars later and more than three decades after locating the problem, the railways remain in state hands and in dire shape. But the donors remain undeterred; in 2005, as part of a donor-backed reform strategy, the government again agreed to allow a foreign company to take over management.

Disincentives to Reform on Both Sides
How does such a charade continue? Understanding why reform often did not occur requires rethinking the common perception that donors were forcing changes onto weak governments that had to accept because they needed the money. In practice, it rarely worked that way. African governments were hardly subordinate and rarely accepted donor demands, even if politicians often liked to blame the international organizations in public. Indeed, in many ways it was the donors who were in a weaker position.

A closer look reveals that there were strong incentives on both sides for the money to continue to flow, but not the reforms. For many of the government officials (the real decisionmakers, if not the technocrats actually doing the negotiation), the path of least resistance was to agree on paper but find ways to get out of any obligations after the money arrived. Because the status quo was beneficial for those currently in power (or their friends and allies), it was rarely in their own interest to change course. Officials also quickly learned that it was fairly easy to convince the donors why a particular promise went unmet. In fact, some governments found that, like the Kenya Railways example above, you could repromise the same thing many times over. Why implement a policy change if you can "sell" it again, or, better yet, ten more times?

On the donor side, there were also incentives against enforcing the agreements. Staff in the donor agencies are often partly judged based on how much money they are able to disburse. Like some perverse incentives in banking, it was easier for staff to turn a blind eye to nonperformance and to continue with the program. Indeed, the hassles would be much greater for trying to enforce an aid cutoff, which would inevitably lead to political intervention, perhaps including calls from an angry president. Making matters worse, there is heavy staff turnover in donor-country teams. A typical World Bank staff member, for example, will change to a new country team every few years. This meant that government negotiators were often dealing with new people who had not been involved in previous agreements, making them more susceptible to accepting past mistakes and agreeing to promises already made. Governments could merely ride out a testy staff member, while every new one would (perhaps somewhat naturally) be inclined to give a government at least one chance to try again (even if the same deal had been struck with their predecessor).

The Post–Washington Consensus Agenda

The reform period of structural adjustment was not a complete failure. Macroeconomic management has visibly improved almost across the board. For example, nearly every country in Africa has tamed inflation (which is probably the single greatest tax on the poor). But the "structural" part of change has been extremely slow and erratic. Out of this acknowledged disappointment, the mainstream reform agenda has evolved into a more nuanced version, integrating sequencing and trying to end the sham of "buying reforms." More generally, however, the policy agenda has grown substantially. There are a few lingering debates about the merits of all ten of the Washington Consensus suggestions (most notably over the best type of exchange-rate policy and the optimal pace of trade liberalization) and a move toward more flexibility to allow countries to experiment with different policies. But most of the changes have not been to replace the Washington Consensus, but rather to add to it. In other words, the old agenda is mostly considered necessary but not sufficient for countries to grow faster and reduce poverty. The new "Post–Washington Consensus" includes a much wider range of policies and ideas, including: consultation with civil society, promoting transparency, tackling corruption, providing social safety nets, giving help to those hurt by reforms, and targeting spending on specific poverty-reduction schemes (see Chapter 8 for more on the emerging aid agenda).

New Conditionality

It is also now widely accepted that donor conditionality, at least in the form utilized in the 1990s, does not work. In response to this acknowledgment, conditionality has not been dropped, but rather new ways to induce better policies by governments have been tried. This "new conditionality" comes in two forms.

Inside Leverage: A Hypothetical Negotiation

Crucial to understanding the donor-recipient dynamics of conditionality is that neither side is monolithic. Instead, the process of negotiation is just as vigorous within each side as between them, helping to create conditions that militate against reform.

Consider this hypothetical, but no doubt typical, example: A donor and an African government sit down to negotiate a deal. The government wants cash and the donor wants some policy changes in exchange, let's say to simplify matters just two things: a reduction in military spending and an end to a state trucking monopoly. The finance minister and the donor-country team leader haggle over the conditions. The donor official says there is no way they can agree to the aid until the government cuts its military budget and sets a timetable to allow private trucks to carry crops. The finance minister says he agrees but that the defense minister is very powerful, the country has legitimate security concerns, and that the trucks ensure that the poor farmers can get their crops to market (though unspoken, both sides know these claims are only partly true and that the president's cousin is getting rich off the trucking deal). In the end, they reach some compromise, say a 10 percent cut and a five-year phase-in for private trucks. On the basis of the deal, the aid is delivered. But the military budget is not cut, and perhaps is even increased, while no steps are taken to liberalize the trucking market. A year later, the donor-country team leader (let's charitably assume it's still the same person) and the finance minister meet again. The donor official, who is under pressure both to spend his budget and to get the policy changes, wants to know what happened? The finance minister says, yes, he knows, he's trying his best, but he is up against powerful forces. In fact, the finance minister claims he actually succeeded in stopping the military budget from increasing by even more and has managed to get the president to consider changes in trucking. He just needs more time. The country team leader now faces a dilemma. He thinks that continuing the aid may help to strengthen the finance minister, who he believes probably supports the policy changes. He also knows that if aid is cut off, the defense minister and the president's cousin win and the reforms definitely stall. He also knows that headquarters wants to know why his budget is not being spent fast enough. What to do? All too often, the easy choice is to keep the aid flowing and wait until next year, when the whole thing starts again.

This hypothetical example hopefully shows the various dynamics at play in a simple way. In reality, there are numerous actors that complicate matters even more, including multiple government officials (each with their own agendas), perhaps more than twenty different donor agencies (who can often be played off one another), and a range of domestic interest groups vying for influence, such as labor unions, business, and NGOs. The point is to suggest that the popular model of donors imposing their will onto weak African governments is simplistic and misleading. Thinking about the dynamics, politics, and incentives of reform also helps to understand why, after almost three decades of structural adjustment, many of the same issues are still on the table.

• *Performance.* Donors have largely moved from giving aid based on promises to giving aid based on past performance. Instead of sitting down and asking "What are you going to do if we give you more aid?" the donors are now asking "What have you done to deserve more aid?" The change is subtle, but important. Whether it will make a substantial difference, or whether donors will stick to the shift, remains to be seen.

• *Process.* Another big change is a shift from "policy conditionality" to "process conditionality." In the past, countries were judged mostly on what policies they pursued, with the idea that donors could help identify the policies most appropriate for each country and then induce them to follow the more enlightened path. While there is still considerable agreement around the Washington Consensus, the exact mix for each country, and the difficult questions of how and when, led donors to adapt. The conditions for loans or grants now are usually linked less to specific policies and based more on how policies are decided, including new demands for consultation with "stakeholders," which include representatives of civil society, local businesses, and regular people. Again, there are limits as to how far this works in practice, and it is far too early to know if the results will be any different.

For Further Reading

The best books on the incentives and disincentives for reform in Africa are Nicolas van de Walle's *African Economies and the Politics of Permanent Crisis, 1979–1999* (2001) and William Easterly's *The Elusive Quest for Growth* (2001). Peter Lewis's review article "Economic Reform and Political Transition in Africa: The Quest for a Politics of Development" (1996) is also an excellent overview of the main issues.

A large literature on the politics of adjustment appeared in the 1990s. Among the best on Africa are *Hemmed In: Responses to Africa's Economic Decline,* edited by Thomas Callaghy and John Ravenhill (1993), and *Economic Change and Political Liberalization in Sub-Saharan Africa,* edited by Jennifer A. Widner (1994). For a view of these issues beyond Africa, see Tony Killick's *Aid and the Political Economy of Policy Change* (1998), Stephan Haggard and Robert Kaufman's *The Politics of Economic Adjustment* (1992), and Dani Rodrik's "Understanding Economic Policy Reform" (1996).

For an explanation of the dynamics behind Africa's "partial reform syndrome," see David Gordon's "Conditionality in Policy-Based Lending in Africa: USAID Experience" (1992). To see how one country managed to outmaneuver the donors, see Paul Mosley's "How to Confront the World Bank and Get Away with It: A Case Study of Kenya" (1992). Among the large literature on Ghana's experience are Donald Rothchild's *Ghana: The*

Political Economy of Recovery (1991) and Jeffrey Herbst's *The Politics of Reform in Ghana, 1982–1991* (1992).

Two qualitative articles on the demise of conditionality are Joan Nelson's "Promoting Policy Reforms: The Twilight of Conditionality?" (1996) and Paul Collier's "The Failure of Conditionality" (1997). One cross-country quantitative assessment is David Dollar and Jakob Svensson's "What Explains the Success or Failure of Structural Adjustment Programs?" (2000).

The original "Washington Consensus" comes from John Williamson's "What Washington Means by Policy Reform" in *The Progress of Policy Reform in Latin America* (1990). Subsequently, and partly because he felt his term has been misunderstood and misused, he has written several follow-up pieces to update and clarify the term (all of these can be found on the Institute for International Economics website). Much more on the evolving aid and policy agenda can be found in the "Further Reading" section of Chapter 8, but the seminal report sparking World Bank structural adjustment lending in Africa was *Accelerated Development in Sub-Saharan Africa: An Agenda for Action* (1981), while *Can Africa Claim the 21st Century?* (2000) lays out the more recent agenda and strategy.

8

The International Aid System

FOR MANY PEOPLE "DEVELOPMENT" IS MOSTLY ABOUT AID.
Interaction between the developed and the developing world is intimately shaped by the financial and political relationships surrounding the transfer of money. Billions of dollars flow from rich countries to poor ones every year (and vice versa). But the international aid system is deeply dysfunctional and is rife with contradictions and unintended consequences. More importantly, development is about much more than aid. In fact, there is growing evidence that there are other kinds of things rich countries can do—trade, migration, technology, private finance—that might do much more to reduce poverty than aid. Nevertheless, for most of Africa, aid has become the largest single source of financing, and will remain a central component of development promotion efforts on the continent for the foreseeable future.

Indeed, in the early years of the twenty-first century, aid is popular again. After Cold War justifications for foreign aid evaporated, aid to low-income countries declined precipitously in the mid-1990s. Aid proponents scrambled for a new rationale and the outcome was the fight against global poverty—for humanitarian and strategic reasons. The push for more aid gained new life after the September 11, 2001, terrorist attacks, and there were renewed efforts from antipoverty advocates to capitalize on the growing sentiment that low-income countries were both threats and opportunities for the West.

Africa is among the prime targets of much of the aid business, as the region with the worst poverty and so far seemingly the least responsive to past aid efforts. This chapter will give a basic overview of the types and institutions of aid, as well as the major issues confronting those trying to fix a broken system, including figuring out how much aid is the right amount and how it can be delivered better. Aid is another development topic dominated by acronyms and lingo that can seem impenetrable to outsiders. This chapter should help you to understand that USAID gives US aid and how CIDA is different from SIDA, even if the two are pronounced the same. It should even help you make sense of why ODA for the MDGs from IDA use the CPIA to implement PBA in support of the PRSP.

Origins of the International Aid System

Even before World War II was over, planning for European reconstruction had begun. The major allies met in Bretton Woods, New Hampshire, in the summer of 1944 to help create a more stable international economic system after the war. The outcome of that conference was the creation of the International Monetary Fund (IMF) and the International Bank for Reconstruction and Development (IBRD, the main component of the World Bank)—what are now known as the "Bretton Woods Institutions." The purpose of the IMF was to help coordinate rules about policies toward money and exchange rates and also to create an organization that could make short-term loans to countries facing a temporary crisis. The IBRD/World Bank was to act like a bank and make long-term loans to finance reconstruction of the roads, bridges, and other things destroyed during the war.

In addition to the creation of these global, multilateral institutions, the United States also had its own assistance plan for Europe. Dubbed the "Marshall Plan" after then-US secretary of state George Marshall, it was a large package of aid given to the Western European countries from about 1948 to 1951, about half of which went to Britain and France. Although there is some debate today about whether the money was the important part of the help or not, the Marshall Plan was successful in the sense that Europe was able to rebuild and get back on its feet. Around the same time, the United States also started giving aid to Greece and Turkey as part of US strategy to counter communist expansion. As the Cold War became more intense, the use of foreign aid also accelerated. In 1961 the US Agency for International Development (USAID) was established, marking the birth of the modern era of foreign aid as a tool of US foreign policy.

In addition to geostrategic concerns, the other driving force behind the growth of foreign aid and bureaucracies to hand it out was decolonization. The dismantling of the British and French Empires led to new foreign aid programs, especially in Africa in the early 1960s. For the former colonial powers, this was initially aimed at smoothing the transition to independence, but soon took on other strategic purposes, such as preventing Soviet influence or promoting continued European influence on the continent. France in particular saw its aid programs to former colonies as part of maintaining French global status. Such historical justifications are evidenced by the strong links between language and colonialism to contemporary aid allocation; donors tend to give much more aid to countries with which they have had a past relationship.

More recently, poverty reduction has become the primary rationale for aid to Africa. This is partly for moral or humanitarian reasons (to relieve avoidable suffering and promote economic opportunity) and also for a new security agenda (based on a supposed relationship between poverty and emerging transnational threats). Promotion of Western economic interests is a third-order concern for aid to Africa since the markets are so small, with the exception of a few oil-producing countries. Although poverty concerns were always in the background, they became the main purpose only after the fall of the Berlin Wall. Given this new reasoning, issues of aid effectiveness—that is, the ability of aid to produce economic growth or to reduce poverty rather than just buy off allies—became urgent questions.

Various Types of Aid

There are many different types of aid. The most basic distinction is by donor, which can be either private aid (given by individuals, churches, charities, or other nongovernmental groups) or official aid (given by governments). Within the official aid category there are further donor breakdowns into either bilateral aid (from a single government, such as Germany or New Zealand) or multilateral aid (from an institution owned by many governments, such as the World Bank or the African Development Bank). Another difference can be by recipient, as aid can be channeled to governments (such as the government of Benin) or to private organizations (such as CARE or Nigeria's Society for Women and AIDS in Africa). Aid can be given for specific projects (to build a school in Nairobi), for a sector (to support Malawian healthcare), or as budget support (a payment into Ghana's treasury for general use).

Official Development Assistance

The most commonly discussed type of aid is "official development assistance" or ODA. ODA is official aid given for nonmilitary purposes and is either a grant (an outright gift) or a soft loan (a loan with low interest rates and often with long repayment periods). ODA is usually given in "net" terms, which subtracts principal repayments from past loans that flow in the other direction (which is why some countries could receive negative net ODA if their repayments of old loans are larger than new aid).

The usual ODA data that gets reported every year—and provides the numbers for most studies on aid—comes from the Development Assistance Committee (DAC) of the Organization for Economic Cooperation and Development (OECD), which is a club of donors. Although ODA data is self-reported by each donor, the DAC provides a common definition and reporting standards for ODA and a source for comparable figures. Despite these attempts to clarify what counts, not all aid is what it appears. Some of it is given out to help finance activities in African countries, such as to pay for medicine in clinics or books in schools. But much of what counts as ODA is spent on "technical assistance" (mainly consultants), administrative budgets for aid agencies, and even things such as the Peace Corps or English lessons for new migrants. There is thus much behind the headline figures.

Major Donors: The Bilaterals

Each rich country has some foreign aid program. The most common donor group is the DAC, which has twenty-two members. In addition, there are a growing number of "new" non-DAC donors, including China, Saudi Arabia, and South Korea. Most of the donors have a specific agency that manages the bulk of their nonmilitary assistance (see Table 8.1). But this also differs quite a lot, and each country has its own system for helping poor countries. (As we will see below, this can create

Table 8.1   Bilateral Donors, DAC Members

Country	Lead Aid Agencies
Australia	Australian Agency for International Development (AusAID)
Austria	Austrian Development Cooperation (ADC), Austrian Development Agency (ADA)
Belgium	Directorate-General for Development Cooperation (DGDC), Belgian Technical Cooperation (BTC)
Canada	Canadian International Development Agency (CIDA)
Denmark	Danish International Development Agency (DANIDA)
Finland	Department for International Development Cooperation
France	l'Agence Française de Développement (AfD)
Germany	Federal Ministry for Economic Cooperation and Development (BMZ)
Greece	International Development Cooperation Department (HELLENIC-AID)
Ireland	Development Cooperation Ireland (DCI)
Italy	Directorate General for Development Cooperation
Japan	Japan International Cooperation Agency (JICA), Japan Bank for International Cooperation (JBIC)
Luxembourg	Lux-Development
Netherlands	Directorate-General for International Cooperation (DGIS)
New Zealand	New Zealand Agency for International Development (NZAID)
Norway	Norwegian Agency for Development Cooperation (NORAD)
Portugal	Portuguese Institute for Development Support (IPAD)
Spain	Spanish Agency for International Cooperation (AECI)
Sweden	Swedish Agency for International Development Cooperation (SIDA)
Switzerland	Swiss Agency for Development and Cooperation (SDC)
United Kingdom	Department for International Development (DFID)
United States	US Agency for International Development (USAID)

certain problems.) There are also multiple agencies within each donor country, which are only sometimes coordinated.

USAID

The United States, for instance, is particularly fragmented, with at least forty different US government agencies involved in some sort of ODA. The lead agency, USAID, which was created as part of the 1961 Foreign Assistance Act to manage all nonmilitary assistance, handles only about half of total US ODA. USAID is technically part of the State Department, but does not have cabinet-level representation. Many of the cabinet departments, such as Commerce, Health and Human Services, Treasury, Agriculture, and other parts of the State Department, have their own programs that count as foreign aid. Even some activities of noncabinet agencies, such as the Centers for Disease Control, the National Institutes of Health, and the Overseas Private Investment Corporation (OPIC), are included in the ODA figures. In addition, the US Congress plays a very active role in setting the foreign aid agenda, including approval of all budgets, restrictions on how the money can be spent, and often earmarking of funds for specific purposes. In 2004, the United States added another wholly new foreign aid program, the Millennium Challenge Account (MCA), an experimental model designed to help channel money to the "good performers."

DFID

A completely different model is used by the British, where the vast majority of aid is channeled through the Department for International Development (DFID). British "aid" was originally handled by individual colonial offices. In 1962 a separate Department of Technical Cooperation was set up to help administer aid programs to former colonies. Every change of government then brought a new reorganization of the British aid bureaucracy. In 1979 Margaret Thatcher moved lead responsibility to an Overseas Development Administration under the Foreign Office. In 1997 Tony Blair reorganized again and created DFID, promoting the secretary to cabinet level. DFID not only manages most of Britain's bilateral aid, it plays a coordinating and strategy-setting role for other nonaid policies that might affect development, such as UK trade or security policy. The British Parliament can help to shape UK aid policy, but does not have nearly the same amount of influence as the US Congress over what gets spent, where, or how.

Major Donors: The Multilaterals

The large multilateral organizations are central to global efforts to promote African development. This is partly because they are able to gener-

Table 8.2   Bilateral ODA to Africa (in US$ millions, average for 2000–2003)

Rank	DAC Donor	Global ODA	ODA to Africa
1	United States	13,059	2,423
2	France	6,186	2,083
3	United Kingdom	5,650	1,308
4	Germany	6,528	1,200
5	Netherlands	4,158	992
6	Japan	10,131	714
7	Italy	2,332	572
8	Belgium	1,340	504
9	Denmark	2,020	489
10	Sweden	2,311	480
11	Norway	1,830	428
12	Canada	2,016	322
13	Switzerland	1,180	207
14	Ireland	423	197
15	Spain	2,034	152
16	Austria	631	136
17	Portugal	362	134
18	Finland	520	90
19	Luxembourg	178	54
20	Australia	1,199	35
21	New Zealand	159	9
22	Greece	321	2
	Non-DAC Bilaterals	2,429	205

Source: Author calculations based on OECD data.

ate fairly substantial amounts of money, but probably more importantly because of their multilateral status—meaning they are owned by multiple member governments—which gives them extra influence and global reach. The most important for Africa are the World Bank, the IMF, the African Development Bank (AfDB), and the various UN agencies.

The World Bank Group
The single most important global institution shaping the development agenda is the World Bank. It alone provides about one-quarter of all ODA to Africa. But its money is perhaps far less important than its influence and presence. The World Bank has 184 member countries. Although it is based in Washington, DC, it has offices in more than a hundred countries and is increasingly delegating more authority beyond headquarters. It employs more than 10,000 people with a huge range of expertise including economics, health and education policy, infrastructure, and other aspects of development. Its main operations are much

---

Shorthand for the Multilaterals

• *International organizations (IOs)* can be any agency that has multiple member states, such as the UN, the World Trade Organization, or the OECD.

• *Multilateral development banks (MDBs)* are the various banks owned by groups of governments that make long-term loans for development purposes. For Africa, these include the World Bank and the African Development Bank.

• *Regional development banks* are the MDBs with a regional focus. For Africa the most important is the African Development Bank based in Tunis, although there are also subregional ones, such as the East African Development Bank in Kampala or the Development Bank of Southern Africa near Johannesburg. (There is similarly an Asian Development Bank, the Inter-American Development Bank, etc., for the other regions).

• *International financial institutions (IFIs)* is a generic term for any global organization involved in financial transactions, but is often used as shorthand for the World Bank and IMF.

• *The Bretton Woods Institutions* are specifically the World Bank and the IMF.

Table 8.3   Multilateral Donors to Sub-Saharan Africa (in US$ millions, 2000–2003 average)

Donor	ODA to All Countries	ODA to SSA
International Development Association (World Bank's IDA)	5,712	2,793
European Union (EU)	6,454	2,094
African Development Bank (AfDB)	504	479
UN High Commission for Refugees (UNHCR)	614	262
UN World Food Program (WFP)	392	230
UN Children's Fund (UNICEF)	659	197
UN Development Program (UNDP)	346	155
UN Technical Assistance Program (UNTA)	509	111
UN Population Fund (UNFPA)	286	84
UN International Fund for Agricultural Development (IFAD)	171	77
Other UN Agencies	626	87
Arab Agencies	104	61
Nordic Development Fund	43	22
Global Environment Facility	112	20
International Monetary Fund (IMF)	152	15

Source: Author calculations based on OECD data.

like any bank: it borrows money in private markets and then relends it to governments. In addition, it also provides advice to borrowing governments and has a (mostly independent) research department that does some of the most cutting-edge and innovative analysis of development issues and trends.

The World Bank Group (often just called "the Bank") is actually several organizations under one umbrella. The two main components are the International Bank for Reconstruction and Development (IBRD) and the International Development Association (IDA).

• *IBRD*. The IBRD is the original "World Bank" and lends money to middle-income countries, currently those that are either fairly rich (the 2004 threshold was US$865 per capita income) or can borrow from regular capital markets (perhaps because of oil or some other reason investors think they are creditworthy). In Africa, countries such as Botswana, South Africa, Gabon, or Mauritius are IBRD, which means they can borrow from the World Bank and get advice, but they pay close to commercial interest rates (there are exceptions, like borrowing for HIV/AIDS).

• *IDA*. IDA is the "soft window" set up in 1960 for low-income countries. As the Bank expanded from European reconstruction into promoting development for the former European colonies, it was thought these very poor countries would need to be able to borrow at cheap fixed-rate interest rates. The current terms for IDA loans are extremely favorable: forty-year loans at 0.75 percent, plus there is a ten-year grace period. IDA is also increasingly using more grants, which are outright gifts with no repayment. To pay for grants or loans with such cheap rates, the main shareholders give money to IDA every three years as a subsidy. These pledges are called the "IDA replenishment" and the fourteenth such period, called IDA-14, started in July 2005. (IDA-15 will begin in July 2008, and so on.) The vast majority of African countries are IDA members.

In addition to the IBRD and IDA, the World Bank Group has other affiliate components. The most important are:

• *International Finance Corporation (IFC)*, which makes loans not to governments but to private companies in developing countries. The IFC has a dual mandate to both promote development (by helping private firms grow and investing in private projects such as power or energy) and make profits.

• *Multilateral Investment Guarantee Agency (MIGA)* acts like an insurance company that provides protection for private investors in risky markets, with the intention of encouraging greater capital flow into projects that would promote development.

• *International Centre for Settlement of Investment Disputes (ICSID)* is a fairly small organization that mediates between governments and investors when there is a dispute. The purpose is to use the World Bank's influence to resolve differences and increase the confidence that investors would have recourse where local courts may not be strong enough.

The International Monetary Fund

The International Monetary Fund (IMF) is the sister organization to the World Bank, and sits only a few feet across 19th Street in downtown Washington, DC. The primary purpose of the IMF (known commonly as just "the Fund") is to provide countries with short-term loans when they face an immediate crisis. Its role in low-income countries that are facing long-term development problems rather than financial emergencies is somewhat ambiguous. Beginning in the mid-1970s, the Fund began to make medium-term loans to countries with deeper problems. Kenya was the first such country, getting an "extended fund facility" in 1975. In the mid-1980s, the "enhanced structural adjustment facility" (ESAF) was launched, which allowed low-income countries to borrow from the Fund. In exchange for the ESAF loan (which was for ten years at 0.5 percent with a five-and-a-half-year grace period) countries would have to agree to meet certain targets and make changes. These differed from country to country, but usually included some limits on the budget deficit and money supply (to contain inflation) and promises to reduce the government's involvement in the economy through lowering trade barriers, freeing up the exchange rate, or selling off state companies. At regular intervals, the Fund would review the country's progress and report on whether it was "on-track" or "off-track."

The reason these judgments were so important was not simply access to the Fund's capital. In fact, ESAFs were usually fairly small in dollar amounts. The key part of getting an IMF agreement and sticking to the conditions was that the other donors, including the World Bank and most bilaterals, used the Fund as the signal for whether the country was basically heading in the right direction or not. Thus, the Fund's main role in Africa has been to monitor country policies and activities and act as a gatekeeper to other donor funds. The consequences of a "no" vote by the Fund are more significant than just a small loan; it could cut off a country from most of its external financiers.

In practice, this authority by the IMF has been double-edged. Since

The World Bank's Deepening Agenda, 1960s to Present

Officially, the mandate of the World Bank Group is to reduce poverty and increase living standards around the world. It does this by making loans, providing advice, and conducting research covering a wide range of development activities. But what it has done in practice has changed significantly over the past four decades.

The dominant ideas about development in the 1960s, reflected in Bank strategies, emphasized the role of state planning to generate a "takeoff." The Bank was therefore initially focused on helping to build large infrastructure projects, such as the massive Akosombo Dam in Ghana constructed in the early 1960s. But these big projects did not have the intended effect of spurring the rest of the economy. In the 1970s the Bank's focus shifted toward specific projects to help people, sometimes called a "basic needs" approach, which was to start projects in healthcare or education. These were somewhat successful, especially international efforts to combat river blindness in West Africa. A related strategy, called "integrated rural development," also emerged that tried to support agriculture and link farming to projects in transport and healthcare. But neither basic needs nor integrated rural development sparked an economic revival. In fact, much of Africa got worse, with a wave of political instability bringing coups and civil wars and economies mostly stagnating.

By the late 1970s and early 1980s, the World Bank began to emphasize policies and management. The idea was that if neither big enclave projects nor small targeted projects were working, then the broader environment must be the problem. It was true that many African economies had high inflation and much of the public spending was put into wasteful projects. Among the most notorious is construction with public money in the mid-1980s of the world's largest church, a replica of Saint Peter's in Rome, in Yamoussoukro, Côte d'Ivoire, the birthplace of then-president Félix Houphouët-Boigny. Less grandly, but perhaps no less damaging, millions of dollars flowed into nonproductive and inefficient state projects, such as steel plants that produced no steel or collective plantations that produced few crops. Of the money allocated to social services, little of it ever arrived where it was supposed to go. Most African states had gotten deeply involved in the ownership and management of the economy, to the benefit of the politically connected, but with terrible results for the rest of the population.

The response by the Bank was to shift again, this time toward structural changes. Part of this was to try to fix policies ("get prices right") and to remove the state from activities where private ownership and management were thought more efficient (such as with shoe factories). The advent of "structural adjustment" meant that World Bank loans were tied to various policy changes, including control of public spending, the removal of price controls, the lowering of trade barriers, and the selling off of loss-making, state-owned companies. There were a number of

(continues)

(Continued)

success stories from these changes, such as the recovery of Ghana and Uganda, both of which bounced back strongly in response to reforms, seeing growth pick up and poverty rates decline. For many countries the changes were partial and the overall results of reform were uneven and disappointing. It was also increasingly evident that the Bank's strategy of attaching conditions to loans was not working. Countries rarely fulfilled their promises and the Bank usually failed to enforce its own conditions. As a whole, Africa and the Bank continued to disappoint.

The next wave was the rise of the "governance" agenda. If changing policies was not enough or if governments were half-hearted about reform, the next idea was that there must be a problem with the state itself. But since the Bank is not mandated to deal with "political" issues, the initial governance projects were small technical steps, such as civil-service reform. Over time this expanded to include more substantial changes in the operations of the state, such as budget management, decentralization, and corruption. The purpose was to reorient the state to be more "development-friendly" and less prone to the waste and graft of the past.

By the 1990s, the Bank's agenda grew even broader, including deeper involvement in the budget, the promotion of civil society, and even cultural and social issues. The buzzwords for the twenty-first century are not about policy change or technical reform, but the mega-concepts of ownership, participation, and transparency. Its current agenda is in many ways so wide and diffuse that there are now calls for the Bank to draw back and focus more narrowly on what a bank can reasonably achieve.

the donors are so reliant on the Fund, it wields enormous influence beyond its immediate size. This means that IMF negotiators can play a major role in setting a country's agenda and also be the primary judge of that country's performance. But because a Fund withdrawal from a country has such significant implications, the negotiators have been hesitant to exercise that option. This has created resentment against the Fund on both sides. Countries complain that the Fund is too powerful and has too much influence on their economic policy. (Some of this criticism is fair, much of it is not.) At the same time, the IMF has been criticized for failing to enforce its own conditions and being gullible, allowing countries to drag reforms on for decades, always accepting new promises but never following through (see Chapter 7).

In 1999, the ESAF was renamed the Poverty Reduction and Growth Facility (PRGF). Although the idea is that the new PRGF is supposed to be more focused than the ESAF was on poverty issues and less on macroeconomic targets, in practice it operates in much the same way. Recently, the Fund, under criticism for allowing poor countries to run up IMF debts, has also been experimenting with new programs that do not have any loan component but are just a surveillance agreement. Countries set their own targets and the IMF agrees to make regular progress reports, but no money changes hands. Nigeria and Uganda were among the first countries to test out this new option.

African Development Bank

The African Development Bank (AfDB) is a bank for African governments (including North Africa). It was established in 1964 to be a regional player, much like the World Bank, but with much more local control. It has seventy-seven member nations, fifty-three of which are African and twenty-four that are "nonregionals." Like the World Bank, it has a hard window for middle-income borrowers and a soft window for the low-income countries. Unlike the other financial institutions, however, African countries wield considerable voting power (although not enough to completely override the nonregionals who finance the AfDB). In practice, the AfDB has faced many problems that have undermined its ability to play a more significant role. In many ways, the AfDB has tried to replicate much of what the World Bank does, but with fewer resources, personnel, and overall capacity, with predictable results. Its closeness to its borrowers is supposed to be a strength, but it is also a weakness, in that the organization has been more susceptible to political interference, which has adversely affected its performance. The AfDB has also had difficulties related to its location. Based in Abidjan, Côte d'Ivoire, it was forced to temporarily relocate to Tunisia when civil war broke out and the then-head of the bank faced death threats. In 2005, new leadership was installed and another reorganization begun.

UN Agencies

There are multiple agencies of the United Nations (UN) involved in various aspects of promoting security and economic development in Africa. For the most part, the activities and roles of these agencies reflect the broader strengths and weaknesses of the UN system: they have credibility as multilateral organizations but their ability to implement projects or provide policy advice is usually very weak. One reason for their unfulfilled promise is the staffing quota system, which allows member governments to use UN appointments as patronage, often installing people with few qualifications into high-paying jobs. UN funding is, unlike that of the MDBs', wholly reliant on the donors, making it vulnerable to shortfalls and volatility. More broadly, the UN agencies reflect UN membership: ideologically diverse, often quarrelsome, and almost always bureaucratic. The UN agencies are also long on talk—reports, conferences, summits—but short on action or real analytical input. These may be unavoidable qualities for an international organization trying to represent nearly two hundred member governments, but they are barriers for building an effective response to complex developmental problems. There are many UN agencies involved in one way or another with African development, and the main programs or specialized agencies include:

• *UN Development Program (UNDP)* is the lead development agency that can play an important coordinating role in some places, but its own ability to manage projects or shape the development agenda is extremely limited.

• *Economic Commission for Africa (UNECA)*, based in Addis Ababa, Ethiopia, is one of the five regional UN commissions that does a limited amount of analytical and advocacy work on behalf of the continent.

• *UN High Commission for Refugees (UNHCR)* has been crucial in providing support for people forced to flee their home country and facilitating their return.

• *World Food Program (WFP)* is the leading official organization for delivering emergency food aid and is very active in Africa.

• *UN Children's Fund (UNICEF)* has been important in raising awareness of childhood diseases and other issues, and in coordinating immunization campaigns.

• *Food and Agriculture Organization (FAO)* is supposed to help improve agricultural policies, but is mainly a talk-shop on food policy.

• *UN Population Fund (UNFPA)* provides advice for countries on population data and management issues.

• *World Health Organization (WHO)* was set up to help national governments improve their own health policies. Recently it has taken a lead role in organizing a global response to transnational health issues, such as Avian flu.

• *UNAIDS* is the UN body that deals with the HIV/AIDS pandemic. It plays a mostly public-information and advocacy role, although it does get involved at times in programs and monitoring (see Chapter 10).

• *UN International Fund for Agricultural Development (IFAD)* finances agricultural development projects through low-interest loans and grants, usually for food production.

• *UN Conference on Trade and Development (UNCTAD)* is a mostly ineffectual group that is supposed to promote trade and investment in developing countries. It has sometimes been schizophrenic about whether trade and investment are good for the poor or not, but its most useful function is to provide annual data on foreign investment (see Chapter 13).

• *UN Department of Peacekeeping Operations (DPKO)* has been extremely active with peacekeeping in Africa, with nearly half of the UN's global operations on the continent (see Chapter 4).

Nongovernmental Organizations

Nongovernmental organizations (NGOs) have become increasingly important players in the aid business, both in delivering services and setting agendas. Many of the donors subcontract to private groups to actually implement projects. USAID is one of those most often using this approach, with hundreds of companies set up mainly to compete for government contracts (they are sometimes called "beltway bandits"). USAID even publishes a list of all of its contractors and projects in an annual "yellow book" (a great source for job hunting). There are local NGOs based in African countries that also can receive contracts (or subcontracts) from donors. NGOs have also become increasingly active in lobbying for policy changes and other development issues. Debt relief is perhaps the most prominent example, but NGOs are now actively engaged on a range of aid issues including proponents for larger budgets and for changing the way donors distribute aid.

The rise of NGOs as a force in aid is in many ways positive. Local groups (or private foreign groups with affiliates on the ground) are often better able than large bureaucracies to execute projects. They are often closer to the people they serve, better able to adapt to local conditions, and often simply more efficient because they are smaller than the big donor agencies. US politicians also tend to prefer using NGOs because they are thought to be less corrupt than governments, and many gain favor because they are church affiliated. But the use of NGOs is not without its problems as well. Using hundreds of separate groups makes aid even more uncoordinated, not only with other donors but also with the plans and priorities of the host government. Ironically, because many NGOs have gotten more involved as contractors, they have also become more reliant on public money—and thus perhaps are no longer truly "non" governmental. (Some of them are now derisively referred to as MGOs for "mostly governmental organizations.")

NGO lobbying activities are also fraught with problems. They can raise important issues, and also tend to be more media-savvy and politically connected than disorganized groups of poor people in foreign countries. But because NGOs often claim to speak for certain populations (such as "the poor" or "Africans"), they are thus self-appointed and not accountable to their stated constituencies. Many of the NGOs also come with ideological baggage, such as skepticism toward capitalism or opposition to certain kinds of technology, which often proves unhelpful for those they purport to be serving.

Recipient Governments

The most central players in the aid business—even though they are too frequently overlooked—are the recipient governments themselves. The aid business is rife with talk of "partnership," but much of the haggling, strategizing, and planning goes on among and between donors. This is true despite the fact that most donors recognize that the most important factors in development success are the attitudes, intentions, and actions of the host governments. In fact, the primary responsibility for promoting development lies with African governments, even if neither donors nor recipients acknowledge this.

It is hard to generalize about African governments as they include such a wide array of abilities and skills. The government of Botswana, arguably Africa's most "developmental" state, is very different from the government in Congo or Chad. Much of Africa's public sector is simply not geared toward promoting development or reducing poverty, but rather toward private gain or political survival (see Chapters 3 and 7). Yet the ability to manage money, deliver services, or even provide basic security all affect the results of aid efforts.

Aid Intensity and Dependency

Contemporary sub-Saharan Africa is by far the most aid-dependent region of the globe at any time in history. Total aid to Africa has climbed over the past four decades, as has Africa's share of global ODA (see Figure 8.1). This trend has also recovered from a dip at the end of the Cold War, including a jump from about $13 billion in 2001 to over $23 billion in 2004. Recent pledges from the major donors for even greater aid increases to the continent suggest these figures will rise even further over the next decade or so.

In addition to rising overall levels of aid, the relative importance of aid to Africa is very high. In 2003 total ODA to Africa was equivalent to over 5 percent of GDP, and if South Africa and Nigeria (two large economies that receive relatively little aid) are excluded, the total for the remaining countries jumps to over 10 percent of GDP. Historically, this is an unprecedented scale for any region. The US Marshall Plan to reconstruct postwar Europe, for instance, never amounted to more than 3 percent of any recipient European economy, even at its peak. In addition to the regional average, there are many countries with even larger shares of aid. Table 8.4 shows the "aid intensity" ratio, ODA as a percentage of total GDP, for each sub-Saharan country. The last column of Table 8.4 also shows ODA per capita or how much each country receives per person.

"Big Push" vs. Dependency

The debates over how much aid is the right amount for Africa have been ongoing for the past half century. On the one hand, proponents of more aid to the continent often argue that poor economies are trapped in poverty, and only an even bigger push can help get them out. This was a popular view of development in the 1950s and has recently come back into favor among those lobbying for large new increases. The traditional skeptics of aid have worried that too much help would make countries dependent and discourage them from standing on their own feet. More recent critics point to the high level of aid and dismal performance in most of Africa, charging that aid itself is one reason that Africa remains poor. They argue that Africa already gets lots of aid—including many countries who have been aid-dependent for several decades—and believe increased aid flows may make matters worse. Both views are prevalent today, with supporting examples on both sides (Botswana and South Korea on the pro-aid side, with Congo and Zambia supporting the anti-aid camp).

At the root of these differing perspectives are not only selective use

Figure 8.1 Aid to Sub-Saharan Africa as a Share of Total Aid, 1960–2004

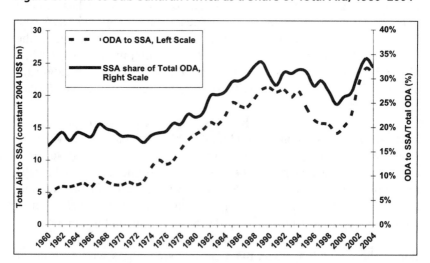

Source: OECD DAC.

Table 8.4 Aid to Africa, by Recipient, 2003

ODA/GDP (%)		ODA per capita (US$)	
Congo, Democratic Republic of	94.7	Cape Verde	306
São Tomé and Príncipe	63.8	São Tomé and Príncipe	240
Guinea-Bissau	60.8	Seychelles	107
Eritrea	52.8	Congo, Democratic Republic	101
Burundi	37.7	Guinea-Bissau	98
Sierra Leone	30.2	Mauritania	85
Malawi	29.0	Namibia	72
Mozambique	23.9	Eritrea	70
Ethiopia	22.6	Sierra Leone	56
Mauritania	21.7	Cameroon	55
Rwanda	19.7	Mozambique	55
Cape Verde	17.3	Zambia	54
Gambia, The	17.0	Tanzania	47
Niger	16.6	Malawi	45
Tanzania	16.2	Mali	45
Uganda	13.7	Lesotho	44
Zambia	13.0	Ghana	44
Mali	12.0	Senegal	44
Ghana	11.9	Benin	44
Burkina Faso	10.6	Equatorial Guinea	43
Madagascar	9.9	Gambia, The	42
Chad	9.4	Comoros	41
Benin	8.4	Rwanda	40
Comoros	8.0	Niger	39
Cameroon	7.1	Uganda	38
Senegal	7.0	Burkina Faso	37
Guinea	6.5	Angola	37
Lesotho	6.5	Madagascar	32
Central African Republic	4.2	Liberia	32
Angola	3.6	Burundi	31
Sudan	3.5	Guinea	30
Kenya	3.5	Chad	29
Namibia	3.4	Swaziland	24
Togo	2.5	Ethiopia	22
Zimbabwe	2.1	Congo, Republic of	19
Congo, Republic of	2.0	Sudan	19
Côte d'Ivoire	1.8	Somalia	18
Swaziland	1.5	Botswana	17
Seychelles	1.3	Kenya	15
Equatorial Guinea	0.7	Côte d'Ivoire	15
Nigeria	0.6	Zimbabwe	14
Botswana	0.4	South Africa	14
South Africa	0.4	Central African Republic	13
Gabon	−0.2	Togo	9
Mauritius	−0.3	Nigeria	2
Liberia	not avail.	Gabon	−8
Somalia	not avail.	Mauritius	−12

Sources: Estimates based on data from the OECD, IMF, World Bank.

and interpretation of evidence, but also a philosophical divide about the way to achieve human progress. Aid proponents generally believe that interventions with external assistance can be transformative and that major changes can be possible in a short period with the right amount of money, know-how, and effort. They also put great faith in the ability of public institutions to make life better for all. Skeptics, even those that acknowledge the value of aid in some circumstances, tend to think that aid can only support changes going on inside countries already, and that development is mostly about slow, incremental societal evolution. They also usually perceive the state not as driving changes, but rather as creating space to allow individuals and private groups to act within the natural forces of the market.

Another issue with aid has been the linkage to governance. Aid proponents argue that aid can be used to induce governments to behave better, pointing to the widespread use of aid as leverage to encourage elections in a number of countries in the early 1990s. They also believe that aid can be designed in ways that support civil society, either by forcing governments to consult their populations as a prerequisite for receiving aid (see PRSP below) or by funding NGOs directly. Political scientists have tended to make the counterargument that aid has supported antidevelopmental political systems by providing resources for patronage. Evidence that this continues is the common use of aid funds to buy expensive four-wheel-drive vehicles for public officials and the use of donor-sponsored "training" or travel allowances as a way to top up salaries. In many cases, aid provides a lifeline for otherwise bankrupt regimes and has undoubtedly (if usually indirectly) funded the buildup of militaries and other means of repression.

The International Aid Target: 0.7 Percent

One of the answers to "how much aid?" has been the international target for rich countries to spend 0.7 percent of their national income on development aid. Many of the donors have pledged to reach this level by some future date, but in practice only a few donors have done so, all of them small northern European nations (see Table 8.5), and only a portion of this aid goes to sub-Saharan Africa (SSA). Campaigners have long used the 0.7 percent target to lobby for more aid, and there are common complaints from poor countries that the donors have not met their promised goal. But there are also several popular misunderstandings about the 0.7 percent target (and questions often raised by the countries near the bottom). First, the target was first set in the early 1960s using a model based on global conditions at that time. Over the following decades that model (known as the "financing gap") has lost credibility. Just as importantly,

Table 8.5   Donors and the International Target (average for 2000–2003)

Rank	Donor	ODA/GNI (%)	Percentage of total to SSA
1	Denmark	0.97	24
2	Norway	0.84	23
3	Netherlands	0.82	24
4	Sweden	0.80	21
5	Luxembourg	0.76	30
6	Belgium	0.44	38
7	Ireland	0.35	47
8	Switzerland	0.35	18
9	France	0.35	34
10	Finland	0.33	17
11	United Kingdom	0.32	23
12	Germany	0.27	18
13	Australia	0.26	3
14	Austria	0.26	22
15	Spain	0.25	7
16	Portugal	0.25	37
17	Canada	0.25	16
18	New Zealand	0.24	5
19	Japan	0.24	7
20	Greece	0.20	1
21	Italy	0.16	25
22	United States	0.12	19

Source: Author calculations based on OECD DAC Database.

the world has changed considerably: many then-poor countries have gotten rich, private capital flows have grown, and poor countries have saved more of their own resources. All of these changes suggest that the assumptions that went into arriving at the 0.7 percent target are no longer true. Perhaps more important than the origins of the specific number, there is supposedly a political consensus to reach this figure, notably several UN resolutions promising to move toward the target and an endorsement of the target by the high-profile Pearson Commission in 1970. But none of these recommendations was a binding agreement. Indeed, the United States, in every administration since John F. Kennedy, has explicitly avoided committing to any specific aid target.

The Millenium Development Goals
A more recent attempt to boost donor aid flows has been the Millennium Development Goals (MDGs). As part of the effort to rationalize aid after the Cold War, aid bureaucrats at the OECD came up with a list of global targets in the mid-1990s. Over time, this evolved into eight goals, with

eighteen targets and forty-eight indicators. In 2000 at the UN, the largest-ever gathering of heads of state unanimously adopted the Millennium Declaration, committing to reach these goals by 2015. Known as the MDGs (see Table 8.6), these are the yardstick by which current international development efforts are to be judged. In response to the goals, several studies also tried to estimate the costs of reaching the MDGs, most of which suggested a global level of about $100 billion per year (roughly a doubling from the 2000 level). The MDGs have partly been responsible for growing attention to global poverty, and rising aid levels in particular. But it is also probably true that nearly all of Africa will miss nearly all of the goals by 2015, no matter how much money is spent, since the continent is so far behind the rest of the world in these indicators. Whether making such an ambitious target will spur even faster progress or create disappointment will be one trend to watch in coming years.

Table 8.6   The Millennium Development Goals

Goal	Targets for 2015 (from 1990 level)
1. Eradicate extreme poverty and hunger	Halve the ratio of those with income < $1/day Halve the ratio of people who suffer from hunger
2. Achieve universal primary education	Universal primary schooling completion
3. Promote gender equality and empower women	Eliminate gender disparity in schooling (preferably by 2005)
4. Reduce child mortality	Reduce the under-five mortality rate by two-thirds
5. Improve maternal health	Reduce the maternal mortality rate by three-quarters
6. Combat disease	Halt and begin to reverse spread of HIV/AIDS Halt and begin to reverse incidence of malaria and other major diseases
7. Ensure environmental sustainability	Halve the ratio of people without access to safe drinking water and basic sanitation Improve lives of 100m slum dwellers by 2020 Reverse loss of environmental resources
8. Develop global partnership	7 targets related to: trade, debt, youth, technology, drug affordability, and special needs of poor countries, landlocked countries, and small islands

Aid Effectiveness: Does It Work?

The recent resurgence of aid to Africa is partly the result of renewed efforts to help the continent break from its past dismal economic performance. As poverty rates have plummeted in Asia and fallen almost everywhere else over the past several decades, they have been persistent in Africa. About half of the continent's population still lives below the $1-per-day line of extreme poverty (although no one knows for sure; see Chapter 10). Africa's economic growth rates have been meager, with average per capita income growth in Africa since 1970 close to zero. Contrary to the claims of some aid campaigners, this has not been because of a dearth of aid (see Figure 8.2). Partly because of the perceived failure of aid to lead to either rapid economic growth or poverty reduction, there are major changes under way in the international aid system.

Perhaps more of an issue than the total size of ODA flows has been the perception of its ineffectiveness. The ability of aid to promote economic growth (or not) or to reduce poverty (or not) has been the subject of major debate within the development and economics communities. There is no question that some aid has been monumentally successful. There are many cases that show aid-financed interventions leading to significant improvements in quality of life, such as the Onchocerciasis Control Program, which is credited with halting transmission of river blindness in eleven West African countries and preventing 600,000 cases between 1974 and 2002. At the same time, there is no shortage of examples of wasteful projects, which spend huge sums of money and are unable to show any palpable results. The big questions are about aid's record overall, and about the conditions under which aid can be more effective.

The Aid-Growth Debate

There is a particularly charged debate among economists about the relationship between aid and economic growth. On average, there is little evidence that foreign aid generates broad economic growth. The cross-country studies done through much of the 1990s have tended to show no relationship between aid and real GDP growth rates. A series of newer studies, however, has tried to look at this relationship more closely by slicing aid and recipient countries in different ways. Most of the recent studies that control for recipient country characteristics find that aid does lead to economic growth in certain environments, such as where there are "good policies" in place, like low inflation and reasonable management. These results are disputed, however, as they appear to depend on which countries and years are included. More importantly, most of the studies that do show that aid can cause growth also suggest

Figure 8.2   Aid and Growth in Africa (10-year moving averages)

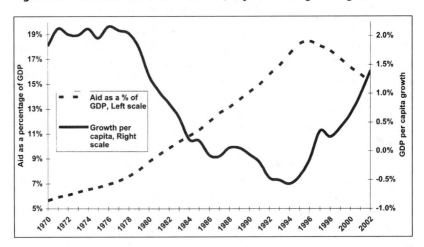

Source: World Development Indicators.
Note: This figure is an updated version of a chart that first appeared in William Easterly, *The Elusive Quest for Growth,* MIT Press, Cambridge, MA, 2001.

that, even where aid appears to be most productive, this is true only up to a certain level (what economists call "diminishing returns"). This suggests that even where aid is thought helpful to bolster incomes, donors cannot keep pouring in more aid to get more growth. In fact, it looks as though many countries in Africa are near or beyond that point already (sometimes called a "saturation point," beyond which additional aid is thought to have zero effect).

Other even more recent empirical studies have found that aid used to pay for certain short-term investments, such as infrastructure, has an even stronger impact on growth. The logic of this approach is that, for example, aid for education would only expect to show an effect after a decade or more, not within the four- or eight-year intervals normally examined. These results, along with political pressure on the industry to show that foreign aid "works," have been seized upon by aid advocates to justify their calls for higher aid levels.

At the same time, the studies trying to figure where and under what conditions aid can be best used have also led to important changes in aid allocation, both among countries and sectors. A few of the key trends are outlined below.

Recipient Selectivity

The allocation of aid to various recipients is a puzzle that researchers have tried to model with limited success. Many of the bilateral donors appear to give aid to countries for foreign policy reasons other than poverty reduction, perhaps to support a friendly government or as a payoff for some other kinds of desired activities. ODA intended for promoting development has tended in the past to be allocated based on somewhat different criteria, where donors are selective about who they think will use the money most wisely—hence, the birth of "conditionality."

In the beginning of the 1980s, donors began attaching conditions to aid, typically a series of promised actions to liberalize the economy (such as privatization) or to stabilize the economy (such as meeting budget targets). In the 1990s, political conditions, such as the holding of free elections or allowing open media, were added to the list (by bilaterals; the multilaterals shied away from political conditions). However, by the mid-1990s it was becoming clear that conditionality was not working (see Chapter 7 for more on conditionality and the politics of reform). Countries were frequently implementing only partial reforms, or finding excuses for not reaching the promised targets. Donor behavior also encouraged nonreform. In only a few cases did countries get cut off for not fulfilling their promises. Credibility on both sides dissolved.

More recently, and partly in response to new research on aid effectiveness, a new kind of selectivity has become common: performance-based allocation (PBA). Unlike conditionality, which relied on *ex ante* promises, PBA is based on *ex post* performance. The World Bank has used some form of PBA since the late 1970s, but its system has been refined and expanded substantially. The International Development Association's (IDA's) method for deciding how much countries get is based on a formula mostly comprised of the Country Policy and Institutional Assessment (CPIA). The CPIA is an internal score of twenty variables for each country judging its economic management, policies, social inclusion, and the quality of its public-sector institutions. That score counts as 80 percent of the formula for determining the size of a country's IDA envelope. (The remainder is based on an internal portfolio score for Bank projects in that country, plus an extra adjustment for its governance rating.) Although the CPIA is not public, countries can find out their own score, and the Bank is moving toward releasing scores. In December 2003, country CPIA rankings were released in quintiles for the first time (see Table 8.7).

The African Development Bank has a PBA system similar to CPIA's, but bilateral donors follow their own internal systems that tend to be much more arbitrary or designed by less explicit weightings. Some countries, such as Canada, announce "priority countries" that receive the bulk of Canadian assistance.

Table 8.7 World Bank Country Policy and Institutional Assessment (CPIA), 2003

All IDA-Eligible Sub-Saharan African Countries, by Global Quintiles				
1st	2nd	3rd	4th	5th
Cape Verde	Benin	Cameroon	Chad	Angola
Mauritania	Burkina Faso	Ethiopia	DRC	Burundi
Senegal	Ghana	Kenya	Republic of Congo	Central African Republic
Tanzania	Madagascar	Lesotho	Côte d'Ivoire	Comoros
Uganda	Mali	Malawi	Eritrea	Guinea-Bissau
	Rwanda	Mozambique	Gambia, The	Nigeria
		Zambia	Guinea	São Tomé & Príncipe
			Niger	Sudan
			Sierra Leone	Togo
				Zimbabwe

Source: IDA.
Note: Liberia and Somalia not scored, but presumably in bottom quintile.

The Millennium Challenge Account

The major exception to the allocation mystery is the US experiment with the Millennium Challenge Account (MCA, managed by the Millennium Challenge Corporation or MCC). The MCA is a new aid program to concentrate assistance in a few countries thought to be performing most efficiently from a poverty-reduction perspective. The MCA determines eligibility for funds based on a set of criteria that are, unlike the CPIA's, publicly available (indeed most of the scores are based on World Bank data). These cover sixteen indicators in three groups: ruling justly, investing in people, and encouraging economic freedom. To qualify, a country must perform above the median in a majority of each group. The board of the MCC then approves the final qualifying list and has discretion to add or delete countries. The final step is for a country to submit a business plan (or "compact") to the MCC for approval, outlining how the extra funds will be used. In the qualifying round for fiscal year 2005, eight African countries cleared the first hurdle (see Table 8.8). For the qualifying countries, the potential gains in aid are huge, perhaps tripling the amount of assistance from the United States, already among the largest donors to each of these countries.

Instrument Selectivity

For many donors, selectivity is used not only to determine how much each country gets, but also in what form. In general, countries thought to be able to handle aid responsibly are given more flexible forms of aid,

Table 8.8   African Countries Qualified for the MCA, FY 2005

Qualified	Threshold (missed by one indicator)
Benin	Kenya
Cape Verde	São Tomé & Príncipe
Ghana	Tanzania
Lesotho	Uganda
Madagascar	
Mali	
Mozambique	
Senegal	

such as budget support. Countries in Africa such as Ghana and Uganda have been receiving increasing amounts of aid from donors as direct budget support and from the World Bank through a poverty-reduction support credit, its most flexible kind of loan. Intermediate-performing countries such as Malawi or Cameroon are likely to receive aid in more constrained forms, such as sectoral support (i.e., aid targeted for one particular sector) or project support (aid for a specific stand-alone project). In the worst-performing countries, such as Sudan or Zimbabwe, where the government is not considered effective at managing funds, donors typically channel aid to projects run and managed by NGOs. Although a growing number of donors are following this spectrum approach in their aid delivery, some bilaterals (such as the United States and Japan) still prefer project aid even in the best-performing countries.

Substance Selectivity

In addition to the country and instrument selectivity used to allocate aid, donors also tend to favor certain kinds of projects at any given time. In fact, donors tend to herd together, following similar trends, such as the near unanimous abandonment in the 1990s by bilaterals of infrastructure and almost exclusive concentration on health and education. More recently there are four substantive areas that are attracting a growing amount of donor attention—and money:

• *The poorest of the poor.* Many donors, including the World Bank and European bilaterals, are increasingly targeting aid to countries with large populations living with low incomes. The UK, for instance, has pledged to dedicate 90 percent of DFID resources to the poorest countries. This is based on both a strategic decision to use aid to specifically fight poverty and a tactical way for aid bureaucracies to protect their decisionmaking from other agencies of government that may have other foreign policy goals (prioritizing middle-income countries of strategic importance, for example). In practice, the poverty focus has meant channeling a greater portion of resources to poor countries and also earmarking assistance for the health and education sectors, which are thought to help the poorest segments within these countries.

• *HIV/AIDS*. The HIV/AIDS pandemic has generated massive resources to specifically fight that disease. Most donors have special HIV/AIDS financing windows, such as the US president's Emergency Plan for AIDS Relief (PEPFAR, which will provide $15 billion over five years) or the World Bank's Multicountry AIDS Program (MAP, about $500 million per year). In addition, there are so-called vertical funds aimed at specific diseases, such as the Global Fund to Fight AIDS, Tuberculosis, and Malaria (GFATM), which has generated about $1 billion more per year. Indeed, the issue for battling HIV/AIDS is to a large extent no longer about raising financing, but about spending it effectively. Many African countries, for instance, are eligible for HIV-related funds several times larger than their entire health budgets (Chapter 10).

• *Postconflict*. Donors are also diverting an increasing amount of resources toward postconflict reconstruction (Chapter 4). This is the result of two factors. First, a growing body of evidence showing a strong relationship between conflict and development has convinced donors that dealing with political instability is a precondition for tackling poverty. Second, the major lesson drawn by the international community from the successful experience in East Timor is that a large and immediate infusion of resources can help to consolidate a positive transition. The World Bank has also accepted this view and shifted considerable resources toward postconflict reconstruction. Indeed, the single largest allocation of World Bank funds to any African country in 2003–2005 has been not to one of the best performers, but to the Democratic Republic of Congo.

• *Infrastructure*. For much of the past decade, donors have been shifting away from financing large capital-intensive projects and toward the social services. Indeed, by the late 1990s almost all of the bilateral donors were completely out of financing roads, power, water systems, and ports. But, faced with growing demands from African governments and the urgings of the World Bank and others, infrastructure is coming back in fashion. In fact, infrastructure is one area where large increases in aid could probably be best and most quickly absorbed.

Fixing "Aid Quality"

Perhaps more important than aid volumes or where it is allocated are the numerous changes in aid "quality" under discussion. In response to disappointing results from aid in the past, the way aid is delivered and the relationship between creditors and recipients have been evolving in response to ongoing complaints about the dysfunctional way the aid business often works.

• *Fragmentation.* One of the most prevalent problems is that many donors tend to have their own projects, fragmenting efforts, often duplicating what others are doing, and going off in ways that the host government might not approve of or even know about. Another common complaint is that donors have their own procedures, forcing African countries to learn dozens of different regulations, reporting requirements, and other bureaucratic mazes. These two problems together create enormous burdens on public officials, who often wind up spending most of their time dealing with donors rather than their own populations.

• *Volatility.* Aid flows themselves can also create instabilities. Since donors rarely tell governments ahead of time how much money they can expect, or they deliver a different amount than was expected, governments are usually unable to integrate donor funds into the normal budget process. Typically, African governments make a best-guess as to what they will get, but they never really know until the money arrives. In addition, the flows often change for unknown reasons, sometimes having little to do with issues in that particular country. Even when they are related to changes in a country, the criteria donors apply are opaque; countries are rarely aware of the criteria by which they are being judged.

• *Agenda setting.* The setting of spending priorities is also an area that generates dilemmas. On the one hand, donors feel that if they are the ones paying, then they have a right to direct the funds to where they think is best. Yet, African governments object to what they see as interference, especially when it might be a former colonial power that they view with suspicion. Recipients also can passively resist by agreeing to the donor preferences, but merely shifting their own money around to different parts of the budget (what economists call "fungibility"). For example, donors usually want to spend on education but not the military. So governments let them pay for schools and books and then just use more of their own money to buy tanks (and if donors still complain, military spending can just be shifted "off-budget" and out of sight). At the same time, donors have realized that few poor countries, even those that are democratic, have systems in place for ordinary people to register their preferences. Even if there are regular elections, civil society rarely has any say or influence on the budget.

• *Lack of feedback.* Lastly, there is a general problem with aid in that it is not linked to results. Unlike a commercial business, which gets feedback from the market of what it is doing right and wrong—allowing companies to change what they are doing or forcing them to close down—there is no such feedback for aid. This is partly because aid projects are rarely evaluated to assess their impact. The usual question is "Was the money spent?" not "Did the project have the intended impact?" This is partly because collecting such data is costly. But it is also because the aid bureaucracies were simply not held accountable for their results.

In response to the multiple, long-identified shortcomings of aid, there are efforts to increase ownership and participation and to make aid more efficient and linked to results.

Ownership, Participation, and the PRSP

There is a growing recognition that recipient governments must be on board if aid is to have the desired economic effect. Development's checkered history of misappropriation, capital flight, and unsustainable projects is partly the result of a donor-initiated agenda in which priorities were foisted on recipients by outsiders. To combat this, "ownership" is the idea that recipients must play the central role in setting priorities. Another aspect thought to encourage better development outcomes is widening participation beyond government officials to ask the people themselves what kinds of development they want.

Both of these concepts are embodied in the poverty reduction strategy papers (PRSPs), a process whereby governments hold consultations with civilian groups and then lay out their investment priorities. The PRSPs were initially introduced as part of the effort to ensure that savings from debt relief were spent wisely. In theory, they provide a central framework for governments to connect with their own populations and for donors to identify the demands of a country's own development efforts. In practice, the consultations have largely been superficial and donors have for the most part continued to fund their own priorities rather than responding directly to the PRSP. Given the extensive financing of African budgets by outsiders, this is perhaps to some degree unavoidable.

Untying Aid

One of the clear positive changes in assistance has been the untying of aid. "Tied aid" is assistance given by a donor that must be spent in the donor country or by hiring companies or nationals from that country. This had the effect, through inefficient procurement and noncompetition, of reducing by an estimated 25–30 percent the value of aid. In response, many donors have moved away from this practice. French aid was nearly 50 percent tied a few years ago; now just 3 percent of its aid is officially tied. The UK ended tied aid altogether in 2001. The United States continues to tie most of its aid (but has stopped reporting such statistics to the OECD).

Budget Support and Pooled Funds
One of the common complaints from African governments has been the high administrative and management costs of multiple donors funding a multitude of different and disparate projects. (The famous story of Tanzania writing 2,400 quarterly reports a year for donors is an urban legend, but the very real problem it highlights is no myth.) One solution to this problem is for donors to pool their resources. The idea is that rather than each donor having its own project and basket of funding, they would agree to a common framework and then contribute to a common fund. Although this is only in the early stages, donors are beginning to find mechanisms for combining funds to reduce overhead and management costs, such as the health-sector pooling in Ghana and Mozambique. Another approach believed to add efficiency (but as yet still unproven) is to provide budget support instead of project or sector aid. The idea is that aid would be fully integrated into the budget by making a general contribution to a treasury (subject to the donors agreeing to the budget and having confidence in the local accounting systems). Several donors, notably Japan and the United States, have preferred to maintain their own oversight and have generally shied away from budget support.

Predictability
Another common complaint of countries is that aid is unpredictable. Donors do not always deliver what they pledge and the amounts tend to change substantially year-to-year. This, combined with the cycle in which donors release money (which rarely matches national budget cycles), makes it very difficult for recipient governments to integrate aid flows into their own budget projections. This is especially problematic in the countries where donors are providing the bulk of public expenditure (i.e., much of Africa), and undermines sensible long-term fiscal planning. In response, donors are considering several options to make aid flows more predictable, such as longer pledge cycles and synchronizing with annual budget processes. Despite much talk, there has been very little progress on this front so far.

Measuring Outcomes
As surprising as it may be to outsiders, development agencies have traditionally not measured the impact of their own efforts. On the one

Table 8.9 Tied Aid by Donor (percentage aid tied, 2003)

Donor	Tied share
Italy[a]	92
Korea	81
United States[c]	72
Austria	49
Canada	47
Spain	44
Australia	33
Denmark	29
New Zealand	19
Finland	14
Netherlands[a]	9
Portugal	6
Germany	5
Greece	5
Switzerland	4
France	3
Japan	3
Luxembourg[b]	3
Belgium	1
Ireland	0
Norway	0
Sweden	0
United Kingdom	0

Source: OECD.
Notes: a. 2001 data; b. 2000 data; c. 1996 data.

hand, this is understandable. When there are multiple donors and groups working in a single area as well as the government, trying to figure out who is responsible for what is extremely difficult. Since no single entity is responsible, then no one really is. Collecting data and tracking progress is also costly, and tallying inputs (such as spending) is simply easier than final outcomes (like infant mortality). Making matters even more complicated, most development indicators (school enrollment, mortality rates, etc.) are affected by many factors, and development efforts may not be among the most significant.

On the other hand, the lack of measurable results has debilitated development efforts because both governments and donors are unable to adjust strategies based on responses or to justify their efforts to parliaments by showing value for money. The MDGs are one attempt to measure outcomes and to try to hold donors and governments accountable. But the issue of attribution is probably unavoidable, again leaving no one truly accountable. The World Bank is investing heavily in data collection and hopes to use new outcome measures as part of improving their efficiency and impact. Whether this will work in practice or affect how donors behave remains to be seen.

Grants vs. Loans

Much "aid" is delivered in the form of soft loans, meaning the interest rates are very low. The original idea behind giving loans was to both create incentives for countries to spend wisely (so they could pay them back) and also to recycle money (so the repayments could be re-lent to other countries). However, it did not work out that way in many cases (see Chapter 9). Given the mounting debts of many low-income countries, and the repeated waves of debt relief, there has been a growing trend to give aid as grants rather than loans. Most of the bilaterals have switched to grants for the poorest countries. The World Bank also began giving grants for postconflict reconstruction, to fight HIV/AIDS, and for some investments in countries with high levels of debt already.

Grant proponents argue that it makes no sense to give loans if the debt is ultimately unsustainable and more debt relief is the likely future outcome. However, defenders of loans suggest that the "credit culture" is useful as it encourages more-effective spending. There are some specific concerns for the IDA as it shifts to grants, notably the recycling issues since IDA relies on "reflows" from old loans for about a third of its current funding.

Output-Based Aid

One interesting innovation in the aid business pushing the idea of basing aid on performance has been the advent of output-based aid (OBA). The way OBA works is that a survey is done at the beginning and then the donors agree to pay the government based on any progress over a set time period. For example, a donor might count access to water in a given city and then agree to pay the government $10 for every house that gains access to water in the next year. If the pricing is done right and the results are able to be fairly counted, the government would have incentives to hook up as many houses as possible. For the donors, they also would know that they would only pay for "successful" hookups and no money would be wasted. If there is no progress, there is no payment. Such approaches are being piloted in a few areas, such as with electricity in Mozambique's Inhambane Province, and will be closely watched.

For Further Reading

There is a vast literature on aid and the aid business. Even though much of it is about global trends and ideas, Africa features prominently in most such work. The research departments at the World Bank and IMF, plus think tanks such as the Overseas Development Institute, World Institute for Development Economics Research, and the Center for Global Development all produce books and papers on aid, much of which is available free online. Working paper series are particularly useful and usually come out months or even years before journal publication. The websites of all the major aid institutions are a treasure trove of information about their policies, programs, and research. The main source of data on ODA is the OECD's DAC (www.oecd.org/dac), whose database is hard to use but is free. There are also quite a few nongovernmental organizations that maintain websites critical of the major financial institutions. Some of these play a useful watchdog role and disseminate alternative views, but too many of them frequently are the source of misleading or unreliable information. Surfer beware.

A discussion of the major aid issues can be found in *Foreign Aid and Development: Lessons Learnt and Directions for the Future*, edited by Finn Tarp (2000).

Two of the best books on aid, both skeptical views that highlight the incentives problems within the industry, are William Easterly's *The Elusive Quest for Growth* (2001) and Nicolas van de Walle's *African Economies and the Politics of Permanent Crisis, 1979–1999* (2001). At the other end of the spectrum is Jeffrey Sachs's *The End of Poverty* (2005), which argues that more aid combined with technical know-how can eradicate poverty in Africa. An amusing (although outdated) critique attacking the excesses of the aid business is Graham Hancock's *Lords of Poverty* (1992). A more recent argument in a similar vein is Michael Maren's *The Road to Hell: The Ravaging Effects of Foreign Aid and International Charity* (2002).

The original justifications for aid were provided by Walt Rostow in *The Stages of Economic Growth: A Non-Communist Manifesto* (1960) and the writings of Hans Singer, compiled in *International Development Co-Operation: Selected Essays by H. W. Singer on Aid and the United Nations System* (2001). The early skeptics were Milton Friedman in "Foreign Economic Aid" in *The Yale Review* (1958) and the many writings of Peter Bauer, for example his *Dissent on Development: Studies and Debates in Development Economics* (1976).

A fascinating paper on how the Marshall Plan has perhaps been misunderstood is Bradford De Long and Barry Eichengreen's "The Marshall Plan: History's Most Successful Structural Adjustment Program" (1991). The 0.7 percent aid target became best known once it was endorsed by the so-called Pearson Commission. Its main report, which also gives a good overview of the aid debates during the late 1960s, is *Partners in Development: Report of the Commission on International Development* (1969) by Lester Pearson and the commission members.

For insights into the US aid program, see Carol Lancaster's

Transforming Foreign Aid: US Assistance in the 21st Century (2000). The authoritative source on the new US Millennium Challenge Account is *Challenging Foreign Aid* (2003) by Steve Radelet. Gordon Cumming looks at European aid policies in *Aid to Africa: French and British Policies from the Cold War to the New Millennium* (2001). For background on British aid policy, see *Britain's Overseas Aid Since 1979: Between Idealism and Self-Interest* (1991), edited by Anuradha Bose and Peter Burnell. For more recent ideas on using aid to reduce poverty in Britain, see UK Department for International Development's white paper *Eliminating World Poverty: A Challenge for the 21st Century* (1997) or the weighty final report of the Tony Blair–chaired Commission for Africa, *Our Common Interest* (2005). The DAC also produces regular reports on aid trends among the various bilateral donors.

The World Bank produces mountains of paper on almost every aspect of aid, as well as being the subject of a mass of literature. A basic place to start is the Bank's own *A Guide to the World Bank* (2003). The authoritative history of the Bank is Devesh Kapur, John Lewis, and Richard Webb's *The World Bank: Its First Half Century* (1997). The critical report for shaping the Bank's strategy in Africa for the 1980s and beyond was the pivotal *Accelerated Development in Sub-Saharan Africa: An Agenda for Action* (1981), which is better known as the "Berg Report," but marked the shift from just projects to focusing on policies and economic management. More recently, *Can Africa Claim the 21st Century?* (2000) set out the agenda for the current period. The annual *World Development Report*, which has a new theme every year, is also reflective of the evolution of thinking and debate inside the Bank.

Sebastian Mallaby's *The World's Banker* (2004) examines the tenure of James Wolfensohn as Bank president from 1995 to 2005 and his effect, both positive and negative, on the institution itself and ideas about development. Another critique of the Bank in recent times is Jessica Einhorn's "The World Bank's Mission Creep" (2001). The *Report of the International Financial Institution Advisory Commission* (2000), better known as the "Meltzer Report" because its chief author was Alan Meltzer, was also highly critical of the way the Bank operated, sparking several recent changes. The agenda for improving the Bank is best outlined in the triennial IDA replenishment reports when the shareholders weigh in, the latest being the World Bank's IDA-14 report, "Working Together to Achieve the Millennium Development Goals: Additions to IDA Resources, Fourteenth Replenishment" (2005). There are surprisingly few books on the African Development Bank, with E. Philip English and Harris Mule's *The Multilateral Development Banks: The African Development Bank* (1996) being a notable exception.

The rise of the NGOs as aid players is part of a bigger trend identified by Jessica Mathews in "Power Shift" (1997) and P. J. Simmons's "Learning to Live with NGOs" (1998). Also useful is Ann Marie Clark's "Non-Governmental Organizations and Their Influence on International Society" (1995). Some critical perspectives can be found in David Hulme and Michael Edwards's *NGOs, States, and Donors: Too Close for Comfort?* (1997) and Sebastian Mallaby's "NGOs: Fighting Poverty, Hurting the Poor" (2004).

Information on the MDGs can be found on the various UN websites. The main costing study for the MDGs is "Goals for Development: History, Prospects and Costs" (2002) by Shantayanan Devarajan, Margaret Miller, and Eric Swanson.

The "aid effectiveness" literature is also substantial. The early studies that suggested aid could lead to higher growth were the seminal works of Paul Rosenstein-Rodan, such as "International Aid for Undeveloped Countries" (1961) and Hollis Chenery and Alan Strout's "Foreign Assistance and Economic Development" (1966). More recently the aid-growth debate has accelerated. The most famous of these is Craig Burnside and David Dollar's study "Aid, Policies, and Growth" (2000), which found that aid did lead to growth in good policy environments. They were challenging the work of Peter Boone, who found no aid-growth relationship in "The Impact of Foreign Aid on Savings and Growth" (1994), and Henrik Hansen and Finn Tarp, who found a positive relationship regardless of conditions in "Aid Effectiveness Disputed" (2000). The latest in this line of literature is "Counting Chickens When They Hatch: The Short-Term Effect of Aid on Growth" (2004), wherein Michael Clemens, Steve Radelet, and Rikhil Bhavnani found that certain kinds of aid did lead to growth. For a good overview of the World Bank's conclusions in this debate see David Dollar's *Assessing Aid: What Works, What Doesn't, and Why* (1998).

The aid-quality debates are perhaps more interesting. Nancy Birdsall outlines the major failings of the donor community in "Seven Deadly Sins: Reflections on Donor Failings" (forthcoming 2007). Tony Killick considers some problems with the new results-based aid agenda in "Politics, Evidence, and the New Aid Agenda" (2004). Andrew Rogerson's "The International Aid System 2005–2010: Forces for and Against Change" (2004) takes a forward-looking view of how the global aid industry may or may not be changing. Tim Harford and Michael Klein suggest ways of applying market forces to the aid system in their accessible *The Market for Aid* (2005). Peter Heller lays out some of the dilemmas facing countries that experience increases in aid in "Pity the Finance Minister: Issues in Managing a Substantial Scaling Up of Aid Flows" (2005). Deborah Brautigam and Steven Knack tackle some of the possible negative effects of aid on states in "Foreign Aid, Institutions, and Governance in Sub-Saharan Africa" (2004).

9

Debt Burdens and Debt Relief

DEBT RELIEF HAS BEEN ONE OF THE SIGNATURE ISSUES OF THE development advocacy community since at least the 1980s. The idea that poor countries owe money to rich ones is often considered repugnant and morally offensive. But the process of reducing the debts of poor countries has been one fraught with problems of incentives and is not without hard choices and dilemmas. This chapter will outline the major concepts around measuring debt, the mechanisms for reducing African debt, and some of the potential implications for the continent and its development.

Debt Stigma

Because of its association with poverty and stress, "debt" has all kinds of negative connotations. But debt itself is not necessarily bad. If managed properly, debt can actually be a very good thing for a country, allowing it to use other people's money to invest in the future. Debt is merely a financial obligation by one actor to pay money to another actor based on some previous transfer of funds. The actor who owes the money is called a debtor and the one to whom the funds are owed is called a creditor. Most countries are both creditors and debtors at the same time, with governments both lending to and borrowing funds from various other entities. In fact, the United States is currently the world's largest debtor—that is, it owes more money to creditors than any other country in the world.

Almost all African countries have borrowed more money than they have loaned, making nearly all of them significant debtors. Africa's debt became a problem only in the 1980s, when the total debt started to mount up at the same time that countries encountered problems paying back older loans. The total amount owed by the continent grew from just $6 billion in 1970 (or about $22 billion in today's dollars after adjusting for inflation) to nearly $200 billion by the mid-1990s. This debt represented less than 15 percent of the continent's total GDP in 1970 but jumped to over 100 percent by the 1990s. More importantly, it was clear that for many African countries their debts were unpayable and that the rising level of debt itself was becoming a barrier to progress on other fronts.

Some Basic Debt Indicators

How much Africa owes changes every day as governments borrow more, make payments, and renegotiate old loans. It makes sense to think about debt as more than a particular amount owed by a country. "Debt stock" is the face value of all the outstanding debt owed by a particular country, typically reported in US dollars or relative to the size of the economy as a percentage of GDP. "Debt service" is how much a country is supposed to pay in a particular year. This is often expressed as a percentage of a country's export earnings that year, also called the "debt service ratio." Looking at just one of these indicators can be misleading because the burden on countries can be very different. For example, saying a country has $1 billion in debt stock does not tell you very much about the country's ability to pay or the structure of repayments. A $1 billion loan for one year at commercial rates, say 10 percent, would mean the country would have to repay $1.1 billion the following year. However, a different $1 billion loan (implying the same nominal debt stock) that is for thirty years at 1 percent would mean the country would have to pay only about $38 million the following year. Most loans to low-income African governments have been closer to the latter example (soft terms) rather than the former (hard terms), meaning that countries often have large debt stocks but relatively small debt service. The World Bank's loans to most poor countries, for example, are for forty years at a rate of 0.75 percent, and countries are given a ten-year grace period during which nothing must be repaid.

One other important point worth keeping in mind when thinking about debt service is that external loans (as opposed to borrowing at home in local currency) have to be repaid in foreign currency (e.g., US dollars or Japanese yen), which means that the loans are repaid indirectly through future export earnings and cannot be covered by just printing more money.

When Debt Becomes a Problem

Whether debt becomes a problem or not depends on how the loan is used. If the money is invested wisely in things that will produce a return, especially exports, then the loan should be repayable. However, if the loan is used for consumption (such as buying luxury goods), is wasted (spent on projects that fail), or disappears (say, into a private Swiss bank account), then there is little chance that the loan will be repayable. Unfortunately, many of the loans taken out by African countries have been of the latter category. In fact, heavy borrowing is not necessarily trouble if the money is spent well and produces future income.

The problem for Africa has been that many countries have built up a lot of loans *and* failed to generate returns to pay the money back, even on the soft aid–like terms. Governments tended to spend a lot more each year than they collected in revenue, so they covered the difference by borrowing, usually from other governments or international institutions such as the World Bank. Critically, much of these borrowed funds were used to pay salaries or were sunk into misguided projects. Thus, when the loans became due, even if it was twenty years later, there were no dollars generated to service the debt.

Another way to think about it is that well-used loans should encourage faster economic growth and hopefully more exports, too. In Africa's case, we can see that did not happen enough to allow repayment of those debts. To give one example, the continent's real GNI growth 1970–2003 was about 1.1 percent per year. If African economies had grown instead over this period at (a still modest) 3 percent, the overall debt burden would be half as much in 2003 (about 37 percent debt stock/GNI versus the actual ratio of 70 percent). This suggests that Africa's "debt problem" is perhaps as much of a story about slow growth as it is about over-borrowing. In other words, looking at the usual debt indicators, it is perhaps not so much that the numerators grew too fast as it is that the denominators grew too slowly (or, for many countries, not at all).

Africa's Creditors

Most African governments owe money to international financial institutions such as the World Bank and other governments, primarily those in Europe, North America, and Japan. This is because aid in the past has mostly been given in the form of a loan, although often with very low interest rates. Such debts are called "official debt." When it is owed to individual governments it is called "bilateral debt" and when it is owed to international or regional organizations it is called "multilateral debt." The final category of debt is to private companies, investors, or banks and this is known as "commercial debt" (see Table 9.1). For example, see Table 9.2 for recent debt figures for Kenya and Mali, broken down by creditor type.

Debt Relief

As early as the 1970s, bilateral creditors began writing off debts to some low-income countries or agreeing to easier repayment plans. For some creditors, it was merely a simple way to transfer more resources to

Table 9.1　Main Types of African Debt

Creditor type	Official debt		Commercial debt
	Bilateral	Multilateral	
Examples	British government	World Bank	bondholders
	Japanese government	IMF	private banks
	Canadian government	African Development Bank	oil companies
			equipment
			manufacturers

Table 9.2　Debt Indicators for Kenya and Mali, End-2003 (in US$ millions unless noted otherwise)

	Kenya	Mali
Total debt stock	6,766	3,129
Long-term debt owed or guaranteed by the government	5,704	2,910
Bilateral	2,029	839
Multilateral	3,250	2,071
Commercial	425	0
Total debt as a proportion of gross national income	48%	75%
Total debt service paid	574	77
Total debt service as a proportion of exports	16%	7%

Source: World Bank.

countries, either as another form of aid or to help a strategic ally. But it was also part of a growing realization that much of the old lending was probably not going to generate returns sufficient to pay back the original loans. The major bilateral official creditors are organized into the Paris Club to provide a framework for renegotiating old debts. Since 1996 there is also the heavily indebted poor countries (HIPC) program set up by the IMF and World Bank to help the poorest countries. Finally, countries can also make agreements among themselves to renegotiate old debts. By the 1990s, there was a growing movement from advocates and pressure groups, such as the Jubilee 2000 campaign, for more debt relief. These mounting calls from the outside, combined with a change of heart among the major creditors and in the international financial institutions, led to progressively more generous debt relief. The Paris Club allowed deeper and deeper cuts in debt with each new set of terms. The HIPC program allowed, for the first time, for debts owed to international financial institutions to be written off.

The Paris Club

Traditionally, the main forum for renegotiating bilateral debt has been the Paris Club of major creditors. This is an informal group that began in 1956 when Argentina asked all of its official creditors to meet to discuss its debt problems. Today the Paris Club has nineteen members including all of the major international economic powers. They meet regularly with officials from debtor countries who want to reorganize their loans, called rescheduling. Although the Paris Club is not a formal legal organization, it has established rules and arrangements by which all members abide. One example of this is "equal treatment," whereby debtors must pay back all creditors equally. In practice this means that decisions taken at the Paris Club must be by consensus because all creditors must accept any changes to loan terms.

There have been several sets of terms agreed to over the years (named after the cities in which the new terms are agreed) that generally treat poorer countries more favorably. Three terms are most commonly considered today for African countries. "Houston terms" are for the lower-middle-income countries, such as Kenya, and merely restructure the payment schedule without any reduction in debt stock. "Naples terms" are for the low-income countries showing strain from their debts that also meet certain conditions, such as having an IMF program in place. Naples is a concessional rescheduling, which includes a write-down of 67 percent of the debt stock owed. "Cologne terms" were added in 1999 for countries in the HIPC program, which qualifies debtor countries for up to a 90 percent reduction. Most recently, the Paris Club also agreed to a new category of so-called Evian treatment, which gives members flexibility to consider each country on a case-by-case basis. (Iraq was the first country to get a Paris Club rescheduling on Evian terms in 2004, which included an 80 percent write-off.)

Many African countries have turned to the Paris Club to help rearrange and reduce their debts. Most of them qualified for Naples terms and received debt relief in this manner. Some countries have gone back to the Paris Club repeatedly. Senegal has returned no less than thirteen times since 1980 and Niger and Madagascar ten times each.

Heavily Indebted Poor Countries Initiative

Even though some form of debt relief was available in the 1980s and early 1990s, advocates for the poor began to call for more widespread debt relief. Campaigns began to urge the rich-country creditors to erase the debts owed by poor countries. In many cases the debt itself was in fact a major burden for the debtor countries, and nongovernmental groups such as the Jubilee campaign lobbied hard for action. One sticking point was the legal terms that did not allow the World Bank or IMF to provide debt relief. By the mid-1990s, it was clear that the debt issue had to be more systematically dealt with, so the IMF and World Bank created the HIPC initiative. This program is for low-income countries that require debt reduction beyond Naples terms. In 1999 the initiative was enhanced and the terms were softened further, including 90 percent bilateral relief on Cologne terms and further reductions through HIPC. The HIPC process calls for countries to first seek a Paris Club deal, then they can apply for HIPC, which determines eligibility based on debt sustainability and some record of good performance. If a country qualifies, it is deemed to reach "decision point," where interim relief is provided. If the country stays on track with its reforms and shows that any savings from debt relief are being used wisely (for instance on schools rather than a new presidential mansion), then the country can reach the "completion point," which is for deeper and permanent debt relief.

In 2005 the major economic powers agreed to even further cuts among the HIPC-qualified countries, with up to 100 percent debt reduction for the qualified countries. The multilateral debt relief initiative (MDRI) expanded the HIPC program to completely erase the remaining debt owed to the World Bank, IMF, and the African Development Bank. In the first year, this included eighteen poor countries, fourteen of which are African. This plan was not without controversy, however, since there remain concerns about whether the MDRI will affect future lending activities of the international institutions. Some antidebt campaigners also hope to expand the initiative to include more countries.

Debt Sustainability

How much debt is too much? "Debt sustainability" is the idea that a country's debts do not grow beyond what can reasonably be repaid. A debt sustainability ceiling is the highest level of debt a country should take on before it becomes a problem. Knowing such a level for a country would obviously be helpful in deciding whether that country should accept new loans or not and whether the country is in need of more relief. But finding that ceiling, or even deciding what is the best measurement technique, is not necessarily straightforward. Because the ability to repay debt is based on future taxes and exports, this may be difficult to forecast, especially if the country's economy is unstable, its future prospects uncertain, and the terms of the loan decades long. Since lenders cannot know the future income stream, they use current conditions as a guide, using some ratio of current debt to the economy (not unlike a mortgage lender who may determine the amount you can borrow based on your current salary). The HIPC framework used two measures. A country would qualify if either its total debt stock (discounted to net present value, which accounts for the interest rate) exceeds either (1) 150 percent of GDP or (2) 250 percent of government revenues. Other analysis of debt sustainability typically looks at the debt service ratio (debt service as a percentage of exports), with anything above 10–15 percent considered high. Because countries that receive debt relief often quickly borrow again, there has been a shift, at least among very poor countries, to give grants instead of loans (see Chapter 8).

Blame for Africa's Debt Problems

There is probably culpability all around for Africa's debt crises. African governments themselves are ultimately most responsible since they are the ones who assumed the obligations by accepting the loans in the first place. They are also the ones that used the initial funds in a manner that was, all too often, not productive, resulting in a situation in which the loans could not be repaid, even on very easy terms.

However, there are two important qualifications to assigning too much blame to Africa's current crop of political leaders. First, many of the loans taken out by African governments are on extremely long terms. World Bank lending, for example, is usually a forty-year loan. These loan terms, which are stretched out like this to give countries extra time to repay, are also much longer than any individual government tends to stay in power. This creates a moral hazard, since governments may take out loans and spend the money now, knowing that they will no longer be around when repayment is due. This also means that the debt obligations for many governments are based on loans taken out by previous governments. This can be particularly troublesome for a new democracy that may find itself having inherited old debts from a previous dictator (e.g., Nigeria) or a country emerging from a long conflict (e.g., Democratic Republic of Congo after the fall of Mobutu Sésé Seko or Liberia after Charles Taylor).

A second caveat is that creditors have not always behaved prudently. They may have made loans to governments in the past knowing that the money was being wasted or stolen. (If Mobutu's lenders were not aware that the money was being misused, they certainly should have been.) Even where such problems may be less obvious, there is evidence that creditors engage in so-called defensive lending, where new loans are given mostly just to pay off old loans. This can create a cycle in which creditors keep lending because of previous loans rather than on the basis of how the new loans will be used, perpetuating the debt spiral.

In fact, both of these important qualifications are reasons creditors do provide debt relief. They recognize that many new governments should not be saddled with debts accrued by previous regimes, and they use debt relief as a way of assisting a new government that they hope will be better. Creditors have also recognized that defensive lending under-mines their own ability to be selective in new allocation of loans or aid, and hope that debt relief will free them from past lending cycles as well.

Debt and Money for Social Services

One of the central claims of debt relief campaigners is that high levels of debt force countries to spend money paying back rich creditors that could otherwise be spent on people. If debt service obligations are low-ered or erased, it does mean more resources are available for the general budget, which in theory could be spent on things such as education and healthcare. Whether this means help for the poor or not depends a lot on what happens next. First, it was clear that many creditors were giving new loans to cover old ones, yet the new lending tended to be much larger than the annual debt payments. If there is no longer a need for defensive lending, new flows to the government from creditors (or donors) may shrink. This will depend on future aid budgets in rich coun-tries and how they choose to allocate their funds. Second, any savings from debt relief goes into the general budget and can be used for any purpose. Since many African countries have significant fiscal problems, and spending on the poor is often a low priority, it is by no means guar-anteed that extra funds will not be spent on civil-service salaries, the military, or pet projects of some kind (such as an airport or stadium in the president's hometown). Despite these potential pitfalls, creditors do try to monitor how new funds are used and there is some evidence that social-service spending has gone up in countries that receive debt relief. The IMF claims that, among the HIPC countries, poverty-reducing expenditure rose from 6.4 percent of GDP in 1999 to 7.9 percent four years later, a level about three times higher than total debt service for those countries. Countries also try to show that the money is being well spent, such as Zambia's announcement in 2006 that basic healthcare would be free as a result of debt relief.

Debt Relief and Conditionality

Some campaigners have raised concerns that debt relief is being used to force countries to make policy changes. It is true that creditors have set conditions on HIPC and Paris Club arrangements. For both of these, countries must have an agreement in place with the IMF. This is done to ensure that overall macroeconomic management is reasonable (e.g., inflation is under control) and that the country shows it is making progress on structural changes within the economy that have gotten them into the problem in the first place (e.g., subsidies to loss-making state enterprises are curtailed). A second condition for HIPC has been to open the budget to input from regular people in civil society (through a process known as a PRSPs; see Chapter 8). A final condition is that some mechanism for tracking expenditure needs to monitor how and where money is being spent. Creditors want this to ensure that any benefits from debt relief are spent in ways that do benefit the poor and in which the population itself has some say. If governments are relieved of their debts and then waste or steal that extra money, not only does that bring no benefit to the people they intended to help, but it also undermines the creditors' own justification for giving debt relief in the first place.

The Costs of High Debt

Antidebt campaigners have often focused on the diversion of resources from antipoverty spending to debt repayment as the main cost of high debt. Economists have tried to explore the link between debt and economic growth, with the concern that high levels of debt might affect economic expansion, what has been called a "debt overhang." The idea of a debt overhang is that the presence of high debt and the strain on the budget undermines the incentives for investment. This might occur because scarce foreign exchange could be used to service the debt instead of financing imports needed for growth, it might lead to underfunding of infrastructure and other investments that could be growth-supporting, or it might discourage private investors from making long-term investments in productivity, such as buying new machinery. All of these are plausible channels for how high debt might impact economic growth. Nevertheless, the empirical evidence is much more mixed, and the relationship between level of debt and economic growth rate is not very clear.

Beyond growth, there are other ways that high levels of debt could impact policy choices and institutional development. The need to service debt can force governments to seek short-term gains at long-term costs. Governments also face credibility problems when they are forced to go back to the creditors to ask for concessions; unserviceable debt is itself an admission of failure. This can also be embarrassing for creditors as well. Ghana, for example, had already been under the tutelage of the IMF for two decades when they entered the HIPC program in 2003. Lastly, the management of high debt can be very costly for African governments because of the time and effort required of technical staff. Countries might owe more than two dozen different creditors, in multiple currencies, and with different terms for each loan. Going to the Paris Club for rescheduling, which some countries have done more than ten times, is also a lengthy and laborious process that drains the capacity of officials.

Benefits of Relief

It thus seems that many of the possible gains from debt relief may be less than immediately obvious. There will likely be some increase in social-service spending. Governments will be keen to show the creditors that their new savings are being used wisely, and the creditors will want to believe them, not least because they may have to account for the debt relief back home to parliaments, congresses, and taxpayers. But will there be a major gain in economic growth? Probably not. Debt relief, assuming it is not followed by renewed heavy borrowing, could help to create an environment for governments to improve overall fiscal and macroeconomic management, which could have long-term beneficial effects. Debtor governments might be under less pressure to seek short-term solutions and may have more time to devote to other public policy matters, both of which may eventually have a positive influence. But such an outcome is by no means certain, especially since most African countries, even if they have better governments now than they did before, still face major governance challenges.

Odious Debt

Some debts could be considered "odious," which means the loans were undertaken under such conditions that they should no longer be legally binding. It is a term that at first appears to apply to many African governments that might have debts accrued by military dictators or other unsavory governments in the past. With a growing number of democracies across the continent, it might seem obvious that these governments will want to invoke the principle of odious debt to get out of paying old loans. However, there are legal and practical reasons that this has rarely been used.

Any country seeking to invoke the odious debt doctrine must first prove that the debt in question is odious and also untangle its obligations to determine which portion is owed to which creditor and under what conditions those original loans were contracted. In practice, both of these conditions have proven extremely difficult. Legal ambiguity further complicates matters because odious debts are not considered illegal under international law. Currently, there are three accepted conditions for debt to be considered odious: (1) absence of consent; (2) absence of benefit; and (3) creditor awareness. Just as importantly, there are many practical barriers to implementing the odious debt doctrine: untangling the original sources of debt after multiple restructurings; treatment of secondary market holders of debt; and fear of exclusion from future lending.

The first widely recognized application of the doctrine of odious debt was included in the final peace agreement following the US seizure of Cuba from Spain in 1898. The only legal precedent is the 1922 case of *Costa Rica v. Great Britain*. In that case, Costa Rica refused to repay loans made by the Royal Bank of Canada to the former dictator Federico Tinoco, citing the absence of benefit to the population and creditor awareness. US Supreme Court chief justice William Howard Taft agreed. The concept of odious debt attracted renewed attention for countries such as Iraq, Nicaragua, the Philippines, the Democratic Republic of Congo, Haiti, and Liberia. However, given the legal and practical complications of an odious debt claim, concessional treatment through the Paris Club and HIPC has proven more fruitful.

Potential Downsides

Although debt relief is often hailed as a major help to poor countries, there are reasons that debt relief may not always be a good idea. Because debt relief still has to be paid for, it can come at the expense of other spending priorities. In practice this can mean resources are diverted to countries getting debt relief and away from those who do not. A few African countries with low debt, such as Lesotho or Botswana, have argued that this unfairly affects them in that they are being indirectly punished for *not* having a debt problem. Another concern is that debt relief undermines the normal development of a credit culture and could delay the ability of countries to eventually borrow in private capital markets like middle- and high-income countries do. Some African countries were initially hesitant to join HIPC precisely because of this possibility; they had hoped to soon borrow commercially and were worried that seeking debt relief would undermine their creditworthiness. Lastly, debt relief is in practice a temporary measure to help countries, but does nothing by itself to address the causes of the debt problem, which may be linked to deeper difficulties in the economy or in the management of public resources.

The Future of Public Finance

In many ways Africa's debt problems are merely a symptom of broader economic issues. Although the debt itself can become a barrier to progress, debt relief is usually little more than a Band-Aid solution to much deeper financial problems of a country. Now that there are mechanisms in place for indebted countries to get out from under any burden, attention will turn to maintaining access to finance and finding ways to ensure that public spending is more efficient in the future than it has been in the past. Otherwise, Africa will see little chance of growing out of poverty, and could find itself back in a debt crisis yet again.

For Further Reading

The preeminent source for data on the debts of a particular country or region is the World Bank's annual *Global Development Finance* (which used to be called the *World Debt Tables*). IMF country reports also typically include debt information, and some further data can be found via individual central banks or debt management offices. The World Bank and IMF also regularly produce information about HIPC and the debt indicators for the countries in that program. Antidebt campaigners also sometimes report debt information, but these should be read carefully as they sometimes use outdated or mistaken information. The Paris Club is also a good source of information about bilateral debt restructurings.

There is surprisingly little quality academic literature on African debt. One of the early antidebt screeds is *A Fate Worse Than Debt* (1988) by Susan George. A more orthodox rationale for debt relief can be found in Jeffrey Sachs's "Resolving the Debt Crisis of Low-Income Countries" (2002). Paul Krugman compares different options to deal with debt problems in "Financing vs. Forgiving a Debt Overhang" (1988). Some skeptical perspectives include Tim Allen and Diana Weinhold's "Dropping the Debt: Is It Such a Good Idea?" (2000) and "What Has 100 Billion Dollars Worth of Debt Relief Done for Low-Income Countries?" by Nicolas Chauvin and Aart Kraay (2005).

A useful resource is William Easterly's "How Did Heavily Indebted Poor Countries Become Heavily Indebted? Reviewing Two Decades of Debt Relief" (2002), as well as his "Think Again: Debt Relief" (2001). Ravi Kanbur links debt policy to aid dependency in "Aid, Conditionality, and Debt in Africa" (2000). Stijn Claessens et al.'s "HIPC's Debt: Review of the Issues" (1997) gives a preview of the debt sustainability debates. Aart Kraay and Vikram Nehru's "When Is Debt Sustainable?" (2004) is the latest attempt to get at a perennially tricky question. For an overview of the multilateral debt relief initiative, see "Briefing: The G8's Multilateral Debt Relief Initiative and Poverty Reduction in Sub-Saharan Africa" (2006) by Todd Moss.

There are many studies looking at the relationship between debt and economic performance, including Catherine Pattillo, Hélène Poirson, and Luca Ricci's "External Debt and Growth" (2002); Ibrahim Elbadawi, Benno Ndulu, and Njuguna Ndung'u's "Debt Overhang and Economic Growth in Sub-Saharan Africa" (1997); and John Serieux and Yiagadeesen Samy's "The Debt Service Burden and Growth: Evidence from Low Income Countries" (2001). Barbara Mbire and Michael Atingi look at Uganda's case in "Growth and Foreign Debt: The Ugandan Experience" (1997).

The key papers on the odious debt doctrine are Michael Kremer and Seema Jayachandran's "Odious Debt" (2003) and Ashfaq Khalfan, Jeff King, and Bryan Thomas's "Advancing the Odious Debt Doctrine" (2003).

10

Poverty and Human Development*

FOR MANY PEOPLE "DEVELOPMENT" IS NOT SO MUCH ABOUT economic policy or institution building as it is about providing goods and delivering services to the poor. One of the first approaches to embrace this philosophy was the "basic needs" strategy popular in the 1970s. Strands of this strategy have survived in contemporary development practice and have infused mainstream popular ideas about development. Charities advertising on television, for instance, talk about how your donation can put an orphan in school or give medical care to a pregnant woman, not more efficiently raise public revenue or battle local corruption—which may be among the prime reasons that those very same people have no school or decent healthcare in the first place. Nevertheless, assisting the poor and providing social services, especially schools and basic healthcare, are things that governments are expected to do, but often do not do in Africa. Thus many of the external interventions to help reduce poverty are concentrated in these areas. This chapter will cover the basic concepts and ideas related to poverty, including measurement and a preliminary discussion of public-service delivery. The last section of the chapter will discuss the HIV/AIDS pandemic, which has recently become one of the most significant challenges for Africa, not only to public health but also to wider development efforts.

What Is Poverty?

If we are interested in reducing poverty, defining and measuring it is a first step. But this is much more complicated than it seems because poverty is a multidimensional concept of human deprivation. It can be manifested in the absence of adequate food, poor health, and lack of education. It can also be viewed in terms of vulnerability or even exclu-

---

*This chapter coauthored with Markus Goldstein.

163

sion from society. More recent, and significantly broader, definitions also consider poverty to be about the lack of opportunity or capability to affect one's own life.

Poverty Measurement

If defining poverty is hard, getting accurate measures is even harder. The broader the definition of poverty, the more difficult it is to quantify. While dimensions such as opportunities and capabilities may point us to some of the underlying causes of poverty (and thus may be more useful for understanding how people may get out of poverty), they are inherently difficult to gauge with any precision. The simplest and most common way to evaluate poverty is income: how much does a person earn? This is of course a fairly narrow indicator and may not take account of a person's full access to resources (for instance, their assets) or other aspects of their quality of life. However, income is easier to gauge and is almost certainly the best single measure of poverty that we have. This is true not because money is necessarily the most important thing in a person's life, but rather that income gives us a first insight into what a person can purchase and in this way gives us some sense (when we adjust for price discrepancies in different places) of their relative command over resources. This is often directly related to welfare because it includes purchasing basic necessities—which is why there is a strong relationship between income and other indicators such as health and education. This does not mean that better health is always correlated with higher income, but historically and on average it has been.

Another way to measure poverty is to look at other "quality of life" indicators. Typical examples include life expectancy (on the not unreasonable assumption that longer life is better than shorter), literacy (education beats ignorance), or caloric intake (every person requires adequate nutrition to function). One approach that tries to combine several dimensions into a single indicator is the UN's annual Human Development Index (HDI), which scores countries based on a combination of life expectancy at birth, adult literacy rate, gross school enrollment rate, and GDP per capita. While a broader measure than any single one of its subcomponents, the inputs into the HDI raise a host of issues about which are the right components and how to weigh their relative importance (which matters more: health or education, and who is to say?). In the end we have simply another rough estimate of an amorphous concept.

Thresholds, Headcounts, and Gaps

Once the dimension of measurement is chosen, the next step is to find a way to distinguish the poor from the nonpoor by setting a threshold or a "poverty line." The first issue is whether this should be absolute (set at a fixed limit, like $1 of income per day) or relative (such as a proportion of the national average). In developing countries, absolute poverty lines are generally set based on an estimate of the cost of purchasing a minimal amount of calories plus some additional amount for nonfood necessities. Relative poverty lines, on the other hand, are usually set as a fraction of average income—for example, people are defined as poor if their income falls below 50 percent of the average income in a country. Relative poverty lines will move as income in a country grows, while absolute poverty lines will not (once adjusted for changes in prices).

When looking at poverty *within a country*, absolute poverty lines give us a sense of how many people cannot afford a basic set of goods. This is by nature a somewhat arbitrary number, but is at least based on an idea of what is needed to survive. When looking to compare *across countries* the number is even more arbitrary, designed to simply apply a threshold in a range of diverse situations, for example the common global measure of extreme poverty of $1 per day (normally adjusted for local costs, using what is known as purchasing power parity exchange rates). A universal level is useful for comparing across countries or regions, but does not really tell much about a true poverty line in any one country. Indeed, country-specific or "national poverty lines" tend to vary widely from the $1 or $2 a day measures. For example, in Ethiopia the national poverty line adopted by the government in 1999 is equivalent to about 30 US cents per day. By contrast, the national poverty line in the United States for a family of four was $19,157 in 2004, or $13 per day per person.

Once a poverty line is agreed, the next step is a summary figure that captures the extent of poverty in a given population, such as a country or a province. A logical choice is the percentage of people who fall below the line, which is known as the "poverty headcount index." While simple and intuitive, this measure is limited in that it does not tell us anything about *how poor* the poor are. To try to get at how far below the poverty line poor people are, a "poverty gap index" is used that gives the average distance below the poverty line as a ratio of the poverty line for the whole population. We can use this number to calculate how much it would theoretically cost to bring every poor individual up to the poverty line (assuming we could target this assistance perfectly). However, as with the headcount, the poverty gap measure has significant problems, because it is difficult to be accurate and because the poor are not static. In fact, it seems that people move in and out of poverty all the time, which can make getting a precise picture close to impossible.

Measuring Inequality Among the Poor
Another problem with both the headcount and the gap index is that neither gives a sense of the income distribution among the poor. For exam-

---

Income vs. Consumption

One thing to note in the two figures given as examples above is that for Ethiopia the figure is measured in terms of consumption, while for the United States it is measured in income. Indeed, most poverty in developing countries is measured in consumption (what people spend) rather than income (what they earn). There are both conceptual and practical arguments for this difference. Income is what you earn from working, but in the end what people consume is determined by a host of things in addition to income, including transfers from friends and families, savings and borrowing, investment, and the sale or purchase of assets. Hence, consumption tells us what people are actually "eating" while income tells us what comes from their paycheck. In practical terms, however, consumption is usually the way to go. In most developing countries, especially in Africa, income comes from a range of sources at different times and in different forms. For example, a farmer in southeastern Ghana may be growing maize that she harvests twice a year, cassava that she can harvest at many points in the year, and running a small food-selling business on the side (for which she keeps no paper records). Even if the fieldworker from the Ghana Statistical Service convinces her that he is not the taxman, she will be unable to recall her income for the last month. Given how much her income varies over the year, we will get a better picture of her welfare by measuring her consumption, which is likely to be more stable over the course of the year. However, it would also be tough for her to remember exactly what she and her family ate for each meal for the last two weeks. Hence, while surveys often turn to consumption, they end up measuring this in terms of expenditure—what households bought. Some do use actual consumption (for example, by having survey workers help households fill out a diary) but this method tends to be a very expensive way to collect data.

---

ple, you could have one country where half of the poor people have zero income and the other half have income equal to the poverty line. This country would have the same poverty gap as a country where all of the poor had an income equal to half of the poverty line. These two different countries are likely to need very different policy responses to poverty, yet the poverty gap does not help us with this. Hence, a frequently used third measure is the squared poverty gap. In this measure, the distance between the income of poor individuals and the poverty line is squared and the average of this is used to compute the poverty index.

Another way to look at this issue, and one that is often used for a whole population and not just the poor, is to measure the equality of the distribution of income. There are many ways to do this, including looking at the percentage of the population with incomes at many different levels, such as by quintiles. The most commonly used measure that gives a simple summary number is the "Gini coefficient." The Gini coefficient ranges from 0 to 1, with zero being perfect equality (all people in the country have the same income) and 1 being perfect inequality (all of the income is earned by one person and no one else earns anything).

Table 10.1 shows these measures for Burkina Faso. The headcount shows that 46 percent of the population in the whole country fell below the poverty line in 2003. It also shows that Burkina Faso is typical for Africa in that the poverty headcount is significantly higher in rural areas than urban ones. The poverty gap and the squared poverty gap show that the poor in the countryside are even poorer than the poor in the towns and cities—not only are more of the folks in the rural areas poor, but their poverty is also much more severe. On the other hand, the Gini coefficients suggest that overall income distribution is much more unequal in urban than rural areas.

Warning on the Data

Before taking any of these numbers too seriously, it is worth thinking a bit more about how they are determined. There are both conceptual and practical issues that should be kept in mind whenever such numbers are thrown around. Conceptually, simple numbers like those from Burkina Faso below mask a number of tricky and not-so-obvious issues. Generally these figures come from household surveys that use a single household as the unit of analysis and then divide by the number of people. But, looking at food intake as an example, this does not account very well for economies of scale (the average per person cost of cooking for two is much more expensive than for ten). There are also different nutritional needs within a family, and any food or income is rarely shared equally within the household. In fact, the intrahousehold distribution can be very significant (if one or two members of the family hog most of the food and money), leading to big distortions in the poverty figures (one study on the Philippines suggested this effect could be as high as 25 percent).

Table 10.1   Poverty in Burkina Faso, 2003

	National	Rural	Urban
Headcount	46%	52%	19%
Poverty gap	0.153	0.176	0.051
Poverty gap squared	0.068	0.079	0.019
Gini coefficient	0.444	0.376	0.484

Source: World Bank

How Poverty Data Are Collected

It is also worth considering how these data are actually collected.

• *Census.* In the rich world the census is the usual form for collecting such information. Although many African countries conduct a regular census, they are infrequent and usually ask only a few simple questions. More worrying, census data is notoriously unreliable. For political reasons, such as the allocation of parliamentary seats by population, there is often a lot of overcounting. This is one reason why estimates of the number of Nigerians can vary from 100 million to 140 million people!

• *Household surveys.* The main way in which poverty is measured in most developing countries is through household surveys—literally sending people around to conduct tallies and interviews in person. These surveys come in a range of forms; the ones best suited to measure income poverty are those that include details on expenditures or consumption, work, health, and education of all household members. The more information collected, the more useful it can be for helping to set policies. However, the more involved a survey, the more costly and time consuming it becomes. More-intrusive questions are also more likely to generate false responses (imagine a stranger arrives at your door asking questions: you might answer how many people live here truthfully, but be less forthcoming about income or who is sick). In recent years, a number of countries have experimented with much shorter surveys in order to track changes in the years between larger, more comprehensive, multitopic surveys.

• *Health surveys.* A common variant is a demographic and health survey. These try to measure the health status and behavior of the population. Although they rarely ask about income or expenditure, they sometimes include questions about household assets.

While the census attempts to reach each member of the population, health and household surveys use "random samples" or a subset of the population that, because it is selected at random, is supposed to be representative. While survey designers are careful to try to limit distortions, such biases are usually unavoidable. This can result in some populations, especially small marginalized groups that are extremely poor, not being well captured in the national poverty picture. In addition, as these surveys tend to use fixed residences to select people for interviews, they rarely cover nomadic populations such as herders or people who live on the streets. Recent studies have tried to merge census data with household surveys to create "poverty maps," showing where poverty is concentrated in more detail.

Africa and Global Poverty Trends

Keeping in mind the limitations of the poverty data, Table 10.2 shows that, according to World Bank estimates, there has been a sharp divergence between Africa and the rest of the world over the last twenty years. Africa has seen a significant rise in the absolute numbers of people living below the poverty line and a rise in the relative numbers. In 1981 Africa even had a lower poverty headcount index (42 percent) than East Asia (58 percent) and South Asia (52 percent), but two decades later, both those regions had seen dramatic decreases in the number of relative poor (and in East Asia, a massive drop in the absolute poor as well). In fact, Africa is conspicuous for now having the largest headcount index of all regions (46 percent) and being one of the two regions of the world (along with Europe and Central Asia) to see this increase. From the perspective of a development practitioner, the 4 percentage point rise in population living below the poverty line is certainly worrying. But the absolute figures are even scarier, suggesting an additional 150 million people living in poverty.

Performance in Other Poverty Indicators

Tables 10.3 and 10.4 show Africa's performance relative to the other regions of the world in terms of nonincome dimensions of poverty.

The Trouble with Poverty Estimates:
The Case of Côte d'Ivoire's Doors

Researchers who conduct household surveys try their best to gather as much information as possible and to vigilantly construct the survey so the results reflect reality as accurately as possible. But this is inherently tricky and even extremely careful exercises can reveal some unexpected surprises. While working on a living standards survey in Côte d'Ivoire, analysts found a sharp decline in household size, from 8.3 people in 1985 to 6.3 in 1988. Since household data is always adjusted for the number of people living under one roof, this change would make a huge difference in the poverty estimates. Had there really been an average decline of two people for each Ivorian house within just three years? Since this was so unlikely, the researchers looked into it further and discovered that the earlier surveyors were using doors rather than actual households to identify their sample, giving an overall bias toward larger houses. After figuring this out, the analysts were able to come up with a way to correct the data. But had this error gone unnoticed, the poverty figures would have been seriously misleading. But what errors did they, and those who conduct all the other surveys, perhaps miss?

Table 10.2   Global Poverty by Region, 1981 vs. 2001 (below $1/day)

	Absolute numbers (millions)		Relative numbers (percentage of population)	
	1981	2001	1981	2001
East Asia & Pacific	796	272	57.7	14.9
Europe & Central Asia	3	17	0.7	3.6
Latin America & Caribbean	35	49	9.7	9.5
Middle East & North Africa	9	7	5.1	2.4
South Asia	475	431	51.5	31.3
Sub-Saharan Africa	163	313	41.6	46.4

Source: World Bank.

Table 10.3   Global Education Indicators by Region

	Primary school completion (percentage)		Literacy (percentage)	
	1990	2002	1990	2000
East Asia & Pacific	97	97	80	90
Europe & Central Asia	88	90	96	97
Latin America & Caribbean	88	96	85	89
Middle East & North Africa	79	84	54	68
South Asia	74	80	47	56
Sub-Saharan Africa	50	59	50	62

Source: World Bank.

The first shows sub-Saharan Africa making progress in education, with the average primary-school completion rate jumping from 50 percent in 1990 to 59 percent by 2002, and literacy also making strong gains. While these are substantial increases over a short time period (and keeping in mind that literacy in Africa a hundred years ago was close to zero), the continent remains far behind most other regions of the globe.

In terms of health, however, Africa lags much more significantly. Table 10.4 shows the data for two commonly used health indicators. The infant mortality rate of 101 means that one in ten children born in Africa in 2003 died before their first birthday. Life expectancy in Africa has risen from only forty-one years in 1960, peaking at fifty years in 1990, but has worsened in recent years—due mainly to the scourge of AIDS— and now is just 45.8 years, far lower than all other regions.

Table 10.4 Global Health Indicators by Region

	Infant mortality rate (per 1,000)		Life expectancy (years)	
	1990	2003	1990	2002
East Asia & Pacific	44	32	67.2	69.4
Europe & Central Asia	39	29	69.3	68.5
Latin America & Caribbean	43	28	67.9	70.7
Middle East & North Africa	58	43	64.3	68.6
South Asia	89	66	58.5	63.0
Sub-Saharan Africa	110	101	50.0	45.8

Source: World Bank.

Income and Other Variables

The different ways to measure poverty are often interrelated, such as the strong correlation between income and health. In Benin, for example, a major survey found that the access and quality of care received by the poorest fifth is much worse than that of the richest fifth; only half of the poorest children have complete vaccination compared to nearly three-quarters of the richest. The poor also face greater health risks: 16 percent of the children in the bottom 20 percent reported having diarrhea within the last two weeks, compared to only 9 percent of the richest 20 percent. These factors can add up to a significant human toll: child mortality in the richest fifth is half that of other households.

This association also seems to be true across countries, as several studies have shown that wealthier countries score better on a wide range of health variables. More mysterious, however, is the relationship between economic growth and such variables over time. There are some indications that global changes, such as the creation of vaccines in helping to explain reductions in child mortality rates, may be more important than changes in the income levels of any particular country. It also seems that the world is getting more efficient at turning new income gains into welfare gains: globally, it now takes just one-tenth the relative income to have the same life expectancy as it did in 1870. This means that Africa has still seen broad improvements in health and education indicators even though it is far behind, has much less income than other regions, and has not been growing economically.

Causes of Poverty

There are no simple answers as to why people are poor. There are many possible reasons why Africa in particular seems to have such deep and persistent poverty—yet none are satisfactory. Although it is somewhat tautological, the discussion and data in Chapter 6 suggest that the most obvious reason that so many Africans are poor is that their economies have simply not grown fast enough. The causes of such a lousy economic performance are complex and, frankly, not very well understood. Among the most common structural explanations are Africa's unlucky history, bad geography, and inhospitable climate. The macroeconomic reasons tend to highlight misguided policies and immature institutions (see Chapter 6). In addition, some observers have pointed to specific problems such as environmental degradation, lack of access to land, the burden from disease (especially malaria, tuberculosis, and more recently HIV/AIDS), or the prevalence of conflict (Chapter 4). Some other popular, but mostly discredited, ideas about the causes of poverty include high external debt (Chapter 9) and even the recommendations of the international financial community such as structural adjustment (Chapter 7). In reality, the diversity of African conditions suggests that a different combination of causes may be at play in different environments, including within the same village or even the same family.

The "Poverty Trap" Idea

A commonly proposed reason for the seemingly intractable conditions in Africa is the so-called poverty trap. This is the idea that people with extremely low incomes are caught in a series of short-term emergencies just to survive, and thus they can never make choices that might allow them to eventually improve their lives. A classic example of this is that a poor family that cannot grow enough food to feed itself is unlikely to grow enough to have a surplus to sell in order to buy fertilizer to improve its crop, thus it becomes stuck. There is also a theory about a country-level poverty trap, where a whole society may be too poor to grow fast. The idea here is that countries cannot afford to make investments, such as in roads or schools, that might allow their economies to grow quickly and help to raise incomes, so they too become stuck. It seems indisputable that both poor people and poor countries face extra challenges and that their choices can be affected by extreme deprivation. But the actual evidence of a poverty trap seems much less clear and can create a fatalist approach to development in which the poor are hapless souls with no chance (and thus no responsibility) for self-improvement. Instead, the millions of people who have successfully made the transition out of poverty (including the ancestors of every now-rich person) suggest otherwise. Each now-rich country, including the recently industrialized states in Asia, is also evidence that no such country trap exists.

Poverty Reduction and the Aid Business

The aid business—donor agencies, international financial institutions, thousands of NGOs, an army of consultants, and more—are all supposed to be working to reduce poverty in Africa. This is partly about transferring money from the rich world to poor countries, but also about the spread of ideas and values. Much of the aid industry is driven by greed, self-interest, or geostrategic concerns, but there is also a strong streak of humanitarianism involved. Especially after the fall of the Berlin Wall and the dissipation of Cold War reasons for maintaining aid programs in Africa, the aid business rediscovered its purpose in poverty reduction. The latest manifestation of this is the Millennium Development Goals, a series of targets the development community has pledged to meet by 2015 (see Chapter 8 for more on the aid system and the MDGs). In general, there are two broad, and not mutually exclusive, strategies for combating poverty: boosting growth and delivering services directly to the poor.

Pro-Poor Growth

Because of the depth of poverty in Africa and huge numbers of people living on meager incomes, it is logical that increased growth is a necessity. In a country where the average person's income may be well below the international poverty line—as in Burundi, Ethiopia, Liberia, and Niger—it is clearly a case where better sharing of the pie is not enough; a larger pie is needed. On the one hand, most African economies would do well simply to raise their growth rates. In countries that have seen an increase in growth—Ghana in the 1980s or Uganda in the 1990s, for example—there has also been a drop in poverty. Growth-oriented strategies have tended to shift from public-led investment (the state setting up, financing, and running businesses) to establishing conditions that would allow private firms to thrive by improving governance and increasing the competitiveness of the environment (see Chapters 6 and 13). The idea is that not only are private companies and farmers likely to make more efficient economic decisions, but that it is ultimately their taxes upon which the state will rely. This is, of course, still a strategy in the works, but the main idea that higher growth is needed in Africa has become indisputable.

At the same time, not all growth is the same when it comes to reducing poverty. For instance, an increase in GDP from offshore oil production may or may not filter down to the poor (via taxation and royalties through the budget to public services for people). The experience of such growth benefiting the poor in Africa is fairly dismal. On the other hand, growth that is based on a broader range of economic activity, such as farming and manufacturing, can have a direct impact on poverty through higher incomes, increased employment, and other gains that people receive from joining a thriving economy. This kind of more inclusive activity is sometimes called "pro-poor growth" because the impact on poverty is greater. The problem for African governments and policymakers has been to find practical ways to best connect the poor to the economy and allow them to participate in the benefits from economic growth, without either undermining growth itself or allowing such policies to be hijacked by political interests. As detailed in Chapters 6 and 7, there are no easy answers to this conundrum.

Social Services Delivery Approach

The other approach to poverty reduction, in addition to encouraging higher growth, is to provide services directly to poor people. This means intervening to provide access to healthcare, education, clean water, sanitation, roads, banking services, and emergency relief during crises. The development community has also increasingly taken a wider view of helping the poor by seeking ways to allow them to participate in decisions that shape their lives. Simply asking people about their priority needs before embarking on new projects in their area is one simple innovation, while the poverty reduction strategy paper (PRSP) process is perhaps the best example of an attempt to do this on a grand scale (see Chapter 8).

But the need for things such as donor-mandated consultation with people and massive external financing (and often management and implementation) of public services raises some serious questions about why such steps are necessary in the first place. It is true that in most of Africa these services rarely benefit the poor.

1. *Skewed spending.* Public spending is often captured by elites instead of reaching the poor. The World Bank found in Guinea about 50 percent of public health spending went to the richest fifth of the population and only 5 percent to the poorest fifth. In response, donors are increasingly insisting on more pro-poor spending and mechanisms such as the PRSP as a condition for continued funding.

2. *Lack of accountability.* Even if the budget is made more equitable on paper, the poor tend to lose out as the money is often diverted or wasted with few ways for the poor to voice their complaints. Here, the purported solutions tend to lean on financial tracking and finding ways to increase the incentives for service providers to actually deliver what they promise.

3. *Low demand.* Demand for services can also be in short supply

among the poor for a huge range of reasons: maybe the schools are dreadful and the teachers never show up, the clinics may be too far away and include hidden fees that the poorest cannot afford, or perhaps the children are needed at home to work. Although there have been some attempts to copy Mexico's *opportunidades* (originally called *progresa*) initiative that pays poor families to send their kids to school, there are few quick solutions to this problem—other than broad-based growth that increases demand over time.

Financial Tracking

One of the most prominent trends in health and education circles is resource tracking, a direct reaction to the frequent disappearance of funds supposedly budgeted for building schools or paying nurses. The high level of donor involvement and money in these sectors has added attention, especially when aid agencies need to report back to their parliaments about how their resources are being spent. In addition, a growing number of civil-society watchdog groups have demanded more-open and accountable systems. As a result, a number of innovations have emerged, including simple public notification. In some countries the mere publication of the budget has been a major step toward better transparency (in some countries, such as Angola, the budget is still considered a state secret!). Perhaps the most famous case is Uganda, where the World Bank analyzed the fraction of education spending that actually found its way to the schools and discovered that 78 percent was missing. In response, the Ugandan finance ministry began giving money directly to school headmasters and posting the amounts on school doors for all the community to see. The "leakage" all but disappeared. Other approaches from donors have included setting up special accounts, for example an HIV/AIDS account, that can be externally audited. While such approaches can help to ensure money is not lost, it is a Band-Aid solution that does not address wider problems with the bureaucracy.

Key Public Health Issues

Given the problems with public health in Africa, much of the development community's attention has focused here. There is a huge literature on public health and the links to other development issues, but here we highlight just three issues that are central in shaping policy development today.

• *Access to and quality of care.* The provision of healthcare services in Africa is constrained by a range of barriers. Physical access is a prob-

---

Scaling Up

"Scaling up" is a common phrase used to describe a perennial problem in development: How do you take a small successful project and make it bigger? For example, donors and NGOs have found they can, with the right resources, people, and attention, establish a single clinic to serve poor people in an area and help to increase their health status. But how do you "scale up" the clinic to make an effective public health service for a whole nation?

---

lem for rural areas where the nearest clinic may be far away (the average distance to medical facilities in Chad is over 14 miles), or where there are too few facilities for large urban populations. Despite substantial donor inflows, most public health systems in Africa are drastically underfunded and unable to afford even basic equipment, drugs, and supplies. There are widespread staffing shortages as well, the result of low salaries and generally miserable working conditions. As a result, the overall quality of healthcare in Africa tends to be inferior.

• *Building functional health systems.* Africa's public health needs are great, but even where the resources can be made available, the capacity to manage them and create a performing overall system is lacking. Donors recognize this, but are frequently drawn to support specific projects so they can track and identify their contribution rather than contribute to a larger (and often dysfunctional) system.

• *Vertical vs. horizontal approaches.* Vertical programs are those that target a particular disease or goal—such as eradicating malaria—and then design and implement the program on its own. This has been the approach favored by many donors, for example in the battle against HIV/AIDS, because the resources and systems are isolated from the broader problems with the national health systems, services can be delivered more quickly, and donors can more easily influence outcomes and track results. (Although this approach has its limits; see the HIV discussion below.) A horizontal approach is to tackle the broader healthcare system and try to improve its overall effectiveness. While this strategy seems a more sensible and sustainable approach, it is also much harder to do, results are much more out of the control of funders, and there is little clarity about who takes credit or blame.

Brain Drain?
One of the commonly heard reasons for the shortage of healthcare workers in developing countries is that they have all migrated to rich coun-

tries. It is certainly true that there are many doctors and nurses from African countries working in Europe and North America, lured by exponentially higher pay and better working conditions. In some cases, deliberate policies in Europe, such as the explicit recruitment of foreign healthcare workers, have increased the lure to move abroad (the UK, for instance, once actively recruited African nurses for its own national health service, a policy it has since ended). At the same time, the full range of reasons for emigration of skilled professionals is far from clear—in many cases getting a medical education in the first place is seen as a ticket to a better life abroad. More importantly, the lack of working nurses and doctors is probably due to homegrown factors much more than to foreign poaching. For example, there are only two thousand Kenyan nurses working in the UK, but there are at least five thousand qualified nurses in Kenya who are either unemployed or working in another profession. Thus, the outflow of health professionals is perhaps more a symptom of a broken system at home—low salaries, lack of medicine and equipment, and few prospects for advancement—than a direct cause of Africa's poor health.

HIV/AIDS

The HIV/AIDS pandemic is in some ways the greatest challenge for Africa today—and has effects far beyond public health. The UN estimates that out of the roughly 40 million people living with HIV worldwide, two-thirds are in sub-Saharan Africa. The recent death rate on the continent from the disease has been nearly seven thousand per day. After many years of neglect, fighting the spread of HIV/AIDS has now become one of the highest priorities on the global agenda. Even as the money raised for HIV/AIDS programs has mushroomed, the battle to help the infected and stop the spread of the virus has revealed deeper problems with public health and development systems.

Demographics of the Plague

Statistics often report on the prevalence among pregnant women, not necessarily because they are the most vulnerable to the disease (although they may be), but rather because HIV testing data is usually collected regularly at prenatal clinics and then extrapolated to the wider population. This is not without its problems (for example, basing conclusions on a small slice of the population), but is generally more accurate than household surveys, in which self-reporting of HIV status will no doubt result in massive underestimation and voluntary testing with high rates of refusal. Nevertheless, the transmission of HIV/AIDS among the African population has followed certain discernible patterns:

• *Age and education.* HIV/AIDS runs especially high among the young. In Africa, fully one-quarter of all those infected with HIV are in the fifteen to twenty-four age group. The linkage between HIV infection and education is less clear. In the early years of the pandemic, prevalence rates were higher among more educated groups. More recently, HIV infection rates have been higher among less educated groups.

• *Gender.* Of all infected adults in Africa, an estimated 57 percent are women. Among young people fifteen to twenty-four years old, the disease is even more biased, with young women and girls accounting for 75 percent of those infected.

• *Region.* Southern Africa is the worst-hit region, with several countries above 20 percent adult prevalence (Botswana, Lesotho, Namibia, South Africa, Swaziland, and Zimbabwe). This regional concentration is in part because of employment and migration patterns that keep workers apart from their families for long stretches of the year, encouraging prostitution and then the spread of the virus during home visits. Adult HIV prevalence rates are also thought to be near 20 percent in parts of war-affected Central Africa. West Africa has generally lower infection rates, with many countries reporting below 2 percent prevalence.

Table 10.5 HIV/AIDS in Africa, 2005 Statistics

Adults and children living with HIV	25.8 million
Number of women living with HIV	13.5 million
Adults and children newly infected with HIV	3.2 million
Adult prevalence	7.2%
Adult and child deaths due to AIDS	2.4 million

Source: UNAIDS.

Prevalence vs. Incidence

"Prevalence" is the number of cases of a given condition for a given population, regardless of when the condition was acquired. For example, the HIV prevalence rate is 16 percent in Mozambique as of 2005, meaning that proportion of the population is infected. "Incidence" is the number of new cases in a population over a given period. For example, Mozambique's incidence rate is about five hundred new cases per day. Because prevalence is a stock and incidence is a flow, the former reflects accumulated changes in the latter over time. Thus, changes in incidence would not necessarily be reflected in the prevalence rate for some time.

• *Heterosexual transmission.* HIV is transmitted most commonly in Africa through (hetero) sexual contact, putting young girls in particular at risk, especially since marriage and sexual patterns in many parts of the continent result in older men with multiple much-younger partners.

Multiple Costs of AIDS

The loss of working adults, especially women, has a devastating effect on households, and long illnesses drain family savings and strain social networks. Increased sickness and time spent caring for family members is likely affecting the labor supply and productivity. Over the long term, losses of skilled and capable people pose a further risk by breaking the normal process of passing information between generations. If, for example, the knowledge about how to farm a particular area that was learned over many generations is lost, it could have a ruinous effect on a family and its production. Collectively, this phenomenon could affect an entire region or country.

In the hardest-hit countries, the public sector, already generally weak, has been further impaired by HIV/AIDS, with reports of some countries training several people for one position because the chances of one or more of them dying are so high. The demographics of the disease can lead to a "hollowing out" of the population, where there are many young and old, but fewer of working age. In addition to lost labor and skills, the AIDS epidemic can have perverse effects in other areas. As AIDS curtails how long people live in many countries—for example, life expectancy in Botswana has dropped from fifty-eight in 1980 to only thirty-eight today—the incentive to invest in children's education is reduced. This, combined with higher costs associated with caring for sick family members, can have an effect on school attendance—and the future of Africa's next generation.

Despite these likely channels for detrimental effects of HIV/AIDS having a major long-term impact on African development, the actual evidence for a lot of these costs is weak. The data show that people are dying, but tracing the broader effects on society and the economy is diffi-

Table 10.6   Prevalence Rates, Selected Countries, 2004

Botswana	39%
South Africa	22%
Tanzania	7%
Ethiopia	4%
Senegal	<2%

Source: UNAIDS.

cult. A number of economists have tried to estimate the bearing on GDP under various scenarios, and nearly all show negative consequences, but the scale differs from a small effect to 1.5 percent per year (which can accumulate over time into a huge impact). One model, for instance, suggests that the South African economy will be 17 percent smaller in 2010 because of AIDS.

Strategies for Combating AIDS
The battle against HIV/AIDS is being waged on many fronts, including prevention, counseling and testing, and treatment.

• *Prevention.* The main initiatives for prevention are public education (via clinics, schools, churches, billboards, and even theater and music) and condom distribution. The evidence of how well these work in changing behavior is, however, still far from clear (see discussion of the ABC Program below). Some of the recent HIV therapies are also used to prevent pregnant mothers from passing the virus to their babies.

• *Counseling and testing.* Testing is a key aspect of prevention (since knowledge of HIV status is crucial in discouraging risky behavior), as well as treatment (in order to identify the target populations). There are now rapid tests available that can provide results within thirty minutes, but there are still debates about how aggressively to test (such as whether the test should be mandatory or given on an opt-out rather than opt-in basis). Prenatal clinics are still the main location at which testing occurs, although voluntary testing centers for the general population are becoming increasingly common across Africa. There is also some evidence that people are reluctant to be tested if there is no treatment; alternatively, testing tends to increase once therapy is made available.

• *Treatment.* The ability to cope with HIV infection has been transformed by new treatment, especially the arrival of antiretroviral (ARV) therapy (sometimes called highly active antiretroviral therapy). In Africa, access to ARVs has grown tremendously in recent years as the price of these medicines has fallen dramatically and external financing has become available. Fortunately, the positive results of ARVs in Africa are almost identical to those found in the United States and Europe, where such treatment first became available.

Issues with ARVs in Africa
While the advent of ARVs has transformed the campaign against AIDS, there are some particular challenges in this approach for Africa. For ARVs to work, patients have to stick to a strict regimen and take these medicines for the rest of their lives. This requires a functioning and

effective healthcare system, which is often lacking in Africa. The risks of failure are also extremely high. If patients stop taking ARV treatment, not only will they die, but they risk creating and spreading a treatment-resistant strain of HIV. On a continent where the health sector still has trouble delivering one-time vaccines, the task of providing and monitoring the use of ARVs for the millions of people in need will take a huge investment in health systems, including skilled personnel, equipment, and facilities.

The ABC Program

One of the highest-profile efforts to contain HIV/AIDS has been a public relations campaign to change people's behavior, known as the ABC Program. The acronym stands for: Abstain, Be faithful, use a Condom. It was heavily promoted by Uganda's president, Yoweri Museveni, and has attracted support from several donors, especially after being cited as one of the reasons that Uganda has seen a decline in HIV prevalence, including a reported drop among pregnant women in Kampala from 30 percent to just 10 percent. The program has, however, been highly criticized on several grounds. Some have questioned whether the improvement in Uganda can be attributed to ABC or not, while there has also been some concern that an emphasis on abstinence (preferred by some donors) might detract from other efforts to finance treatment or other strategies.

Who Pays?

Although the international community was off to a slow start, funding for HIV/AIDS programs has risen rapidly. Global funding for such interventions in poor countries had grown to $6 billion by 2004, nearly as much as allocated to support general healthcare. In some African countries, the response has been even sharper, with a handful of the donor favorites seeing donor HIV/AIDS funds swamping the overall health budget. The main sources of international support are the bilateral agencies, the Global Fund, and the World Bank. In addition, there are local sources, including the regular budget of each country, a growing number of initiatives by private companies, and the resources of NGOs. Ultimately though, many of the final costs are borne by individual households.

Key Global HIV/AIDS Institutions

There are multiple (and often overlapping) high-level international programs to fight HIV/AIDS. Among the most prominent are:

• *WHO*. The World Health Organization (WHO), the public health arm of the UN, works directly on HIV/AIDS by developing recommendations for national protocols, screening drugs, and monitoring the spread of the disease.

• *UNAIDS*. As its name suggests, UNAIDS is the lead UN agency specifically tasked with coordinating the global response and helping to develop ways for countries to manage related money. In practice, it mostly plays an advocacy and publicity role.

• *Bilaterals*. Each of the major bilateral donors (see Chapter 8) provides some HIV/AIDS funding or has its own programs.

• *PEPFAR*. In January 2003, President George W. Bush announced the United States would spend $15 billion over five years to fight HIV/AIDS in Africa and the Caribbean. Known as the President's Emergency Plan for AIDS Relief (PEPFAR), it is by far the largest single bilateral program. PEPFAR has involved a range of initiatives for treatment and prevention, targeting fifteen "focus countries," of which twelve are in Africa. Although PEPFAR has a single coordinator, its implementation has been done through USAID, the multilateral Global Fund, and nongovernmental groups.

• *Global Fund*. The Global Fund to Fight AIDS, Tuberculosis, and Malaria (GFATM or commonly just called the "Global Fund") was founded in late 2001 to fight against those three devastating diseases. While it has been an important vehicle for raising money, it has also been an innovative experiment in changing the way international aid is delivered. Rather than establish its own country programs, the Global Fund works more like a light foundation, making grants to local initiatives while demanding high accounting and performance standards.

• *World Bank MAP*. In 2000 the World Bank created an extra grant window, the Multicountry AIDS Program (MAP). Most of the affected countries in Africa have since received MAP funding, which can be for a range of projects as long as it is coordinated with a country's national HIV/AIDS strategy.

Constraints in Battling AIDS
The barriers to fighting HIV/AIDS are in some ways similar to broader problems in public health, without the scarcity of resources. The international community has mobilized billions of dollars and for many African countries the main challenge now is to spend such sums wisely. The sudden wave of cash can actually be a problem for a health system that does not have budget systems in place to track money, ways to buy and distribute large amounts of drugs, or enough trained personnel to staff the clinics. Pressure to spend money quickly also raises the chances of corruption and waste (thus putting future funding at risk). The common donor preference to fund HIV/AIDS initiatives but not general health-

care means that there are severe imbalances, with some parts of the healthcare system flooded with cash and others starved of it. In both Uganda and Zambia, for instance, external AIDS funds have recently been nearly twice as much as all other public health spending.

Expanding healthcare systems based on donor money also carries long-term risks because such funding is volatile and uncertain. Any effort to improve healthcare, for example, would almost certainly mean hiring more workers and building more facilities. This implies long-term commitments to provide salaries and maintenance, yet donor funds are notoriously fickle and could easily dry up in the future. Especially worrisome in such a decrease is the possible deadly effect on HIV/AIDS treatment. Given that AIDS patients must continue ARV therapy to stay alive, interruptions caused by funding gaps would literally mean scores of deaths. Such concerns do not suggest people should not be put on ARVs, but rather that there is a potentially tragic mismatch between the long-term financing needs of HIV/AIDS care and the short-term financial cycles of the donors.

Lastly, there are still major cultural barriers to fighting HIV/AIDS. Even in the face of mass deaths, there is still a widespread stigma attached to AIDS in Africa, as well as a common reluctance to discuss sexual issues in public. Although there is some initial evidence that such attitudes are slowly changing, this will remain a problem for those on the front lines.

For Further Reading

The major annual publication on poverty is the UN's *Human Development Report*, which includes all the data on the Human Development Index. The scholar most responsible for broadening the definition of poverty is Nobel Laureate Amartya Sen, especially his *Development as Freedom* (1999). Deepa Narayan's three-volume *Voices of the Poor* (2000) gives detailed accounts of the lives of poor people, the constraints they face, and makes a case for increasing influence. An excellent overview of the issues related to poverty on the continent is *African Poverty at the Millennium: Causes, Complexities, and Challenges* by Howard White, Tony Killick, and Steve Kayizzi-Mugerwa (2001).

Data on income and other welfare indicators in individual countries and for regional aggregates can be found through World Bank databases, especially *World Development Indicators*. The Bank also produces periodic *Poverty Assessments*, but only for a small number of countries. Publicly released assessments since 2000 are available for Benin, Burkina Faso, Ethiopia, Swaziland, and Uganda. The World Bank also warehouses different surveys taken in its *Africa Household Survey Databank*, most of which is accessible on the website. The UN and the AfDB also track progress toward some of the Millennium Development Goal indicators, but the quality of their numbers is even shakier than the figures produced by the World Bank. The article on the sample bias problem cited above is "Correcting for Sampling Bias in the Measurement of Welfare and Poverty in the Côte d'Ivoire Living Standards Survey" by Lionel Demery and Christiaan Grootaert (1993).

The seminal paper on the relationship between income and health is Lant Pritchett and Lawrence Summers's "Wealthier Is Healthier" (1996). One analysis of the causes of health outcomes is Lucia Hanmer, Robert Lensink, and Howard White's "Infant and Child Mortality in Developing Countries: Analysing the Data for Robust Determinants" (2003). John Strauss and Duncan Thomas review the evidence in "Health, Nutrition, and Economic Development" (1998). Charles Kenny suggests that the income gaps are less important than the narrowing of other quality-of-life indicators in his provocatively titled "Why Are We Worried About Income? Nearly Everything That Matters Is Converging" (2005).

A recent argument in favor of the poverty trap is "Ending Africa's Poverty Trap" by Jeffrey Sachs (2004). An economic analysis that disputes the existence of a poverty trap is Aart Kraay and Claudio Raddatz's "Poverty Traps, Aid, and Growth" (2005). The paper on household allocation and how it may severely affect the poverty numbers is Lawrence Haddad and Ravi Kanbur's "How Serious Is the Neglect of Intra-Household Inequality?" (1990).

The major report on service delivery is the Bank's *World Development Report 2004: Making Services Work for Poor People* (2005). Ruth Levine documents seventeen successful health interventions in poor countries in *Millions Saved: Proven Successes in Global Health* (2004). Michael Clemens disputes the attribution of brain drain as the reason for poor health in Africa in "Do No Harm: Is the Emigration of Health Professionals Bad for Africa?" (2006). Anne Mills and Kara Hanson edited a special edition of the *Journal of International Development* entitled "Expanding Access to Health Interventions in Low and Middle-Income Countries: Constraints and Opportunities for Scaling Up" (2003). Maureen Lewis examines systemic problems in "Governance and Corruption in Health Care Delivery" (2006).

UNAIDS's *Report on the Global AIDS Epidemic* (2004) provides data on the spread of the disease and an overview of efforts to stem the tide. UNAIDS also produces regular *AIDS Epidemic Updates* with more recent information. *AIDS in the Twenty-First Century* by Tony Barnett and Alan Whiteside (2003) is also a useful volume.

Paul Farmer and colleagues made a case for more active treatment in low-income countries with "Community-Based Approaches to HIV Treatment in Resource-Poor Settings" (2001).

Alex de Waal asks "How Will HIV/AIDS Transform African Governance?" (2003). Markus Haacker's substantial edited volume *The Macroeconomics of HIV/AIDS* (2004) has many contributions looking at various ways the epidemic is affecting various economies and societies. A good summary of previous studies as well as a model of South Africa can be found in "The Long-Run Economic Costs of AIDS: Theory and an Application to South Africa" by Clive Bell, Shantayanan Devarajan, and Hans Gersbach (2003). See also Channing Arndt and Jeffrey Lewis's "The Macro-Economic Implications of HIV/AIDS in South Africa: A Preliminary Assessment" (2000). Other potential effects are addressed in "The Impact of HIV/AIDS on Labour Productivity in Kenya" (2004) by Matthew Fox and colleagues and "Educational Attainment and HIV-1 Infection in Developing Countries: A Systematic Review" (2002) by James Hargreaves and Judith Glynn.

Maureen Lewis lays out some of the limits to spending money to stop the crisis in "Addressing the Challenge of HIV/AIDS: Macroeconomic, Fiscal, and Institutional Issues" (2005). Martha Ainsworth and Warnya Teokul also advise caution in "Breaking the Silence: Setting Realistic Priorities for HIV/AIDS Control in Less-Developed Countries" (2000). Michael Kremer proposes some ideas for encouraging an AIDS vaccine in "Pharmaceuticals and the Developing World" (2002).

PART 3

Regionalism and Globalization

11

Regional Institutions and NEPAD

THE AFRICAN CONTINENT IS CARVED INTO A PATCHWORK OF dozens of separate states. Because of the colonial origins of current borders, drawn up mainly to suit the strategic compromises of European powers sitting around a table in Berlin in 1884, the lines dividing countries have little relevance to the realities on the ground (see Chapter 2). This leaves the continent with both huge, unwieldy, and probably ungovernable states, such as Sudan and the Democratic Republic of Congo, and tiny unviable states, such as Djibouti (which is really little more than a port) and The Gambia (which is just a sliver of two river banks cut into the heart of Senegal). Even the borders of most middle-sized African countries make little sense. The seemingly obvious answer to this problem is regional cooperation and integration. In practice, however, these ideas have rarely been put into practice. The continent has a range of regional institutions and arrangements, some with very ambitious plans, that seek to promote greater regionalism. This chapter lays out the background for these trends and also describes some of the key regional institutions relevant to the continent's economic and political development.

Frozen Borders
Ideas to redraw Africa's borders along more logical lines have gone nowhere. The usual reason given for keeping borders frozen is the risk that opening such a Pandora's Box will inevitably unleash violent conflict, mass bloodshed, and will further balkanize the continent. In fact, there have been almost no cases of substantial border changes over the past half century except for Eritrea's secession from Ethiopia in 1993. Yet this example bodes poorly for more comprehensive efforts since that was a mutually agreed split and nevertheless ended in a bloody border war just five years later (Chapter 4). Perhaps more important than the fear of violence, Africa's political leaders themselves have little incentive to yield control over their own states or to cede authority.

Fragmentation Effects

The result of frozen borders is that cohesive social or linguistic groups are often split between different countries or lumped together. The large number of African states also means that most countries are small. Out of forty-eight sub-Saharan countries, twenty have less than 5 million people, or about the population of metropolitan Detroit. Economically, the effects are especially evident as African economies are fragmented into relatively tiny and undiversified units. The GDP of at least thirty sub-Saharan economies is $5 billion or less, or about equivalent to the capitalization of a midsize US company. This can prevent economies from achieving the critical mass needed to provide a production and consumer market large enough to thrive and compete internationally.

The borders themselves are an economic problem since every one is a potential barrier to the flow of people and goods. Africa, with a total economy roughly the same size as metropolitan Chicago, is split up into four dozen individual states. (Imagine the impact on life in Chicago if it were divided into forty districts each with border security, customs, and other such hassles.) In fact, Africa's ludicrous borders leave fifteen countries landlocked, forcing them to trade overland through neighbors at huge additional cost and making them highly vulnerable.

Many states also mean many governments. This is highly ineffi-cient, because each government needs to re-create similar structures and institutions—armies, health ministries, central banks, parliaments—each with their own overhead costs and staff. Large numbers of states can also create collective action problems, where cooperation is required to deal with common concerns. But the legacy of Africa's borders means that multiple states have segregated interests into smaller entities not designed to work well with each other.

Pan-Africanism

The early solution to these problems of African social, economic, and political fragmentation predates independence. Ideas of unity and racial solidarity became powerful motivators among the early nationalist caus-es emerging among exiles in Europe and among African American thinkers in the United States (see Chapter 2). A coterie of independence leaders—especially Kwame Nkrumah and Julius Nyerere—proposed regional institutions in order to promote continent-wide political union. Nkrumah even envisioned a "United States of Africa" that would oper-ate as a single government with a federal structure. Although his plan never came to fruition, it did lead to the creation of the Organization of African Unity (OAU), and the ideals of pan-Africanism live on today in many forms.

More Practical Regionalization

While Pan-Africanist dreams went unfulfilled, a range of regional organizations have emerged with more practical goals in mind. If the United States is no longer considered a model for the continent, the European Union certainly is. As in the EU, the forms of cooperation that tend to work best have specific practical applications as their basis rather than grandiose goals that may run into impassable political roadblocks. In particular, African regional groups have tended to focus on economic integration, with the best example being monetary unions. This brings direct benefits such as sharing a single central bank, but also helps to facilitate trade and other exchanges by eliminating the need to manage and exchange currencies. (Of course, monetary union also limits the flexibility of any individual government on monetary policy, which is why many countries prefer to keep their own national currencies.) Cross-border trade has also been a rationale for regional cooperation, with multiple institutions dedicated primarily to promoting a freer flow of goods among its members. Beside economics, security is the other main area where regional groups have been most proactive. West African regional peacekeepers have played leading roles in suppressing conflicts in Liberia and Sierra Leone, while many of the other regional groups may have started because of economics but have found themselves forced to deal with security issues.

Rhetoric vs. Reality

One trend that appears obvious to any observer of Africa—and a source of frequent frustration—is that the rhetoric of regional integration has almost always been far ahead of reality. Regional summits and institutions often make grand claims of rapid and ambitious plans that are either never implemented or severely delayed for a long list of reasons. This is partly because integration is difficult to achieve anywhere on the globe and requires compromises among a group of countries with a sense of common purpose and a high level of trust. In Africa the number of players tends to be high, trust low, and the incentives for actual progress absent (if not in opposition). The regional organizations themselves are often, like their member states, underfunded and lacking in managerial capacity. They have no ability to raise their own revenue, so they remain dependent on contributions from members or donors. Despite the lofty talk, they are also given almost no real authority. It appears that progress is most frequently made when there are a fairly small number of members (like the three-country East African Community), their purposes are narrow (such as exchanging information about food stocks), or when one country takes the clear lead (as

Nigeria did for West African peacekeeping). In fact, there appears to be an inverse relationship between ambition and effectiveness. Despite these problems, Africa does have a wide array of regional organizations of various scope and ability that are making some modest inroads in promoting integration.

Africa's Pan-Regional Organization: The African Union

The African Union (AU) is the closest thing the continent has to an "African UN," although its founders like to think of it more like an early version of the EU. It was launched in 2002, replacing the Organization of African Unity (OAU), which had been meeting since 1963 but developed a reputation as an ineffectual talk shop. The AU, like its predecessor, has high ambitions for Africa: a single central bank, a single currency, a continental court, and common policies on defense and communications. The AU expects to eventually establish a peace and security council modeled on the UN Security Council that would approve intervention by a standing AU military force in cases of genocide, coup, or gross human rights abuse. A Pan-African parliament was officially launched in 2004, but it is far from clear if it will ever have any meaningful powers. The formal institutions of the AU, however, may be beside the point. The main purpose of the group is to provide a regular forum, including an annual heads-of-state summit, for all fifty-three African leaders (it also includes North African countries) to meet to discuss common problems and strategies.

In many ways it is still unclear whether the new AU will be substantially different from the old OAU. The offices in Addis Ababa are the same and it shares many of the same aims and structures. More importantly, the primary reasons that the OAU failed remain in play: the refusal by member states to cede any real authority or resources. Although each country is supposed to pay regular dues, many do not. More critically, governments generally do not want to voluntarily hand over legal powers or economic policies to a supranational body. Governments understandably want to keep control for themselves, and the smaller countries fear being overpowered by the larger countries, especially South Africa, which had taken a lead role in reviving the AU and promoting the economic agenda. Perhaps most controversially, issues of national sovereignty are highly sensitive and governments want to keep the principle of "noninterference" even if it is no longer officially enshrined in the AU charter. Despite these lingering issues, there are some early positive signs that the AU will be different. External donors seem willing to finance the AU in a way not seen in the past. In its early test of new security and human rights mechanisms, the AU responded fairly robustly by sending observers and troops to Darfur in Sudan in 2005 and played a useful role in helping to enforce a peace agreement in Burundi.

NEPAD

The New Partnership for Africa's Development (NEPAD) is a somewhat amorphous entity. Technically it is the economic strategy of the AU. But it also has its own secretariat in Johannesburg and multiple arms that sometimes make its exact relationship with the AU confusing. It was formally launched in 2001 and emerged from competing regional economic plans by South Africa's Thabo Mbeki and Senegal's Abdoulaye Wade. NEPAD's main areas of work are regional infrastructure, agriculture, market access, education, health, and the environment. A signature project is the African Peer Review Mechanism, which is a voluntary program to try to monitor agreed standards of government behavior (see Chapter 5).

In practice, the concept of NEPAD is a bargain with donors: Africa will improve its governance in exchange for more aid, trade, and investment from the West. So far, it has been considered slow-moving and unable to avoid some of the coordination problems of past regional initiatives. It has also been criticized for not enforcing its own standards, especially in the case of Zimbabwe, where NEPAD's pronouncements about good governance do not seem consistent with the reasons given by Mbeki and others for not condemning human rights and political abuses by Robert Mugabe's regime. Nevertheless, NEPAD holds the potential as a platform for organizing investments that include multiple countries, such as regional power-pools, highways, or telecommunications.

Key Regional Groups

Africa has a multitude of regional groups that promote similar agendas of economic and political integration. Despite what looks similar on paper, they vary in effectiveness.

SADC

In 1980 all of the so-called frontline states in southern Africa formed a group called the Southern African Development Co-ordination Conference. Its purpose was to help countries work together to reduce their economic reliance on white-ruled South Africa. Although it mostly failed in this task, it did provide a united front against the apartheid regime. Once the end apartheid became clear, the group reinvented itself as the Southern African Development Community (SADC) with the mission of promoting regional integration and economic development. SADC now includes all southern African countries, including Mauritius, the Democratic Republic of Congo (DRC), and its predecessor's target, South Africa. In its new role, SADC has been fairly successful in promoting regional trade and hopes to launch a formal free-trade area (meaning that there will be no taxes on goods traded among themselves) for all members at some point. SADC has also been important in coordinating regional energy policy, playing a role in the ongoing project to connect a vast electricity grid across the subregion. There are also long-term plans for a regional development bank, a common currency, and a regional parliament, although these are all far off.

Two other areas where SADC is relevant are security and governance, although the record on both is less than encouraging. Member countries have agreed to a mutual defense pact, but a standby army has never materialized. More of a problem, SADC has not been able to establish clear guidelines for when the defense pact should be invoked. Zimbabwe, Angola, and Namibia used it in 1998 (over South African opposition) as justification for sending troops to DRC to protect then-President Laurent Kabila. But that same year South Africa's call for SADC intervention to put down a possible coup in Lesotho went unheeded (South Africa sent its own troops, but not under SADC cover). In 2004 SADC also agreed to a set of election codes in an attempt to help define "free and fair" and to promote better overall governance. But at its first major test, parliamentary elections held in Zimbabwe in March 2005, SADC failed to uphold its own standards in the face of obvious electoral misconduct.

Overall, SADC is one of the more effective regional institutions in Africa. Nevertheless, its ability to continue to play a positive role will depend on South Africa promoting its agenda without scaring off the other members. Much of the economic plans are being driven by South Africa, which makes sense given its size and sophisticated economy, but most of the other countries are wary of being dominated by their much larger neighbor. Progress toward integration will also depend on finding ways of accommodating members who may need to proceed at different paces. South Africa and its immediate neighbors, for example, have more capacity to contribute to regional initiatives and are likely to be willing to push much farther and faster on trade liberalization than, say, Angola or DRC.

SACU and CMA

The Southern African Customs Union (SACU) links Botswana, Namibia, Lesotho, and Swaziland (sometimes called the "BNLS" states) and South Africa. The idea of SACU, and of all customs unions, is that countries pool any taxes collected on trade coming into the union from outside, and then the money is distributed according to a treaty. Since poverty measures are part of SACU's revenue-sharing formula, in practice this arrangement acts as a subsidy to the smaller BNLS states, with

South Africa both administering the scheme and making regular payments to the other members. This is especially important for Lesotho and Swaziland, which rely on SACU for at least half of total government revenue. SACU is also relevant to trade, guaranteeing preferential access for BNLS goods in the South African market and providing a platform for international free-trade agreements, such as have been agreed with the EU and discussed with the United States, India, and Mercosur (a South American trade zone).

The same group of countries, excluding Botswana, also form the Common Monetary Area (CMA). This allows use of the South African rand, or a local parallel currency valued the same as the rand, and free movement of cash among the group. The CMA provides financial stability for the smaller countries and they benefit from lower inflation managed by the South African Reserve Bank (SARB, its central bank). In exchange for this, however, the smaller countries have ceded monetary policy control to the SARB. Botswana has opted to manage its own currency (the pula) and monetary policy, but in practice maintains a rate partially pegged to the rand.

EAC

The East African Community (EAC) has just three members: Kenya, Tanzania, and Uganda. The group had a rough start, having tried to form a union in the 1970s, but efforts collapsed in 1977, at least partly because its members were about to go to war. (Tanzania invaded Uganda two years later in order to overthrow Idi Amin.) In 2001 the EAC was relaunched with ambitious plans for reductions in trade barriers, coordination of economic policies, and other forms of integration. In a short time, the EAC has made some progress, including the harmonization of standards and coordinating bodies for legal and financial transactions. A customs union agreement was signed in 2004, but it will be only slowly implemented and the list of exceptions is lengthy. In practice, there is political concern that Kenya, whose economy is generally more advanced than the other two, will be overly dominant in the region. Like many of the other regional groups, the EAC also plans to create a currency union, a regional stock market, a parliament, and a joint court, although whether any of this will occur is still to be seen. There is some talk of expanding the EAC, with Rwanda and Burundi as potential future members.

The African Franc Zones

Fourteen African countries are members of the franc zone, which means they share a common currency, the Communauté financière d'Afrique (CFA) franc. The CFA franc was created just after World War II, but

France's former colonies kept the monetary arrangements in place after independence. (Equatorial Guinea and Guinea-Bissau were not French colonies but joined the franc zone in 1984 and 1997, respectively). The countries are divided into two zones, a six-country Central African group and an eight-member West African one (see Table 11.1). The main purpose of the zones is to provide the CFA as a currency fixed to the French franc and guaranteed as convertible by the French treasury. Since the introduction of the euro in 1999, the CFA has been pegged to the new European currency, but France retains special rights within Europe to manage the CFA-euro relationship. In exchange for this deal, the African authorities cede control over their own monetary policy (exchange rate, interest rates, money supply) to the French and a regional central bank. In January 1994 this pact was severely tested as the French authorities devalued the CFA for the first time in nearly half a century. Despite persistent rumors of more devaluations, this has so far not occurred again.

In addition to monetary union, both the regional groups, Communauté économique et monétaire de l'Afrique centrale (CEMAC) and Union économique et monétaire ouest-africaine (UEMOA) have broader integration agendas, including trade liberalization and promo-

Table 11.1   The African Franc Zones

Franc zone	Communauté économique et monétaire de l'Afrique centrale (CEMAC)	Union économique et monétaire ouest-africaine (UEMOA)
Members	Cameroon Central African Republic Chad Congo (Brazzaville) Gabon Equatorial Guinea	Benin Burkina Faso Côte d'Ivoire Guinea-Bissau Mali Niger Senegal Togo
Central bank	Banque des Etats de l'Afrique centrale (BEAC) in Yaoundé, Cameroon	Banque centrale des Etats de l'Afrique de l'ouest (BCEAO) in Dakar, Senegal
Currency	CFA franc	CFA franc
Regional stock market	None	Bourse régionale des valeurs mobilières (BRVM) in Abidjan, Côte d'Ivoire

tion and synchronization of tax and business laws. In general, the West African UEMOA has been more effective and gone farther than its Central African counterpart. It launched a regional stock exchange in Abidjan, Côte d'Ivoire, in 1998, and it eliminated tariffs on internal trade and harmonized import tariffs in 2000. Despite these steps, the region has been hit hard by political instability and civil war in Côte d'Ivoire, the group's largest economy. CEMAC has managed to launch a nominal regional court, but faces even bigger political troubles. Several of its members have suffered internal strife, and leaders of some of the smaller, richer nations have resisted integration. Indicative of the barriers, CEMAC has been planning a regional stock market since the mid-1990s, but the members have been unable to move forward, in part because of disputes over where it will be located. CEMAC was able, however, to muster a small peacekeeping force to deploy in the Central African Republic in 2002.

ECOWAS

The Economic Community of West African States (ECOWAS) is a group of fifteen countries, including all eight UEMOA members plus Cape Verde, The Gambia, Ghana, Guinea, Liberia, Nigeria, and Sierra Leone. (Mauritania was a member but withdrew in 2000.) The main purpose of ECOWAS, launched in 1975, is to promote trade within the region through a customs union and a common market. It has a full-time secretariat, a regional parliament, and a court, all based in Nigeria's capital, Abuja. On its own, it has no real power, other than to convene its members. Since UEMOA already has a monetary union, the remaining (mostly English-speaking) members agreed to form a second monetary union in 2000, but its implementation remains far from certain. Although the delays are technically because most members have failed to meet the required financial targets, it is also because of political factors. There remain high levels of distrust, and the smaller countries are concerned that Nigeria will be overly dominant.

Like many of the other regional economic groups, ECOWAS was forced to also deal with security issues among its members. In fact, ECOWAS is probably best known for its multiple peacekeeping operations, including in Liberia (1990 and 2003), Sierra Leone (1997), Guinea-Bissau (1998), and Côte d'Ivoire (2002). Although the early interventions were mostly Nigerian-led, both Senegal and Ghana have been increasingly willing to commit troops and leadership to peacekeeping, giving it a real regional character. ECOWAS plans a permanent standby force in the future and has received help from Western militaries in the form of training and supplies.

Some Minor Regional Groups

In addition to these larger regional organizations, there are many others of less importance, some of which overlap in membership and mandate. Among the more notable are:

• *The Common Market for Eastern and Southern Africa (COMESA)* aims for a huge free-trade area and a single currency across much of the African continent. With nineteen diverse members, it has not been able to manage much progress and its future as an organization is in doubt. It has managed to persuade eleven of its members to remove tariffs on each other, but the organization has been hampered by factions and defections. Lesotho, Tanzania, Mozambique, and Namibia have all quit the group, while South Africa politely declined to join.

• *The Intergovernmental Authority on Development (IGAD)* was originally set up in 1986 to deal with drought and desertification in the Horn of Africa. Its early plans to coordinate funding for agricultural development and environmental projects came to very little, but IGAD has had some successes in mediating political disputes among its seven members: Djibouti, Ethiopia, Kenya, Somalia, Sudan, Uganda, and (since 1993) Eritrea. Given that each of the members faces severe internal conflict and several have fought all-out wars against each other, it is not hard to understand why security quickly overshadowed the economic agenda. IGAD has, however, played central roles in brokering cease-fires in Sudan and encouraging reconciliation in Somalia.

• *The Indian Ocean Commission (IOC)* includes the African island nations of Madagascar, Mauritius, Seychelles, and Comoros. Its work focuses mostly on environmental management and emergency response, with programs to coordinate fishing, weather forecasting, and oil spill contingency planning. Its initial economic goals have been overtaken by other regional blocs, notably SADC.

• *The Comité permanent inter-Etats de lutte contre la sécheresse dans le Sahel (CILSS)* is an organization of Sahelian countries to coordinate food security and to cope with drought and desertification. CILSS has research and training institutes in Niger and Mali and produces regular statistics on members' food production.

• *The Mano River Union (MRU)* includes Liberia, Sierra Leone, and Guinea. It shares similar aims with other regional groups, but the MRU is possibly the least meaningful of all of them. A nonaggression treaty signed in 1986 was ignored by all sides, and each country has faced violent internal conflict, each involving guerrillas partly encouraged and financed by the others. The MRU rarely met, although fragile peace in all three members recently has revived the idea.

Africa and Other International Groups
African countries are represented in a whole range of international groups that also promote regionalization. Those with a substantial African influence and most relevant to development include:

• *United Nations.* Just by their sheer number of sovereign states, the African bloc makes its presence felt in the General Assembly. It also is a major focus of the UN's various agencies, including the United Nations Development Program and the Economic Commission for Africa (see Chapter 8).
• *Commonwealth.* This group of mostly former British colonies has many African members and holds annual meetings to try to promote better governance among its members. Its mandate remains unclear and its relevance in the future is far from obvious.
• *G-24.* The Group of 24 represents leading developing countries seeking to influence international policies on monetary and development finance issues. Its sub-Saharan members are Côte d'Ivoire, Ethiopia, Gabon, Ghana, Nigeria, South Africa, and the Democratic Republic of Congo.
• *G-77.* The Group of 77 is a larger caucus (despite its name, it now has more than 130 members) that tries to coordinate common negotiating positions for all developing countries on major international economic issues within the United Nations system.
• *NAM.* The Non-Aligned Movement is an international organization of over 100 states that consider themselves neutral in global affairs. NAM started in 1961 at the height of the Cold War with the idea that poor countries were caught in the middle of a larger battle between global powers. In reality, it was far from impartial with a distinctly leftist ideology and Cuba and Yugoslavia among the leading proponents. With the demise of the Soviet Union, NAM still continues to meet today, but is not an influential forum.
• *IOR-ARC.* The Indian Ocean Rim Association for Regional Cooperation is a fairly new organization to promote trade, investment, and tourism for countries with an Indian Ocean coast. It has eighteen members including Kenya, Madagascar, Mauritius, Mozambique, South Africa, and Tanzania.

For Further Reading
Each of the international organizations maintains websites with information about their plans and agendas. Each also produces regular reports on their activities and meetings, including frequent declarations of intent. The aca-

demic literature on regional organizations is fairly thin given the immense attention Africa has put on them. One recent overview of efforts at regional integration is *Assessing Regional Integration in Africa,* published by the UN Economic Commission for Africa (2004). Percy Mistry analyzes why African regional organizations so often fail to live up to their lofty aims in "Africa's Record of Regional Co-Operation and Integration" (2000). Richard Gibb examines the impact of South Africa's emergence on regional efforts in "Southern Africa in Transition: Prospects and Problems Facing Regional Integration" (1998). "Explaining the Clash and Accommodation of Interests of Major Actors in the Creation of the African Union" by Thomas Kwasi Tieku (2004) looks at the transition of the OAU to the AU. Rachel Murray looks at both organizations' record in *Human Rights in Africa: From the OAU to the African Union* (2004).

An overview of the intentions and agenda of NEPAD is Kempe Ronald Hope's "From Crisis to Renewal: Towards a Successful Implementation of the New Partnership for Africa's Development" (2002). Ian Taylor takes a comprehensive but much more critical look at NEPAD in *NEPAD: Toward Africa's Development or Another False Start?* (2005). For a look at the plan's effect on an individual country, in this case Tanzania, see Samuel Wangwe's "NEPAD at Country Level" (2002).

Recent discussions on SADC are contained in *SADC Regional Integration in Southern Africa: Comparative International Perspectives,* edited by Christopher Clapham et al. (2001). Colin McCarthy's "The Southern African Customs Union in Transition" (2003) looks at the challenges facing SACU. Chibuike Uche explores the limits of the ECOWAS agenda in "The Politics of Monetary Sector Cooperation Among the Economic Community of West African States Members" (2001).

12

Africa and World Trade

TRADE, THE SIMPLE IDEA OF A VOLUNTARY EXCHANGE OF GOODS or services, is also one of the most complex development issues. Trade is, of course, one of the most important ways in which Africa interacts with the rest of the world. Indeed, Africans have been actively involved in long-distance specialized international trade for more than a millennium. The early impetus for European circumnavigation and exploration of the continent was partly about expanding trading opportunities. Africa's position in the global trading system has, however, eroded over the past fifty years. Boosting trade is now thought vitally important to Africa's current development prospects, both as a possible explanation of disappointing development so far and as a potential way to improve incomes. Increasing opportunities for trade is often considered an efficient way to reduce poverty, such as the common refrain "trade not aid" as a development strategy. This chapter will lay out the main ideas behind trade theory, the relevant policy issues, an overview of the key programs and institutions, and a guide to the bewildering array of acronyms used in the global trade bureaucracy, such as the difference between GATT, GATS, TRIPs, and TRIMs.

Africa's Long Trading History

Trade has been an essential part of most African societies, and the continent has a long history of long-distance international trade. Commerce along the Nile River basin has almost certainly been going on for thousands of years. The trans-Saharan trade route, moving goods overland via caravans of camels from the North African coast on the Mediterranean across the Sahara Desert to the West African coast, was active from perhaps as early as the eighth century. This growing trade was not only driven by economic interests, but also was undoubtedly linked to the expansion of Islam and the increasing availability of domesticated camels. Early trade included the exchange of gold, salt, and slaves. Empires in what are now Ghana, Mauritania, and Mali became important trading centers, with Timbuktu as the best-known trading city, which both generated great wealth and became a crossroads of cultures. Another significant trade route was along the East African coast, where trading occurred with Arabia and parts of South Asia.

The arrival of Europeans was both a boon and a bust to African trade. Portuguese shipping opened new European markets to Africa and vastly expanded the range of tradable goods. By the early sixteenth century, European trading posts were set up along many of Africa's coasts. Although the prime focus was West Africa, the Portuguese also seized control of Zanzibar in the early 1500s. Many of the early trading posts were initially viewed as restocking facilities for ships headed to Asia, but trade with local African groups gradually expanded. The French and British also began setting up posts along the West African coast in the early seventeenth century, and Jan van Riebeeck founded the Cape Colony on behalf of the Dutch East India Company in 1652. The combination of new shipping capability and conflict in the Sahara Desert led to a steady decline in the overland routes. Colonization helped to improve trading infrastructure, such as the construction of roads and railways, but the European powers also manipulated trade to their advantage, setting up zones of monopoly control and practicing aggressive mercantilism. Voluntary trading with Africans also gradually grew into more exploitative arrangements as colonialism began to take hold. The colonial economies were shaped to meet the needs of Europe, reflected in trading patterns that were highly uneven. But, as with other forms of economic intervention, most African postcolonial governments maintained trade barriers and other restrictions on cross-border exchange (see Chapter 7).

Africa's Postcolonial Trade

Much of Africa's current trade is concentrated in a handful of countries and in particular sectors. South Africa alone is responsible for about one-third of all African exports. Oil is also a dominant export product, accounting for nearly all the exports from some large countries such as Nigeria and Angola. Mining and primary commodity products make up the vast bulk of the rest of the continent's exports. Some countries, such as Ghana, have seen modest growth in so-called nontraditional exports, which include manufacturing, services, and some niche agriculture such as flowers or fruit.

Despite some limited successes, Africa's share of global trade has, however, declined substantially in the postcolonial period. In the early 1960s, sub-Saharan Africa was the source of more than 4 percent of

Figure 12.1   Sub-Saharan Africa Exports, 1965–2004

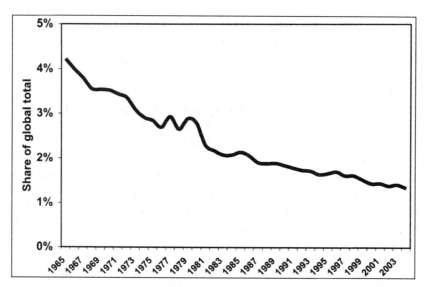

Source: World Bank, *World Development Indicators.*

global exports. This figure dropped steadily over the past four decades and is now less than 1.5 percent (see Figure 12.1). One possibly instructive fact is that Africa's trade-to-GDP ratio is fairly high. In 2003, for example, total trade was about 53 percent of GDP, which is a lower ratio than in East Asia or Europe, but significantly higher than Latin America and South Asia. This suggests that Africa's declining trade numbers might not really be a trade problem per se, but rather a visible symptom of wider economic malaise. Africa's global trade share may have dropped mostly because the continent's economies have not grown as fast as those in the rest of the world.

Africa's disappointing trade performance could also be the result of some specific trade factors. Among the most commonly cited are deteriorating terms of trade, unfair global rules, and domestic competitiveness. In the past, African governments have tended to blame poor trade performance on trade barriers in developed countries, particularly in areas such as agriculture and textiles. By contrast, the IMF, World Bank, and other donors have tended to emphasize economic and policy weakness in Africa as the major barrier. A growing body of evidence suggests that both matter but anticompetitive domestic policies are probably the greater hindrance. Regardless, for policymakers these need not be mutually exclusive and they all suggest some policy changes that might allow

Africa to overcome its barriers and expand trade. In turn, this would likely increase opportunities and job creation, allowing trade to contribute to economic development and increased incomes. But before looking at the various mechanisms and options for trade policy reform, it is worth reviewing why trade might be important in the first place.

Trade, Growth, and Poverty

There are many reasons to think that more trade might be good, in that it allows countries to produce and export things that they can make efficiently and to import things they cannot. For nearly all African economies, which are small and relatively undiversified, this should be particularly important. Domestic producers may require larger markets to reap the gains of "economies of scale" that can only be achieved through seeking external customers. And by importing goods, Africans can benefit from the technological progress and economic advances in other countries. Of course, you must do one (export) in order to be able to afford to do the other (import). Getting the environment right to do more of both is the critical policy question (see the discussion on comparative advantage below) and the source of much controversy.

What do the data say? Based on cross-country analysis, higher levels of trade also seem to correspond with higher rates of economic growth. A statistical link between trade openness and growth is difficult to establish because there are many other factors that are hard to disentangle. Yet several high-profile studies by prominent economists have found strong statistical correlations between trade and growth levels. Skeptics have, however, raised questions about the methodology of many of these studies and the validity of such conclusions. Nevertheless, the bulk of evidence does appear to show that trade and growth often go together. Certainly, countries that have grown fast for prolonged periods of time, such as the East Asian tigers, also seem to have higher rates of growth of exports than other countries. The direction of causality, of course, remains open to debate.

There may also be a pro-poor element in expanding trade, although the link between trade and income growth is empirically unsettled and detecting the connection to poverty reduction is far from obvious. In theory, increased trade should improve consumer choice, lower the costs of goods, and enlarge the range of possible tradable goods, including those bought and sold by the poor. Some macroeconomic trade models show huge gains in the battle against poverty from free flows of goods, such as one estimate that total global free trade would lift 500 million people out of poverty. (Such models are instructive in thinking through the potential channels from trade to poverty reduction and to give a sense of scale relative to other policies, such as increased aid. But they also make a host of assumptions and must be treated with caution.) Several microeconomic studies have found mixed results, with the poor gaining from certain kinds of trade, but also facing a host of other kinds of barriers that prevent them from reaping the gains of greater participation in the global economy.

The Concept of Comparative Advantage

Classical trade theory is based on the concept of "comparative advantage," the idea that total efficiency and welfare are maximized by specialization in the products and sectors for which each country has a relative advantage. *Comparative* advantage is often mistakenly thought to mean *absolute* advantage, but they are distinctly different, and this mixup leads to much confusion. The notion of comparative advantage suggests that each country should focus on producing the kinds of goods and services that it does best relative to other goods and services it might produce less efficiently—not relative to what other countries might produce more efficiently. Thus the comparative advantage of, for instance, Uganda, is to concentrate on the kinds of things it does best relative to itself rather than relative to Nigeria or Belgium. The crucial implication of this theory is that two countries can trade to their mutual benefit even if one of them is more efficient than the other at producing everything, as long as each emphasizes what it does most efficiently and trades for what it does not. Prices for goods and currencies will help to set the balance by determining the relative amounts each should produce to trade for the other.

If comparative advantage is correct—and it is accepted nearly unanimously by economists—then the implication is that completely free trade is both the most efficient and welfare-maximizing. Although there is some ideological resistance to the idea of free trade, the vociferous disputes over trade policy tend rather to focus on how political and economic realities differ from the model and on various strategies and mechanisms for managing transitions toward more optimal trade relationships. In other words, there is little debate over whether free trade is the right long-term goal, but much disagreement on how to get there and who should pay for the cost of adjustment.

Free Trade

Free trade is the idea that governments should not erect barriers that prevent or restrict the exchange of goods and services across national borders. There are three broad rationales for free trade, or at least moving toward more open borders:

• *Moral argument for free trade.* Adam Smith, John Stuart Mill, and later Milton Friedman all made their case for open trade at least partly on the liberal premise that expansion of freedom was an inherent good in itself. Proponents of this view begin by questioning whether governments should have the right to interfere in the free exchange of goods between private individuals. The liberal view in general is that, unless there is a compelling case for intervention where the benefits clearly outweigh the costs, states should not interfere with markets.

• *Economic argument for free trade.* The economic efficiency argument, most eloquently argued by David Ricardo, is based on the idea that markets are a better determinant than states of economic outcomes. This is closely linked to comparative advantage and that economic efficiency is welfare-maximizing. A similar argument about the inefficiency of discrimination might also ask if it makes sense to impose extra costs on exchange between people across borders when similar barriers are not imposed on exchange between people of the same nationality. Given that Africa's borders are particularly arbitrary and unconnected to the socioeconomic organization of the people on the ground, this seems particularly pertinent. Should the lines drawn up by European officials sitting at a conference table in Berlin more than a century ago determine which people are allowed to trade with each other today?

• *Political argument for free trade.* Finally, there is a political argument that because economic policy, including most trade intervention, is typically captured by political elites, that liberalization reduces the value of political connections. Even if the original justification for erecting a trade barrier may be developmental, Africa's record of using such policies to promote trade has been dismal, in part because such privileges are usually accorded to those with close ties to the political leadership while costing the rest of the population (through higher prices and less choice). As such, trade barriers are less of a policy designed to promote development or exports and more of a rent doled out by the state. Thus, removing trade barriers could also be justified on fairness grounds.

Unfree Trade as Development Policy

There are some instances where trade intervention is still considered useful to promote development. In the past, economic development theories have supported the establishment of certain kinds of trade barriers as a tool to encourage industrialization and other developmental goals. One approach, especially popular in Latin America and parts of Africa, is called import substitution industrialization (ISI). The idea of ISI is for a country to start by assessing its main imports, and then to erect barriers against those products to try to encourage local firms to produce them instead. In theory it sounded like a good way to reduce imports and enhance a country's self-reliance. In practice, ISI was a near total failure, as the protected domestic industries rarely were able to become efficient without market pressure and the impact on the balance of payments was sharply negative. Instead, such measures encouraged smuggling and a black market for basic consumer goods. (General rule of development: something has gone horribly awry when ordinary people turn to illegal markets to get everyday goods.)

The strongest case for using trade barriers to promote development appears to be the so-called infant-industry argument—that is, the state will provide temporary protections for new industries to allow them time to "grow up" and become competitive on international markets. The historical evidence from North America, Europe, and more recently from East Asia, all suggests that infant-industry protections can be a helpful boost to allow states to develop certain sectors. Some advocates for trade protectionism argue that Africa should follow a similar path—and indeed, protection levels in Africa are among the highest in the world.

Asia's Experience

Africa's experience with trade protectionism, however, has not produced anywhere near the kind of results as happened in East Asia where exports rose dramatically. This may be because the application of the infant-industry strategy depends on other conditions. Four lessons in particular appear to be important for the success of East Asian trade policy where most Latin American and African examples failed:

• *Temporary and credible.* The protections for industry were usually seen in Asia as only temporary measures. Firms supported by the state were expected to gradually wean themselves off these crutches, and those that did not were allowed to fail.

• *Outward orientation.* East Asian trade promotion strategies (although some were initially import related) quickly oriented protected firms toward the export market. One of the key benchmarks for Korean firms to retain state support, for example, was meeting explicit export targets. This allowed the tigers to avoid the ISI trap.

• *Technical expertise.* The teams of bureaucrats who designed and implemented trade policy—often called "technocrats"—were highly skilled and able to assign enough protection to support the targeted industry, but not so much that it undermined competitiveness.

• *Technocratic autonomy.* The technocrats responsible for identifying potential sectors and firms for support and then being able to enforce conditions were in general insulated from political pressures. This allowed them, for the most part, to punish firms and withdraw support from those that failed to meet targets without fear for their own jobs or that their decisions would be overridden by politicians.

Replication in Africa

Negative experiences with trade intervention in many other regions have frequently been attributed to the failure to meet one or more of these conditions. In Latin America, for instance, protected firms tended not to make the switch from import-substitution to export-orientation. In many African countries, protectionist measures tended to favor industries connected to political elites (what economists call "rent-seeking") and to be applied in haphazard and noncredible ways (see Chapter 7). Overall, it appears that the environment for meeting these conditions may be difficult in many places—that East Asia is more the exception than the rule. If so, then the use of trade protectionism to promote development needs to be carefully considered and formulated. Even in the case of successful infant-industry protection, it must be accepted that these measures come at a cost to general welfare since all consumers, including the poor, will pay higher prices. At times, this might be acceptable if the costs are kept to a minimum, they are seen as temporary, and the ultimate benefits are substantial. However, policymakers must weigh these costs vis-à-vis other policy objectives and the constraints of limited resources. For example, if protection of a particular industry raises food costs for domestic customers, this could negatively affect other policy efforts at poverty reduction. On the other hand, if it leads to the establishment of a viable and competitive new industry that provides new jobs, better services, and tax and export earnings, then it may very well have been a cost worth paying. Unfortunately, examples in Africa of the latter are extremely rare.

Types of Trade Barriers

There are four broad kinds of trade protectionism used by most countries.

• *Subsidies* are payments made by governments to producers. There are multiple kinds of subsidies, including price supports (to provide a minimum guaranteed price for a particular product), export subsidies (to help exports to undercut foreign competitors), or payments for set-asides (which might pay farmers *not* to farm). Subsidies usually come out of the treasury, so they are transfers from taxpayers to producers.

Some subsidies that encourage greater production also reduce global prices for those goods.

• *Tariffs* are taxes on goods when they arrive at the border. Tariffs tend to be very product-specific, and usually are designed to keep out competitors and to favor domestic producers. The outcome is that consumers of these goods pay higher prices, either by having to cover the tariff (if they buy imported goods) or from the reduced competition (if they buy domestic goods).

• *Quotas* are allocated amounts of goods allowed from a particular country or region. In some cases quotas are combined with tariffs to allow low tariffs up to a certain volume, and then high tariffs kick in above that amount. Quotas and tariff-quotas also allow countries to favor specific trading partners over others.

• *Nontariff barriers* are a catch-all phrase for all other kinds of barriers that may be used to keep out foreign goods. These include a huge range of policies that might have legitimate purposes, but can also frequently be protectionism in disguise. For example, governments maintain the legal right to impose environmental or consumer safety standards on imports, but they can also abuse these provisions to keep competing products out. Similarly, customs border controls are practiced universally, but they can also be misused to harass or exclude foreign competitors.

Protectionism and African Development

These trade barriers are relevant for African development in two ways. First, African governments tend to be among the most protectionist, with high levels of tariffs extremely common. Recent data, for example, suggest that average African protection for agriculture is about 18 percent, slightly higher than the level in rich countries. For manufactured goods, African protection is lower at about 12 percent, but this is more than six times higher than comparative tariff levels in the rich world.

Steps taken to erect trade barriers, which might be justified on the basis of defending domestic companies or farmers, cost consumers every time they buy goods in protected sectors. They also can undermine competitiveness because they raise the cost of imports, which may be important inputs into local industry. Tariffs are also often used to raise revenues, such as when countries impose import taxes on luxury goods (such as cars or electronics) that might not be produced at home. Subsidies are also common in Africa, although decreasingly so as external donors have tended not to support such schemes. Subsidies are nevertheless a drain on the treasury, where tax dollars (or, in much of Africa, reallocated aid) are diverted to selected firms that are either state-owned or favored by the government for some reason. Another instrument that African governments have used a lot in the past, but less so recently, is import licenses. These are state-sanctioned legal approval to be allowed to import certain goods, sometimes with an exclusive monopoly. As one might imagine, access to import licenses was highly prized and allocated under often unclear circumstances. Rather than a legitimate policy to promote local industry or save scarce foreign exchange, they instead usually became favors handed out by the government to friends or allies.

Second, rich-country governments also use these forms of protection in a way that often hurts Africa—even though the negative impact on Africans is an unintentional byproduct of policies usually aimed squarely at protecting powerful domestic interest groups, such as US sugar farmers. Tariffs are imposed on some African goods, with some of the highest tariffs levied against products most often made on the continent. Sugar, rice, dairy products, and textiles are among the most protected global markets through a wide array of tariffs and quotas. Subsidies for cotton and maize producers also reduce global prices, meaning that some African farmers will get less for their goods than they might otherwise. Lastly, nontariff barriers, including bureaucracy and complicated reporting requirements, also collude to keep African products out of North American and European markets. African governments frequently complain about rich-country protectionism, and these issues have been central to global negotiations (see WTO below).

Domestic Constraints

In addition to protectionism, African trade is also hampered by domestic conditions inside African countries. The continent's loss of global export share is partly a reflection of slow-growing and noncompetitive economies. While it is true that global trade rules are often tilted against African producers, most of the barriers they face are homegrown. These include bad regulation or corruption that stifles entrepreneurship, and poor infrastructure, which makes things such as transportation or electricity extremely expensive. In some sectors, African firms lack the trained staff or management experience to compete globally. In others, their local markets are simply too small to allow them to reap economies of scale that might be available to larger countries. (See Chapter 13 for more on Africa's investment climate.) Studies that have tried to calculate the relative importance of global trade rules versus local problems have tended to conclude that it has been these local conditions that are more important. Some evidence of this is that, while certain crops are highly distorted, there are many gaps in Western protection. In fact, many areas where African goods might be expected to have an advantage (such as tropical fruit) are generally wide open. If the global rules were really the main problem, Africa should be dominating these markets.

Global Prices and Shocks

Another problem of Africa's trade is the impact of global prices. Because many of Africa's countries are highly reliant on only a few export products, they can be vulnerable to external trends that affect those prices. One aspect is that some of Africa's main exports have experienced long-term declines in prices relative to the prices of its imports—what is called deterioration in the terms of trade (see Figure 12.2). A perhaps more important concern is that sharp changes in the prices for goods—often for some reason having nothing at all to do with events in Africa itself, like a freeze in Brazil or growing demand in China—can have a shock effect on an African economy. All countries face these risks, but Africa's lack of diversification—most countries rely on only a few primary exports—and limited capacity to respond to external changes make it an unusually vulnerable region.

Liberalization and Free-Trade Agreements

Countries can reduce protectionism unilaterally or through negotiated agreements with trading partners. Unilateral liberalization is when a country reduces the various barriers it has erected on its own. Such steps

Figure 12.2   Copper and Cocoa Prices, 1960–2004

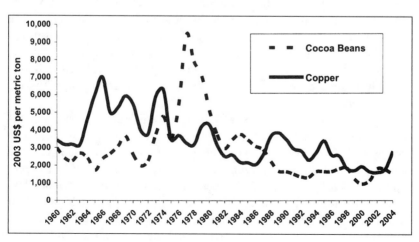

Source: IMF.

have been a central part of economic reform plans and the purpose is to eradicate the greatest distortions in trade intervention. The case for unilateral action is often strong in Africa, especially in services or sectors that are underperforming precisely because of trade policies. Nevertheless, such policy changes can be disruptive by causing political friction, may lead to the closure of some companies, and might have an impact on the budget if tariffs are an important source of government revenues. The key aspect of this approach is that it focuses on domestic conditions and has no effect on the external trading environment.

Countries also negotiate to reduce barriers together, either bilaterally (between two countries) or multilaterally (when groups of countries agree collectively). The largest of these arrangements is the World Trade Organization, which includes 148 countries. Africa participates in these kinds of agreements, especially through its regional organizations, nearly all of which have some trade liberalization component (see Chapter 11).

Reciprocity

An underlying strategy behind most trade agreements among countries is that all sides put something on the table. Trade negotiations are seen as a forum for countries to bargain for concessions on both sides. Although there are some economic arguments for linking trade policy changes to what your partners also do, the main benefit of reciprocity is political. Because changing trade policy necessarily creates some winners and some losers, countries need to try to balance the costs and benefits by getting additional winners to support the agreement. For example, if a country were proposing to lower import tariffs on soap, its domestic soap makers will undoubtedly protest and try to stop any such change. But the government might be able to balance this by getting lower tariffs in another country for a different product, say on cut flowers, which might get backing from flower exporters. In practice, putting lots of issues and products on the table can be complicated, but it also can help to reduce the chance that any one interest group can derail the whole effort.

Special provisions are usually included in large trade agreements that try to take account of different countries' abilities to adjust to change and their level of development. This means that changes need not be symmetrical and, in general, poorer countries are given longer time periods to make agreed changes, and often they have to make less severe cuts (although if their initial levels of protection are higher, their cuts might in fact need to be deeper). For example, a 1999 reciprocal trade agreement between South Africa and the EU allows South Africa substantially longer to implement tariff reductions.

Nonreciprocal Preferences for Poor Countries

A number of international initiatives have tried to use trade barriers to favor certain countries over others and reduce some tariffs in a nonreciprocal way. These are usually called "preferences." The United States and the European Union each have programs to give special access to African goods.

- The *African Growth and Opportunity Act (AGOA)* is special US legislation enacted in 2000 designed to encourage African trade. Its provisions are mostly aimed at boosting Africa's textile sector by allowing clothes and other fabrics into the large US consumer market without the usual tariffs. AGOA has been successful in helping to boost US-Africa trade, but the overall impact has been fairly small and only a few countries have truly benefited.
- The European Union's *Everything But Arms (EBA)* initiative allows many imports into the EU from poor countries (including most of Africa) duty-free. The main exception, as its name suggests, is military hardware. In addition, and to much chagrin in Africa, EBA also has long phase-in periods for bananas, sugar, and rice.

In principle, special preferences for poor countries are supposed to help give them a leg up against competitors, and the fact that they do not insist on poor countries also liberalizing their markets makes them politically popular in Africa. However, in practice, the benefits of preferences are often undermined by "rules of origin" requirements (countries have to prove their exports really are made in their country) and other nontariff barriers that effectively keep African products out. Perhaps more importantly, preferences can be used to defend ongoing protection in rich countries and may lead to the exclusion of poor countries from global agreements. Preferences are also perhaps beneficial for poor countries in the short term, but their sustainability is questionable since the decisionmaking is left mainly in the preference-giver country. In any case, preferences violate certain basic principles of free trade, such as nondiscrimination, and may become increasingly irrelevant.

GATT and the WTO

The largest and probably most important institution for multilateral trade negotiations is the World Trade Organization (WTO) based in Geneva, Switzerland. The WTO was founded in January 1995 to succeed the General Agreement on Tariffs and Trade (GATT), which had been initially set up in 1947 to provide a forum for reducing trade barriers on the principle that countries should all be treated equally. Over time, the GATT grew in membership and scope, giving rise to the need for a more formal international body. The WTO is a multilateral organization of 148 member states with the mandate to facilitate global trade by helping to establish and interpret trade rules.

Since its inception, and particularly after antiglobalization street riots during a WTO summit in Seattle in 1999, the organization has come under severe criticism for being unfair to developing countries. There are certainly many real shortcomings with the WTO, but there is also substantial misinformation about the organization. A few things the WTO is *not* are:

• *Goliath rule maker.* Many people believe that the WTO secretariat decides global trade rules over the will of individual states. But the WTO is less a legislator than a forum for member states to agree to trading rules. Decisions are technically made by consensus (as we will see below, in practice this is often not the case) and all rules must be ratified by member parliaments. The WTO's most important committee is the ministerial conference of trade officials, which takes place every two years (Seattle was the third). The WTO's main teeth is the Dispute Settlement Body, which acts more like a trade court and rules on interpretations of agreements and sets compensatory fines. By size, the WTO is also relatively small, with only about six hundred staff and an annual budget of about $100 million (the World Bank is twenty times larger).

• *Club of the wealthy.* Unlike many international organizations, each member is technically equal. Agreements by consensus mean that small countries can affect rules, especially if they band together. Any country, no matter how small, can mount a challenge in the dispute settlement body (there are of course practical impediments, discussed below). By the nature of the global economy, bigger countries will matter more, because their trade volume is bigger and they have more with which to negotiate. But small countries are likely to have even less influence without an institution like the WTO. Ghana, for example, is unlikely to be able to negotiate dozens of bilateral trade deals with a range of large countries, whereas a multilateral forum offers better opportunities. Indeed, the participation of poor countries in the WTO has substantially improved compared to the GATT, as reflected in the Doha Agenda.

• *Dictator over small countries.* In reality, the demands of WTO membership, which is strictly voluntary, are generally lenient. Typically, joining the WTO (called "accession") requires a series of negotiations for lowering tariffs and agreeing to general nondiscrimination —that is, treating all other members more or less equally. Even so, current WTO rules still allow substantial room for trade policy maneuver including, under certain strict conditions, antidumping legislation and countervailing subsidies.

Special Poor-Country Provisions
In addition to generally easy conditions for joining the WTO, there are also special loopholes designed for low-income countries. First, any country may designate itself as a "developing country," which allows longer periods and softer terms for compliance. All of Africa falls under this category. Second, there is another provision for forty-eight "least-developed countries" (LDCs), as defined by the United Nations, that gives them the option of full exemption for any reciprocity agreed at the WTO. In theory this means that LDCs—which include thirty-three African countries—can maintain trade barriers that they believe help support their development needs and strategies. Whether this is pro-development or not remains controversial. What is clear is that the LDC exemption in practice means that these countries are excluded from some of the main decisionmaking.

Shortcomings of the WTO for Africa
The WTO represents several improvements for African countries and could be a substantial opportunity for poor countries to boost their trade, both through domestic reforms and via a fairer global playing field, such as enhanced market access. Nevertheless, there are several quite serious problems that could continue to undermine Africa's ability to gain from multilateral trade negotiations.

• *Agenda setting.* Although each member is technically equal, the agenda for rounds of trade negotiations remains dominated by the largest economies. As such, the steps taken so far at the WTO are mainly those of most interest to the richest countries. Recent steps to put agriculture on the WTO agenda for the Doha Round reflect the demands for developing countries, but whether this will result in real changes remains to be seen.

• *Capacity constraints.* There are implementation costs to WTO agreements and a huge range of complex issues at stake. Many developing countries have complained that they are having difficulties complying with all the provisions of the WTO, and African trade officials often publicly urged the delegates to adopt a manageable agenda. Although these represent real barriers for LDCs, there is some technical assistance available and scope for regional cooperation and cost sharing.

• *Legal capacity.* The WTO's system is rules-based and member-driven, which should help African countries that might otherwise not have sufficient leverage to reach and enforce trade agreements. But this also means that the approach of the WTO is highly legalistic and that countries must participate to ensure they get benefits. Thus countries with strong legal systems and adequate legal skills are at an inherent advantage. That many African countries lack qualified trade lawyers constrains their ability to both participate in the WTO and to ensure that their interests are promoted. There are also significant costs in maintaining a WTO presence, negotiating trade deals, and implementing agreements. For many poor countries, these costs can be prohibitive. Keeping even a small staff in Geneva is expensive, and few African countries have even a single permanent representative there. The WTO's legalistic mechanisms and the inherent complexity of trade negotiations demand teams of high-quality lawyers, which are difficult to attract and costly to maintain. Indeed, because there are so many meetings and the issues are frequently technical, small-country teams are unlikely to be able to cope adequately. This can be particularly important because concessions and benefits won in general negotiations can be lost when the details are agreed in the latter stages.

Some progress has been made in mitigating these shortcomings. An "Africa group" has been formed to come up with and present unified regional positions, but this is far from adequate and cannot be effective on some issues where there may not be a common position. A few countries, especially South Africa, have tried to exert influence on behalf of the region, but this also has its limitations. A few smaller countries, including Mali, Tanzania, Ghana, and Uganda, have also been occasionally assertive on particular issues (Mali on the cotton issue, for instance), but this remains piecemeal and not fully adequate to serve Africa's interests.

The Doha Round

Global trade talks are organized into multiyear "rounds" usually named after the place where they are launched. The last round of the GATT was the Uruguay Round and ended in 1994. The latest round, begun at Doha, Qatar, in November 2001, is supposed to run until the end of 2007 and, as per tradition, is called the Doha Round. (As of this writing, prospects for a successful conclusion to the Doha Round appear extremely poor.) What makes this round different from the previous ones is the set of issues on the table, especially agriculture, which had been mostly deferred in the previous rounds. In fact, there is an extra emphasis on this round to the sensitivities and needs of poor countries, embodied in the list of topics, the so-called Doha Development Agenda. Its main aspects are:

• *Agriculture.* No other sector is as distorted globally by trade policy as agricultural products, and no sector is also as important to Africa. Indeed, farming provides 70 percent of employment in Africa and is the main source of income for most of the poor. Thus, both African countries and some of the larger agricultural exporters (for example, Australia and Brazil) have long been demanding that the United States, Japan, and Europeans reduce their protectionism. This includes reductions in subsidies, the lowering of tariffs, and the removal of exceptions and loopholes.

• *Non-Agricultural Market Access (NAMA).* This is to continue the work of the previous round to reduce tariffs and quotas in other areas, such as manufacturing. A particular focus of NAMA for developing countries has been on textiles, since that has traditionally been an entry-level light industry that many countries have used to transition from farming to industrialization. It also, perhaps unsurprisingly, happens to be one of the remaining industrial sectors that are highly protected.

• *Development focus.* The Doha agenda continues the practice of allowing low-income countries lesser demands, extra time to comply, and exemptions for the poorest countries.

• *Services.* Doha hopes to make more progress on services liberalization, which includes finance, data processing, and transportation (see GATS below).

GATS

The General Agreement on Trade in Services (GATS) is a treaty of the WTO from 1995 that extends the mandate from trade in goods into trade in services. This late arrival of services to the trade agenda is partly because much of the services sector has been local (think haircuts or schooling). But the growth of many services sectors combined with new technologies has made many services now tradable across borders. Telecommunications, banking and insurance, and transportation are all obvious areas where this might apply. Distance learning and even some healthcare services can now also be done around the globe. Parts of the services agenda have been controversial, with some critics worried about the effects of allowing foreign companies into areas that had traditionally been the purview of governments, such as water or electricity provision. At the same time, some governments resist the GATS agenda since it infringes on sectors that they monopolize. Nevertheless, services is an area that shows considerable promise for Africa, with South Africa developing an information technology sector and even smaller countries such as Ghana getting in on the call center, data processing, and back-office support outsourcing that has become famous in India.

Trade-Related Issues:
TRIPs, TRIMs, and the Singapore Issues

In addition to the normal trade rules dealing with tariffs and subsidies, the WTO's agenda has included a number of "trade-related" agreements, such as those covering intellectual property protection and investment. The WTO's agreement on Trade-Related Investment Measures (TRIMs) are rules that are supposed to help contain discrimination against foreign investors. Since the WTO is a forum about trade, not investment, TRIMs apply only to "trade-related" regulations that affect investment. The TRIMs are only very slowly coming into force and key aspects of their implementation remain to be agreed.

More important for Africa is the Trade-Related Aspects of Intellectual Property Rights (TRIPs) agreement, a treaty that sets minimum standards for intellectual property protection. It was initially intended to protect copyrights, trademarks, and patents and to help crack

---

The Colors of Subsidies

The WTO uses colored "boxes" to determine which subsidies are allowed and which are not. The original idea was, using the traffic light analogy, to set standards:

• *Red box* is for prohibited subsidies, although in practice few fall into this category.
• *Amber (yellow) box* is for subsidies that must be reduced. These include anything that is thought highly trade-distorting and imposes costs on others. Through the WTO, countries agree to limits on how much countries can spend in total in this category.
• *Green box* is for allowable subsidies, mainly payments for environmental programs or regional development initiatives. The key criterion here is that support must be separate (or in WTO-speak, "decoupled") from production. This is supposed to allow governments to help farmers or to protect green spaces, but not encourage overproduction that harms other countries. There is no limit on green box subsidies.
• *Blue box* subsidies were later added at the request of the EU. Any payments that would normally be in the amber box can instead be put into the blue box (and thus not subject to any spending limit) if there are explicit requirements that connect the support to reducing production.

As might be expected, there is considerable controversy over the use of these boxes, with some countries complaining that the blue box is an unfair loophole, or that even blue or green box subsidies can still affect production.

down on illegal piracy and counterfeiting. It has come under fire from several camps of late, however, as being too strong. The main controversy of relevance to African development has been the impact of TRIPs on pharmaceuticals and the use of generic drugs, especially those used to fight HIV/AIDS. The compromise reached has been to allow an exception to combat "public health emergencies," which has enabled African countries to access generic drugs without violating the WTO agreement. Although this was a necessary step to increase access to life-saving drugs, it could also have a negative effect if it undermines the incentives for private companies to invest in new technologies that they think they may later be forced to give away (like a malaria vaccine).

The so-called Singapore issues are four topics of interest to the WTO that have been under discussion since 1996 but that have not yet reached agreement. They are investment protection beyond TRIMs (enhancing the nondiscrimination of investors by nationality), competition policy (antitrust and related issues to control the power of monopolies), transparency in government procurement (standards for how contracts are awarded), and trade facilitation (logistical bottlenecks at the border). Many of the developing countries consider these only of importance to the rich world and have insisted on progress in agriculture before such topics can be addressed. In fact the failure to reach an agreement at the 2003 WTO ministerial meeting in Cancun, Mexico, was partly over the inclusion of the Singapore issues. The only one of these issues that has generated much enthusiasm in Africa has been trade facilitation, since it could lead to help with customs reform and investment in transportation.

Dumping and Food Aid

"Dumping" is a trade term where one country deliberately sells a product below cost in order to undermine or destroy a competitor. The WTO has provisions for antidumping protection and countries can, and have, invoked these to try to stop a flood of cheap goods. The main concern for Africa is whether food aid, which is usually given free, might be considered a form of dumping. Certainly the availability of free food, through an organization such as the UN World Food Program, depresses food prices in the places where it delivers. There are, of course, very legitimate reasons free food may be a good idea, such as during a drought or a conflict when normal food production is interrupted and people face potential famine. But when food aid continues to be delivered in nonemergency situations or arrives at the wrong moment during the harvest cycle, it can undermine the local planting or harvesting. These are well-recognized troubles in the food aid business, and are often the result of bureaucratic or logistical problems that misdeliver food. In practice, delineating between an emergency and nonemergency, or a temporary shortfall and a long-term food security gap, can be difficult. There is also an element of inertia and self-interest, with many of the agencies that deliver food having incentives to keep operating regardless of events on the ground. US politics, where food aid is a de facto subsidy for US grain farmers, also create pressures to keep the ships moving.

Aid for Trade

In addition to helping improve market access, the donor community has several areas where it believes it can intervene to help Africa expand its trade.

• *Trade analysis.* There is still much about trade not well understood. There are significant research efforts to try to trace the links between trade and poverty, with an eye out for ways to both enhance trade volumes and to make it as poverty-reducing as possible. Many of the donors, particularly the World Bank, are also increasing their work analyzing the binding constraints to greater trade for particular African countries as background to help governments formulate their own trade strategies.

• *Trade negotiation.* Given the complexity of trade negotiations and the high cost of participation at the WTO, there is a clear need to assist African countries with the legal and technical skills required to be full participants. The WTO does have limited assistance now for its poorest members, but it is akin to an underresourced and overburdened public defender. Fixing this problem is important not only to encourage wider participation in multilateral negotiations, but also to help improve the credibility of the process by helping the African delegates to feel they are not being sidelined.

• *Shock insurance.* In the long term, diversification will be the best insurance for Africa against trade shocks. In the meantime, donors sometimes respond when poor countries experience shocks, perhaps by granting more aid or releasing some funds early. In 2001, the World Bank gave an extra credit to seven African countries explicitly to help them cope with increased oil prices. But the donors have been thinking about a more systematic approach to try to buffer fragile economies. Schemes are under consideration, and the IMF has even launched a new facility to expressly deal with this problem, where funds are pooled and a release is triggered if prices cross a certain threshold.

• *Trade capacity.* Some aid programs are designed to specifically help increase trade by dealing directly with some of the local constraints. These include investment in ports, roads, airports, and other infrastructure to help bring products to market and to connect African markets to the world. There is also a lot of technical assistance that aims to assist producers to upgrade into more tradable goods (for example, helping farmers shift toward higher-value export crops, such as from cassava to pineapples), help reform bureaucratic procedures that may be stifling potential traders, and to streamline customs at the border. Even some of the investments in education or other social services can be targeted at bolstering specific skills that might help to increase trade.

For Further Reading

The classic texts on how trade is welfare-enhancing are Adam Smith's *An Inquiry into the Nature and Causes of the Wealth of Nations* (1776) and David Ricardo's *Principles of Political Economy and Taxation* (1817). More recent work that defends the virtues of free trade in a sophisticated and nontechnical way and includes a developing-country perspective is Jagdish Bhagwati's *Free Trade Today* (2001). An official publication promoting trade as development-friendly is the OECD's *Open Markets Matter: The Benefits of Trade and Investment Liberalisation* (1998).

Some of the empirical studies that support the idea that trade boosts economic growth include Jeffrey Sachs and Andrew Warner, "Economic Reform and the Process of Global Integration" (1995), Anne Krueger, "Why Trade Liberalisation Is Good for Growth" (1998), and Jeffrey Frankel and David Romer, "Does Trade Cause Growth?" (1999). The most prominent academic trade skeptic is Dani Rodrik, including his paper with Francisco Rodríguez, "Trade Policy and Economic Growth: A Skeptic's Guide to the Cross-National Literature" (1999).

There is a huge literature debating the Asian experience and its application to other developing regions. Among the first to highlight the role of Asian trade and industrial policy were Chalmers Johnson's *Miti and the Japanese Miracle: The Growth of Industrial Policy, 1925–1975* (1983) and Robert Wade's *Governing the Market* (1990). The World Bank's interpretation can be found in *The East Asian Miracle: Economic Growth and Public Policy* (1993). A quick response to this study is elucidated in the three essays in *Miracle or Design? Lessons from the East Asian Experience* (1994) by Catherine Gwin and others.

On the World Trade Organization specifically, the WTO's own website contains a plethora of information, although much of it is WTO-speak and far from accessible. A good overview of the global trading system and the WTO is *The Political Economy of the World Trading System: From GATT to WTO* (2001) by Bernard Hoekman and Michael Kostecki. To read more about the contentious debates over the WTO and its future see Jeffrey

Schott's *The WTO After Seattle* (2000) and *A World Without Walls: Freedom, Development, Free Trade, and Global Governance* (2003) by Mike Moore (the former WTO head, not the filmmaker). *Greening the GATT: Trade, Environment, and the Future* by Daniel Esty (1994) addresses some of the environmental issues. Jean Lanjouw's "Intellectual Property and the Availability of Pharmaceuticals in Poor Countries" (2002) considers the impact of the TRIPs on access to drugs in the developing world and proposes some solutions.

One of the best volumes on the link between recent WTO talks and global poverty, with African case studies, is *Poverty and the WTO: Impacts of the Doha Development Agenda,* edited by Thomas Hertel and Alan Winters (2005). Kimberly Elliott's *Delivering on Doha: Farm Trade and the Poor* (2006) examines the agricultural trade negotiations in particular. One study from the leadership of the IMF on the trade-poverty link is "Trade, Growth, and Poverty: A Selective Survey" by Andrew Berg and Anne Krueger (2003). A global model estimating the gains in poverty reduction from total free trade is William Cline's *Trade Policy and Global Poverty* (2004).

Literature dealing directly with African trade is generally less plentiful. Some of the important studies include *Trade Reform and Regional Integration in Africa,* edited by Zubair Iqbal and Mohsin Khan (1998), and "Open Economies Work Better: Did Africa's Protectionist Policies Cause Its Marginalization in World Trade?" by Francis Ng and Alexander Yeats (1996). For a discussion of the challenges farmers face in transitioning from maize and cassava to pineapple in Ghana, see Markus Goldstein and Christopher Udry, "Agricultural Innovation and Resource Management in Ghana" (1999). A successful case study of export promotion can be found in Morgane Danielou, Patrick Labaste, and Jean-Michel Voisard's "Linking Farmers to Markets: Exporting Malian Mangoes to Europe" (2003). Oxfam has produced several studies looking at the impact of rich-country trade barriers on Africa, especially cotton and sugar.

An edited volume on the impact of global shocks on Africa is Jan Willem Gunning and Paul Collier's *Trade Shocks in Developing Countries: Africa* (2000). A very useful overview of the issues for the continent can be found in "Trade and Trade Policies in Eastern and Southern Africa" by Arvind Subramanian and colleagues (2000).

There is a lot of material available on the US African Growth and Opportunity Act, including an annual report by the US trade representative, "Comprehensive Report on U.S. Trade and Investment Policy Toward Sub-Saharan Africa and Implementation of the African Growth and Opportunity Act," which contains lots of data on bilateral trade between the United States and Africa.

13

Private Investment and
the Business Environment

THE VAST MAJORITY OF THE DEVELOPMENT COMMUNITY'S focus has been on the public sector, looking largely at the role of the African state and what rich-world governments can also do to help. But the history of capitalism and the transition from poverty to wealth in other regions has mostly been about private actors, such as farmers, investors, small businesses, and large corporations. One of the defining features of contemporary globalization has also been the rapid expansion in private capital networks, including growing flows to developing regions. The development community has increasingly, if a bit belatedly, recognized that the private sector and private capital can both play a vital role in promoting economic progress in Africa as well. African governments have taken some steps to try to attract foreign investment, while many of the donors have added programs to try to boost Africa's indigenous entrepreneurs and to help catalyze private-capital flows to the continent. Despite these efforts, the private sector remains a largely marginal player in many countries. If Africa is going to grow out of poverty and create a more prosperous future, it will need more and bigger businesses. To get there will require greater human and financial capital and a better environment to allow businesses to start up, operate, and grow. This chapter will lay out the main types of capital flows, some of the influential actors linking private investment to development, and some of the key private-sector and investment issues on the development agenda.

Types of Capital Flows
A capital flow is the movement of money across an international border. Such flows are normally divided into "official flows" that come from a public source (such as a donor agency like JICA or USAID) and "private flows" that come from private agents (such as a Fidelity mutual fund or the Coca-Cola Company). Private capital is also often

divided again into "foreign direct investment" (FDI) and "portfolio flows." Although the distinction can sometimes be blurred, FDI normally refers to an investment made to gain a long-term stake in an enterprise located in a foreign country. FDI usually implies a fairly large percentage of the target firm and often includes active involvement in management. Such investments often mean the acquisition of an existing enterprise by a foreign company or a new "green field" investment where a foreign company builds a new factory or store from scratch.

A portfolio flow is a different kind of investment that is usually more short-term oriented, more liquid, and involves only a smaller stake in a company. Such investments are often conducted through a stock exchange, which means the investor remains at a distance and is generally passive. (Most countries use 10 percent of a company as the threshold for portfolio flows, with any stake above this classified as FDI, even if the trade occurs on the stock market.) The purpose of the FDI/portfolio distinction is to give a sense of the flow type and whether it can be expected to stick around for a long time.

Private Capital Flows to Africa: A Data Warning

Like much of the economic information on Africa, capital flow data is fairly unreliable. They tend to come from national accounts compiled by the central banks, but there can be large discrepancies. The IMF and World Bank also publish information about capital flows to African countries, but these are also often little more than educated guesses or assumptions based on residuals. Data can be contradictory even from the same institution. The point of looking at such data is thus not to be precise, but rather to get a sense of trends over time and comparisons across countries or regions. From this we can discern that private capital flowing to Africa has generally increased over time, but that it has done so very unevenly. Just as importantly, Africa has not been keeping up with other developing regions in attracting capital.

Official vs. Private Flows

Unlike every other region of the globe, Africa is still dominated by official flows. In 1970 Latin America was the only major developing region where private capital was larger than official flows, but by 2000 Africa was alone in its reliance on official capital (see Table 13.1 and Figure 13.1).

Trends in Foreign Direct Investment

There are four main trends that can be seen in African FDI.

Table 13.1   Official vs. Private Finance in Developing Regions

	1970			2000		
Region	Private (US$m)	Official (US$m)	Ratio pvt/ official	Private (US$m)	Official (US$m)	Ratio pvt/ official
Sub-Saharan Africa	467	1,179	40%	10,356	13,420	77%
East Asia & Pacific	640	1,410	45%	35,946	8,626	417%
Latin America & Caribbean	3,351	1,005	333%	82,672	4,985	1,658%
South Asia	95	1,348	7%	9,701	4,239	229%

Source: World Bank.
Note: "Private" equals net private capital flows; "official" equals net official development assistance plus official assistance.

Figure 13.1   Private Capital Flows vs. Official Aid to Sub-Saharan Africa, 1970–2004

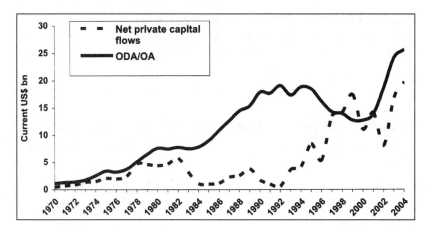

Sources: World Bank; OECD.

1. *Rising modestly over time.* Private investment to Africa has nonetheless increased. In the 1970s, average annual FDI flows to all of sub-Saharan Africa were less than $1 billion, but this jumped to $4.3 billion in the 1990s and $9.3 billion per year for 2000–2002. (Portfolio flows have also risen from close to zero in the 1970s to several billion dollars per year in recent years.)

2. *Shrinking global share.* Despite the modest gains in new investment, the continent has largely missed out on a global investment boom that has seen flows to other regions accelerate even faster. As a result,

Africa's relative share of global FDI, which averaged around 5 percent in the early 1970s, fell to just 1–2 percent by the early 1980s and remained around this level in recent years (see Figure 13.2).

3. *Country concentration.* Private investment to Africa has clustered, with most of the capital going to a handful of countries and only a few sectors. Over the period 1998–2002, for example, South Africa, Angola, and Nigeria accounted for more than half of all FDI to Africa. The top ten countries received 80 percent, leaving just 5 percent of the total for the bottom twenty-seven countries (see Table 13.2).

4. *Sector concentration.* There has been a long-standing concentration in the extractive sectors, particularly petroleum. Nearly all of the investment going to Angola, Nigeria, Equatorial Guinea, Sudan, and Chad is oil-related, with the bulk of the investment in the former three invested in offshore facilities. In addition, much of the foreign investment in Ghana, Zambia, Namibia, Botswana, and South Africa, and more recently Tanzania, has been in large mining projects.

Potential Benefits of Private Investment

The reason that private investment trends are of importance to development is because it is thought that such flows bring substantial benefits.

Figure 13.2   African Inward FDI, 1970–2002 (3-year running averages)

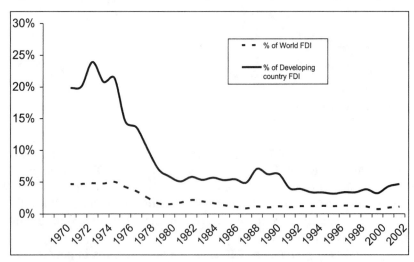

Source: Author calculations based on forty-eight sub-Saharan country figures from UNCTAD.

Table 13.2   Inward FDI: Sub-Saharan Africa, 1998–2002 (average annual)

Rank		Net flows ($m)	Percentage SSA total	Cumulative Percentage
1	South Africa	2,099	24.1	24.1
2	**Angola**	**1,584**	**18.2**	42.4
3	**Nigeria**	**1,074**	**12.4**	54.7
4	**Sudan**	**478**	**5.5**	60.2
5	**Equatorial Guinea**	**384**	**4.4**	64.6
6	Tanzania	344	4.0	68.6
7	Mozambique	283	3.3	71.8
8	**Chad**	**266**	**3.1**	74.9
9	Côte d'Ivoire	260	3.0	77.9
10	Uganda	238	2.7	80.6
21	Kenya	62	0.7	95.0
22–48	Bottom 27 countries	433	5.0	100.0

Source: Author calculations based on UNCTAD data.

Note: Bold indicates mainly oil-related; Chad data is based on 4-year average because of missing data for 2001.

At the macroeconomic level, FDI by definition is new investment capital, contributing to the balance of payments, adding to the country's capital stock, and (assuming the money is not completely wasted) contributing toward future economic growth. There is some evidence that foreign investment can contribute to raising exports for a country and help the economy integrate into global economic networks. At the microeconomic level there is also a range of purported benefits, especially higher productivity through new investment in physical and human capital (machines and training), increased job creation, better management, and bringing new technology into the country. Foreign investment also is thought to have important follow-on effects on local companies ("spillovers") through supply and distribution chains, trading, and outsourcing.

FDI is generally considered more development-friendly than portfolio flows because it is more stable and can often be visibly linked to things such as jobs, buildings, and tax payments. But portfolio flows are also potentially beneficial because they still represent money flowing into a country. To the extent that this raises stock prices, it makes money cheaper for companies to use to expand. There are also indirect gains, such as the impact on corporate governance (companies with shareholders have to live up to higher standards) and helping to link economies into the global financial network, giving access to money for local businesses, and lowering the overall cost of capital.

Historical Skepticism

Despite the growing global competition for investment and Africa's ability to attract only modest amounts, the continent still has a strong historical skepticism toward foreign capital. Much of the prevailing attitude toward foreign investment is rooted in history, ideology, and the politics of the postindependence period. Africa's early experiences with foreign companies as a precursor for colonialism likely continue to affect official and public perceptions. The use of European companies as proxies for colonial ambitions has helped to link in the public's mind international business with imperial expansion. In 1652 Jan van Riebeeck arrived in the Cape, not as a representative of the Dutch Crown, but on behalf of the Dutch East India Company. In the late nineteenth century, Cecil Rhodes claimed swaths of southern Africa on behalf of the British South Africa Company. Through the company, Rhodes secured mining concessions in gold, copper, and diamonds, playing the dual roles of entrepreneur and representative of the British Crown. Harsh conditions and treatment of laborers added to the linking of foreign companies and mistreatment, such as in the mines (e.g., under the Witwatersrand Native Labor Association) or plantations (e.g., Belgian Congo's notorious rubber plantations). As with the lingering effects of the United Fruit Company in Latin America, foreign companies in Africa are still sometimes associated with imperialism and exploitation.

Ideological Resistance

Many of Africa's decisionmakers, including those currently hailed as reformers, have held political positions for decades and were trained on an economic model steeped in anti–foreign investment ideology. Indeed, nearly every African leader, no matter how liberal he is considered today, began his career as a socialist or Marxist. Even as most of Africa's finance ministers have become increasingly convinced that economic openness can be beneficial for their countries and fluent in the language of international capitalism, many of their cabinet colleagues remain unreconstructed economic nationalists. Some of the ideological opposition to foreign investment is part of a general critique of capitalism—and more recently of globalization—and foreign capital remains an easy target.

Nationalist Defiance

Ideas of economic nationalism also affect sentiment toward foreign investment. Zambia's Kenneth Kaunda claimed that "political independence is meaningless without economic independence," a view that continues to shape Zambian investment policy. Even Botswana, one of the African countries that have pursued orthodox economic policies, has not been immune to antiforeigner attitudes. On a more practical level, political elites also do not want to be constrained by foreigners who might control key strategic sectors of the economy or their access to foreign exchange. The flip-side of FDI's stability is that foreign direct investors with a greater stake in the long term might be more inclined to get involved in influencing policy (or getting involved in politics), thus becoming potential competitors for power.

Potential Risks of Foreign Investment

While it is increasingly accepted that there are positive economic gains from foreign investment, there are also a number of possible downsides. Some of these are sensible questions about the actions of private companies in low-income countries, while others are mere conjecture used to attack corporations. Among the criticisms of foreign investment most frequently heard are:

- *Race to the bottom.* The desire to attract foreign investment might encourage countries to reduce labor and environmental protections in a bid to lure companies.
- *Crowd out locals.* Domestic African firms may not be able to compete because of the size, financing, marketing power, or some other unfair advantage that large foreign companies may have.
- *Capital drain.* Foreign firms usually want to take most profits back home, which can lead to future capital outflows.
- *Policy constraint.* Because the interests of foreign firms may diverge from social development objectives, this could affect the ability of governments to promote certain policies.
- *Hot money.* A particular critique of portfolio investment is that investments that can be easily withdrawn can be destabilizing (or that the threat of leaving can constrain policy options).

Barriers to Investment

As a result of historical worries and more immediate political considerations, African governments have constructed a series of barriers to foreign investment and operation. Even though early concerns were directed at large European and small South Asian investors, the more recent influx of investment from East Asia and from South Africa into the rest of the continent has helped to sustain some of these issues. In general, these can be divided into legal and practical kinds of barriers.

• *De jure barriers to investment.* Many countries have a deliberate policy of "Africanization," whereby state intervention is justified in order to transfer ownership of firms from foreigners (or indigenous minorities such as Indians or Lebanese) to locals. In its most extreme cases this can be accomplished through widespread and violent expropriation, such as in Uganda under Idi Amin or, more recently, commercial farms in Zimbabwe. But many countries, including Kenya and Zambia, have pursued less violent but nonetheless explicit forms of encouraging ownership transfer to locals. Such approaches continue in less obvious forms today, such as favoring local investors during privatization. Explicit legal restrictions on foreigners have diminished as part of the liberalization drive, but some limitations still exist, such as limits on the amount of equity of a listed company that can be owned by nonresident foreigners (40 percent in Zimbabwe, 74 percent in Ghana). Many African countries also still have restricted sectors in which foreigners are not allowed to own businesses at all, such as banks and insurance in Ethiopia. Some countries have gone halfway, allowing foreigners in certain sectors, but adding requirements for local employment, inputs, or partnerships.

• *De facto barriers to investment.* Probably more important, there are a range of indirect obstacles related to the business climate that deter investment and are used to keep foreign competitors at bay. These include bureaucratic and other informal impediments, such as ambiguous regulatory approval, delays in customs clearance, visas for expatriate workers, or problems with the legal system. It is not always clear that such barriers are in fact unintentional, but rather are used as deliberate hindrances to foreign investors. Political economists have frequently found that excess bureaucracy, erratic economic policy, and other troubles associated with the business environment can have strong political logic. Because political elites and business elites are typically allied in Africa (or, often, are one and the same), foreign investors could threaten market positions of privileged domestic firms.

Policy Reform
Partly as a result of the growing recognition that private capital can help raise economic growth and contribute toward development, African countries have increasingly engaged in competition to lure foreign investment and also to try to build local financial markets. Most have undergone some types of policy reform designed to both reduce barriers and attract investment.

• *Liberalization.* Nearly all African countries have revised their national laws governing investment, and the vast majority of changes have lifted controls on capital. Explicit restrictions on foreigners, which at one time were the norm, are now mostly an exception.

• *Investment promotion.* In addition to removing barriers, some governments have taken active steps to try to attract investors. In Ghana, for instance, the government has established the Ghana Investment Promotion Centre, which is supposed to be a "one-stop shop" for investors to get information and clearance for their projects. The country also encourages investors though reduced customs duties, tax holidays, and risk guarantees (usually in conjunction with international agencies).

• *Financial sector reform.* One key aspect of the broader economic reform efforts that began in the late 1980s was to try to fix the financial sector. African savings rates tended to be extremely low and private credit was hard to come by. In short, African banks were not acting like banks. The response, encouraged by donors, was to open up the banking sector to competition and try to limit government interference as much as possible, including selling the dominant state-owned banks and allowing private banks to start operations. Ghana, for example, initiated a formal financial-sector adjustment program (called FINSAP) in 1988, which liberalized the sector, closed down the weakest banks, revamped the regulatory capacity of the central bank, and established legislation for a local stock market.

• *Capital market development.* As part of financial-sector reform, governments have sought to develop local capital markets, including local bond and stock markets. Ghana's FINSAP led to the opening of the Ghana Stock Exchange in 1990.

Stock Markets
Africa now has fifteen stock markets with nearly a thousand publicly listed companies (see Table 13.3). Ten of the markets have opened only since 1989, part of the wave of reform that coincided with the emerging markets boom of the 1990s. South Africa dominates the market, accounting for more than 90 percent of the total capitalization (i.e., the value of all the companies listed on the market). But even without South Africa, there are more than five hundred African companies that are publicly listed and whose shares are traded. In 1998, the stock exchange in Abidjan became Bourse Régionale des Valeurs Mobilières (BRVM), the first official regional market. More importantly, many of the markets have begun to cross-list companies from other exchanges, such as the listing of Kenya Airways and East African Breweries on all three East African exchanges (Kenya, Tanzania, and Uganda). Several South African companies are also listed on exchanges in Namibia, Botswana, Zimbabwe, Malawi, and Zambia.

Table 13.3   Sub-Saharan Africa's Stock Markets (through 2005)

	Year Opened	Listed Companies	Market Capitalization (US$ billions)
Botswana	1989	28	2.4
Côte d'Ivoire (BRVM)	1976	39	2.6
Ghana	1989	30	1.3
Kenya	1954	48	6.4
Malawi	1996	10	0.2
Mauritius	1996	38	2.6
Mozambique	1999	2	0.3
Namibia	1992	28	0.4
Nigeria	1961	214	19.4
South Africa	1887	388	565.9
Swaziland	1990	6	0.2
Tanzania	1997	8	0.5
Uganda	1997	7	0.1
Zambia	1994	14	0.9
Zimbabwe	1946	79	1.9
Total		939	605.1
Excluding South Africa		*551*	*39.2*

Source: Standard Bank; African Business Research Limited
Note: Listings include foreign cross-listings; capitalization is domestic companies only.

Despite their relatively small size, African stock markets were established with the strong support of governments and remain fairly popular. There are clearly political and national pride factors behind some of the minor markets, but there are also real economic benefits. Most immediately, the stock markets have been useful vehicles for spreading ownership during privatization (see Chapter 7). In Tanzania, for example, seven of the eight listings are former state-owned companies, and listing them on the Dar es Salaam exchange has allowed trading by smallholders and encouraged wider shareholding.

In the long term, it is hoped that the markets will be used by more domestic firms to mobilize capital for expansion, a trend that seems to be emerging already in Botswana. However, many of the markets remain dominated by local subsidiaries of foreign multinationals, which are able to access capital more easily and more cheaply by turning to the parent company. Over time, as firms become more comfortable with the idea of public ownership and a greater number make the leap in size, more companies may turn to the local market. Similarly, the markets have not yet become a major destination for either local or global investors, but as the markets grow this should also change.

The Capital-Account Liberalization Debate

Although there is near-unanimity among economists that freer trade is beneficial, the debate over freer capital is much more controversial. The main questions are whether, and what type of, capital controls might be useful for developing countries seeking to minimize the instability that may derive from global capital flows. In the late 1990s, the IMF was deciding whether or not to include reducing capital controls as part of its mandate, setting off a heated dispute over the pros and cons of liberalization. While acknowledging the risks, proponents argued that freer movement of money would allow more efficient use and also give savers a greater range of options. But many critics worry that capital markets are more crisis-prone than trade and that by removing controls the countries would find themselves vulnerable and without tools to manage an emergency. The Asian financial crisis of 1997–1998 sharpened the debate further, although the emerging consensus appears to be moving toward limited restrictions on inflows, not on outflows. However, with the exception of South Africa, few African countries face problems of managing the effects of too much private money flowing in.

Multilateral Agreement on Investment

One international effort to address global investment issues was the failed attempt by the OECD to pass the Multilateral Agreement on Investment (MAI) in the mid-1990s. The main provisions of the MAI were to allow foreign investors into most sectors, ensure equal treatment of foreign companies, and remove restrictions on capital. This drew fierce criticism from developing-country governments that did not want to cede these powers. In particular, environmental groups complained that certain other provisions in the MAI, such as the right of companies to sue governments if their assets are devalued, would undermine environmental protection laws. The agreement became a cause célèbre for the antiglobalization movement as well, which claimed the MAI was shifting power from governments to corporations. In the end, the MAI had overreached what was politically possible at the time and effectively died in 1998. Nevertheless, some provisions, such as national treatment, continue to resurface through bilateral investment agreements and at international forums, such as the TRIMs agreement at the WTO (see Chapter 12).

Capital Flight

One of the big issues that used to get more attention than it has recently is money leaving Africa or what is often called "capital flight." A perennial question for those advocating either aid or private investment to Africa has been, "What about all the billions that wealthy Africans are stashing abroad?" There are at least three separate issues of concern with capital flight.

First is the extent of the trend. By its nature, capital flight is hard to measure because such transactions are usually never reported and often deliberately hidden. This leaves only various estimates, but these can be staggering. One credible estimate put the total capital stock held abroad by Africans at $285 billion as of 1996, larger than the debts owed by Africa at that time (suggesting the continent was actually a net creditor to the world).

Second, capital flight means that Africans who can take their money overseas do, suggesting that there are some very powerful market incentives for them to do so. This not only points to the difficult business and investment environment in many African countries (such as the fear of having your assets seized or facing interest rates that are below the rate of inflation), but also is a signal to foreign investors that it is a region to avoid. If the locals are fleeing, the logic goes, then what do they know that we don't?

Lastly, much of the capital flight is undoubtedly tied to illegal activity and corruption. Although there is only anecdotal evidence, the large real estate holdings of Mobutu's family in Belgium and France and the Nigerian cash found in Swiss bank accounts, all point toward some large scams by political elites to siphon off resources from public coffers.

Business Environment

The phrases "business environment" or "investment climate" refer to a broad range of conditions that affect entrepreneurs. One thing that has become increasingly apparent is that these conditions are particularly unfriendly to business in much of Africa. These include legal restrictions (such as requiring multiple licenses), lack of property protection (the state can seize assets), excessive regulations of all kinds, and colossal amounts of red tape and other headaches. The combined effect on business operations is not only onerous and confusing, but can become absurd. In Senegal, for example, an investor trying to open a factory must submit twenty-three different applications, get clearance from thirty-one different agencies, and the process can take up to three years just to clear the paperwork. The worst part is that Senegal is neither unique in Africa nor even close to the worst case. The World Bank has undertaken several efforts to try to document such barriers (such as average number of days to start a business or time spent with officials), not to embarrass governments so much as to give them the information to better make policy as they try to revive the private sector and attract more investment. The results have nevertheless been discomforting. The

Bank's "Doing Business" surveys have found that Nigeria, for example, has massive administrative barriers to trading: it takes eleven documents and thirty-nine signatures to export, while thirteen documents and up to seventy-one signatures are required for imports (see Table 13.4). The net effect of these obstructions is to scare away foreign investors, squash local entrepreneurs, and force many small businesses into the informal black market.

Domestic Entrepreneurship

Although much attention has been focused on foreign investment, it is also clear that local businesses, especially budding entrepreneurs, face considerable barriers. (Anyone who doubts that Africa has entrepreneurial potential should visit the huge Bakara market in Mogadishu and Roque Santeiro in Luanda where, despite being in dysfunctional war-torn countries, almost anything can be found.) Large foreign companies seeking to expand business may get access to high officials, including the president, who may help facilitate their entry. But the average small businessperson in Africa has no such luxury and often is vulnerable to extortion by local officials. Perhaps just as important, most domestic businesses in Africa have little access to credit, fewer resources to buy their way out of problems (such as buying a generator to get around electricity blackouts), and generally lower skills and less management experience.

Another common pattern for African businesses is a segmentation where very small firms tend to be owned by indigenous blacks and the medium and larger firms are owned by ethnic minorities or foreigners. This unavoidably makes business (and policy decisions affecting business) highly political. In addition to the nationalism against foreigners described above, some groups can be seen as dominating the economy,

Table 13.4   Slow Business in Africa

Number of days to...	Nigeria	Chad	Uganda	Africa average	OECD average
Start a business	43	75	36	64	20
Get licenses	465	199	155	252	147
Register property	274	44	48	118	32
Export	41	87	58	49	13
Import	71	111	73	61	14
Enforce a contract	730	526	209	439	226

Source: Doing Business database, World Bank, 2005.

such as people of South Asian descent in East Africa, Europeans in southern Africa, and Lebanese in West Africa. There are also African ethnicities that sometimes concentrate economic power, such as the Bamileke in Cameroon, the Kikuyus in Kenya, or the Ibos in Nigeria, which have similar effects of resentment and hostility that can alter the politics of economic policy.

Microfinance

One of the external responses to the lack of finance for very small entrepreneurs has been microfinance, which has grown exponentially to become one of the most fashionable programs for donors and NGOs. The idea is relatively simple: find ways to get simple banking services (savings and smalls loans) to poor people. The poor typically have no bank accounts and are unable to borrow money, which can prevent them from getting the seed capital necessary to start a business or tide them over during a temporary crunch. Efforts to get traditional banks to extend services to the poor were mostly unsuccessful, mainly because the transaction costs were too high and people lacked the collateral normally needed to secure loans. Enter the idea of microcredit, pioneered and popularized by the Grameen Bank in Bangladesh, which found ways to make very small loans by using soft money (to subsidize overhead costs) and/or alternative ways to ensure repayment (such as grouping borrowers together to use social pressure to prevent default). The concept has seized so much attention because it seems a way to help people help themselves and also to encourage more business activity. As a result, private and public money has been poured into microcredit schemes, especially to help women or other disadvantaged groups. There are thousands of such programs, while the Consultative Group to Assist the Poor is a consortium of the major donors who support microfinance. There are even a growing number of private banks that are exploring ways to try to make microfinance a commercial, rather than philanthropic, venture. Although microcredit has undoubtedly helped many people launch businesses and grow out of poverty, commercial viability remains far from clear and, as with any popular trend, there is a risk that the benefits have been oversold.

Donor Promotion of Private Investment

In addition to donor funding for microcredit to get cash into the hands of the poor, there are also a number of larger initiatives and agencies aiming to help spur big investment capital flows to Africa and assist the private sectors. These include risk guarantees for private investment and trade finance, investment funds sponsored or started by public agencies

---

Remittances

Remittances, the private money sent home by Africans living abroad, are another source of capital for Africa that is often forgotten. There is no hard data on such flows because most of these transactions take place outside formal banking channels (and out of sight of tax collectors). As a result, we have only a rough idea of the size and role of remittances (one estimate puts the inflow to sub-Saharan Africa at $3 billion in 2002). Regardless of their exact size, remittances are thought to be very substantial for countries with large populations living overseas, such as Cape Verde, Ghana, Nigeria, and Zimbabwe. Remittances are thought to be particularly important in poverty reduction because they are cash sent directly to families. Because much higher wages can be found in the rich world (even for the same job), there is a strong incentive for both temporary and permanent emigration—an option taken by millions of Africans—and many of these migrants continue to support family members in their country of origin. For the recipient families, remittances can be a crucial source of income for everyday household spending and investments in schooling, housing, or a business. For the countries involved, it is a source of foreign exchange, and the migrants, if they return, often bring back capital, ideas, and new skills. Some development agencies are trying to find ways to channel remittances for even greater impact on poverty, for example linking them to financial services such as banking.

---

with public money, and technical support for improving local business environments. Within the US government, for example, the Overseas Private Investment Corporation (OPIC) is an agency that provides risk insurance for US corporations investing in developing countries. OPIC also has more than a dozen equity funds, at least three of which are focused on Africa. The US Export-Import Bank provides "export credits" to US companies that want to sell overseas but may be wary about getting paid for goods delivered. USAID has a private-sector promotion initiative, providing technical help and aid for financial-sector reform, while the State Department has directly funded credit ratings for several African countries.

The British government has similar agencies, with the Export Credit Guarantee Department roughly the equivalent of the US Export-Import Bank. The Commonwealth Development Corporation made private equity investments in developing countries (on a commercial basis but with public money and a mandate to promote private enterprise) before it was privatized in 2004 (and is now a private company under the name Actis Capital).

The World Bank Group is involved in promoting private capital in several ways as well. The main low-income window, the International Development Association (IDA), has a private-sector group that works with African governments on a range of reform issues. The International Finance Corporation (IFC) makes direct investments into African companies, while its Foreign Investment Advisory Service provides advice for governments on how to attract private investment. The Bank's Multilateral Investment Guarantee Agency (MIGA) also provides political risk insurance for foreign investors (see Chapter 8).

For Further Reading

The IMF and World Bank provide data on private capital flows using both national accounts from countries and their own estimates of global trends. UNCTAD maintains a database on FDI for each country and issues an annual *World Investment Report*. Data can also be obtained from individual central banks, stock markets, and the growing number of private brokers.

The seminal works on the role of domestic finance in developing countries are Ronald McKinnon's *Money and Capital in Economic Development* (1973) and Edward Shaw's *Financial Deepening in Economic Development* (1973). Empirical research by Robert King and Ross Levine, for example, in "Finance and Growth: Schumpeter Might Be Right" (1993), suggests a strong correlation between financial development and economic growth. Some of the most recent research on the benefits and risks specifically of foreign investment can be found in *Does Foreign Direct Investment Promote Development?* edited by Theodore Moran, Edward Graham, and Magnus Blomström (2005).

Many countries now have their own investment promotion agencies with websites for more information. Amar Bhattacharya, Peter Montiel, and Sunil Sharma ask "How Can Sub-Saharan Africa Attract More Private Capital Inflows?" (1997). Information about African stock markets is contained in the *African Stock Market Handbook*, which used to be an annual report by the IFC, but is now irregularly published by UNDP. For analysis of the rationale behind and impact of stock exchanges in Africa, see *Adventure Capitalism: Globalization and the Political Economy of Stock Markets in Africa* (2003) by Todd Moss and *The Politics of Equity Finance in Emerging Markets* (2004) by Kathryn Lavelle.

All sides in the debate about capital account liberalization are covered in Stanley Fischer et al., *Should the IMF Pursue Capital Account Convertibility?* (1998). Edward Graham lays out a case for the Multinational Agreement on Investment in *Fighting the Wrong Enemy: Antiglobal Activists and Multinational Enterprises* (2000). The seminal paper on capital flight (and the source for the estimates used in this chapter) is "Is Africa a Net Creditor? New Estimates of Capital Flight from Severely Indebted Sub-Saharan African Countries, 1970–96" by James Boyce and Léonce Ndikumana (2001). Also worth a look is Boyce and Ndikumana's "Public Debts and Private Assets: Explaining Capital Flight from Sub-Saharan African Countries" (2003).

The best source of data on African business environments is the World Bank's *Doing Business* reports and databases. For much more detail on an individual country, see the Bank's *Investment Climate Assessments*, which are based on hundreds of firm-level surveys (but are not available for every country). For a policy perspective, see the Bank's *World Development Report 2005: A Better Investment Climate for Everyone* (2004) and James Emery's "Governance and Private Investment in Africa" (2003).

Roger Tangri is very insightful into the barriers government can put up for domestic entrepreneurs in *The Politics of Patronage in Africa: Parastatals, Privatization, and Private Enterprise in Africa* (2000). Thomas Callaghy gives some context in "The State and the Development of Capitalism in Africa: Theoretical, Historical, and Comparative Reflections" (1988). Vijaya Ramachandran and Manju Kedia Shah's "Minority Entrepreneurs and Private Sector Growth in Sub-Saharan Africa" (1999) is a good analysis of the internal ethnic considerations of business policy.

A good starting point on microcredit is *The Economics of Microfinance* by Beatriz Armendáriz de Aghion and Jonathan Morduch (2005). A more skeptical view is taken by Pankaj Jain and Mick Moore in "What Makes Microcredit Programmes Effective? Fashionable Fallacies and Workable Realities" (2003). A related topic to microfinance is the argument to view the poor as potential consumers for a range of products, popularized in the influential *The Fortune at the Bottom of the Pyramid: Eradicating Poverty Through Profits* (2004) by business strategy guru C. K. Prahalad.

Richard Adams and John Page examine the effect of remittances on poverty in "International Migration, Remittances, and Poverty in Developing Countries" (2003). Cerstin Sander and Samuel Munzele Maimbo look specifically at the policy issues in Africa in "Migrant Labor Remittances in Africa: Reducing Obstacles to Developmental Contributions" (2003). Another good source is *Diasporas, Remittances, and Africa South of the Sahara: A Strategic Assessment* by Marc-Antoine Pérouse De Montclos (2005).

PART 4

Conclusion

14

Some Concluding Themes

THIS BOOK HAS ATTEMPTED TO PROVIDE SOME OF THE BASIC information about development in sub-Saharan Africa to smooth the progress of further study. In addition to offering context and some facts to get started, hopefully it has also conveyed some of the complexity of the issues, clarified some of the common confusions, and imparted a sense of humility for the worthy endeavor of helping to bring prosperity to the African continent. Stepping back, the efforts by Africans and the international community to improve Africa's welfare are a colossal, and in some ways unavoidable, undertaking.

At the same time, after half a century of independence, the lack of economic progress on the continent is surely one of the great disappointments in modern history. Perhaps even more worrying, after decades of intense international development efforts in Africa, it is just as striking how little is really understood about how to turn a poor society into a wealthier one. As outlined in this book, there are lots of good ideas and many admirable institutions and initiatives that are undoubtedly saving lives. But as a whole, there is still no clear way to help turn Africa around. Even if it is recognized that external efforts can only do so much and that change must come from within, the development community still does not really know how to encourage that internal process. In short, we simply do not know how to make Chad more like South Korea.

Rather than a source for pessimism, this uncertainty should be a challenge to the next generation of students, scholars, and practitioners. In fact, we have come a long way from the simple-minded solutions of the past of just providing money or roads or loan conditions, and thinking that would be enough. Mindful of these mistakes (and old ideas in new packaging), it is incumbent on the next generation of Africans and development specialists to continue pushing the research envelope and experimenting with new innovations. Indeed, it is in this marketplace of creative ideas—and probably not in a planning committee of some government agency or international bureaucracy—that better ways forward for Africa will be found.

Themes of This Book

As promised up front, this book offers no solutions. It only seeks to help students understand the issues to enable them to ask the right questions as they go on to study or work in Africa. There are, however, some underlying themes that emerge from the book as a whole, themes that hopefully provide context to further probing and learning.

The first message is that history and endowments may be inescapable, but they need not be destiny. Africa certainly has had an unlucky history and faces many unfavorable structural factors that impede its development. But the experience of East Asia or other emerging regions—not to mention the successes of Botswana and Mauritius—suggest that Africa too can do much better. The issue for Africa and for those seeking to help is to find ways to harness what Africa has and seek ways to work around some of its inherent deficiencies.

Second, Africa's development faces a number of inexorable dilemmas. Politics, bad governance, and rotten leadership surely contribute to the continent's problems but, given the necessary role of the state, they also must be central to any major improvements. The next decade for Africa will see increased scrutiny of governance by civil societies, both at home in Africa and around the globe. The implicit bargain struck in recent years is that the international community will provide Africa with greater resources in exchange for better management. Expectations within Africa have also risen with the expansion of democratic freedoms and the opening of political space. And the development practitioners have realized that building institutions is part and parcel of development; the quest for how to apply this in practice will be their next test.

Another quandary is about aid from outsiders. External assistance can be extremely helpful and has undoubtedly saved millions of lives, and there is much the international community can contribute to African development in terms of resources and knowledge. But the aid industry is also a mess of confused ideas, dysfunctional agencies, and as a whole is fragmented and ineffectual. In many ways, the aid business itself is also part of Africa's problem. The next decade or so will bring major challenges for the aid industry, especially to meet the great expectations that have been built up in recent years, such as promises to meet the Millennium Development Goals or to spend the new aid more wisely than has been done in the past. Aid is undoubtedly facing a period of increased scrutiny and evaluation, which will see it fundamentally changed over coming years.

Finally, the challenge of globalization for African development cannot be avoided. Once the hype of both the overexcited globophiles and the hysterical globophobes is peeled away, Africa has some very real opportunities ahead of it, but they come with considerable implications. The potential of global trade and investment to contribute toward African prosperity is substantial— even monumentally transformative— if the conditions are right. At the same time, taking advantage of these opportunities and not allowing Africa to be further marginalized means getting into the "race to the top" by equipping African societies to compete in the global economy. This endeavor is not only a responsibility for African leaders and societies but also for the world, to ensure that the rules regarding trade and development are fair and not fixed to Africa's disadvantage.

The stakes for Africa's development are high. The past half century has seen the greatest advancements in human progress of any time in the history of mankind. The enhancements in welfare, technology, and opportunity for the common person have been transformative for billions of people worldwide. In many parts of the world, poverty and deprivation that had been the norm for the masses since the beginning of time have been essentially erased. But large swaths of the globe remain outposts of destitution, and nowhere is the problem so acute and apparent as it is in Africa. Enormous efforts are under way within the continent and around the world to change all that. But after fifty years, the journey still seems to have barely gotten started.

Acronyms

ABC	Abstain, Be faithful, use a Condom
AfD	l'Agence Française de Développement
AfDB	African Development Bank
AGOA	African Growth and Opportunity Act (US)
ANC	African National Congress (South Africa)
ARV	antiretroviral
AU	African Union
BNLS	Botswana, Namibia, Lesotho, Swaziland
BRVM	Bourse Régionale des Valeurs Mobilières
CAR	Central African Republic
CEMAC	Communauté économique et monétaire de l'Afrique centrale
CFA	Communauté financière d'Afrique (or Coopération financière en Afrique centrale)
CIA	Central Intelligence Agency (US)
CIDA	Canadian International Development Agency
CILSS	Comité permanent inter-Etats de lutte contre la sécheresse dans le Sahel
CMA	Common Monetary Area
COMESA	Common Market for Eastern and Southern Africa
CPIA	Country Policy and Institutional Assessment
DAC	Development Assistance Committee (OECD)
DFID	Department for International Development (UK)
DPKO	Department of Peacekeeping Operations (UN)
DRC	Democratic Republic of Congo
EAC	East African Community
EBA	Everything But Arms (EU)
ECOWAS	Economic Community of West African States
ELF	ethno-linguistic fractionalization
EPRDF	Ethiopian People's Revolutionary Democratic Front

247

ESAF	enhanced structural adjustment facility
EU	European Union
FAO	Food and Agriculture Organization (UN)
FDI	foreign direct investment
FINSAP	financial sector adjustment program
GATS	General Agreement on Trade in Services
GATT	General Agreement on Tariffs and Trade
GDP	gross domestic product
GFATM	Global Fund to Fight AIDS, Tuberculosis, and Malaria
GNI	gross national income
HDI	Human Development Index
HIPC	heavily indebted poor countries
HIV/AIDS	human immunodeficiency virus/acquired immune deficiency syndrome
IBRD	International Bank for Reconstruction and Development (World Bank)
ICSID	International Centre for Settlement of Investment Disputes (World Bank)
IDA	International Development Association (World Bank)
IFC	International Finance Corporation (World Bank)
IFIs	international financial institutions
IGAD	Intergovernmental Authority on Development
IMF	International Monetary Fund
IOC	Indian Ocean Commission
IOR-ARC	The Indian Ocean Rim Association for Regional Co-operation
IOs	international organizations
ISI	import substitution industrialization
JICA	Japan International Cooperation Agency
KANU	Kenya African National Union
LDCs	least-developed countries
MAI	Multilateral Agreement on Investment
MAP	Multicountry AIDS Program
MCA	Millennium Challenge Account (US)
MCC	Millennium Challenge Corporation (US)
MDBs	multilateral development banks
MDGs	Millennium Development Goals
MDRI	multilateral debt relief initiative
MIGA	Multilateral Investment Guarantee Agency (World Bank)
MPLA	Movimento Popular de Libertação de Angola
MRU	Mano River Union
NAM	Non-Aligned Movement

NAMA	non-agricultural market access
NED	National Endowment for Democracy
NEPAD	New Partnership for Africa's Development
NGO	nongovernmental organization
OAU	Organization of African Unity
OBA	output-based aid
ODA	official development assistance
OECD	Organization for Economic Co-operation and Development
OPIC	Overseas Private Investment Corporation (US)
PBA	performance-based allocation
PEPFAR	President's Emergency Plan for AIDS Relief (US)
PRGF	poverty reduction and growth facility
PRSP	poverty reduction strategy paper
RPF	Rwandan Patriotic Front
RUF	Revolutionary United Front (Sierra Leone)
SACU	Southern African Customs Union
SADC	Southern African Development Community
SARB	South African Reserve Bank
SIDA	Swedish Agency for International Development Cooperation
SOEs	state-owned enterprises
TPLF	Tigrayan People's Liberation Front (Ethiopia)
TRIMs	Trade-Related Investment Measures
TRIPs	Trade-Related Aspects of Intellectual Property Rights
UEMOA	Union économique et monétaire ouest-africaine
UN	United Nations
UNCTAD	UN Conference on Trade and Development
UNDP	UN Development Program
UNECA	UN Economic Commission for Africa
UNHCR	UN High Commission for Refugees
UNICEF	UN Children's Fund
UNITA	União Nacional pela Independência Total de Angola
USAID	United States Agency for International Development
WFP	World Food Program (UN)
WHO	World Health Organization (UN)
WTO	World Trade Organization
ZANU–PF	Zimbabwe African National Union–Patriotic Front

Bibliography

Acemoglu, Daron, Simon Johnson, and James Robinson, "Institutions as the Fundamental Cause of Long-Run Growth," in Philippe Aghion and Stephen Durlauf (eds.), *Handbook of Economic Growth,* Elsevier, 2005.

Achebe, Chinua, *Things Fall Apart,* Heinemann, 1958.

———. *Anthills of the Savannah*, Doubleday, 1988.

Adams, Richard, and John Page, "International Migration, Remittances, and Poverty in Developing Countries," World Bank, Policy Research Working Paper 3179, 2003.

Aghion, Philippe, and Stephen Durlauf (eds.), *Handbook of Economic Growth,* Elsevier, 2005.

Ainsworth, Martha, and Warnya Teokul, "Breaking the Silence: Setting Realistic Priorities for HIV/AIDS Control in Less-Developed Countries,"*Lancet*, Vol. 356, 2000.

Allen, Tim, and Diana Weinhold, "Dropping the Debt: Is It Such a Good Idea?" *Journal of International Development*, Vol. 12, No. 6, 2000.

Armendáriz de Aghion, Beatriz, and Jonathan Morduch, *The Economics of Microfinance*, MIT Press, 2005.

Arndt, Channing, and Jeffrey Lewis, "The Macro-Economic Implications of HIV/AIDS in South Africa: A Preliminary Assessment," *Journal of South African Economics*, Vol. 68, No. 5, 2000.

Barkan, Joel, and David Gordon, "Democracy in Africa," *Foreign Affairs*, July-August, 1998.

Barnett, Michael, *Eyewitness to a Genocide: The United Nations and Rwanda,* Cornell University Press, 2003.

Barnett, Tony, and Alan Whiteside, *AIDS in the Twenty-First Century*, Palgrave Macmillan, 2003.

Bates, Robert, *Markets and States in Tropical Africa*, University of California Press, 1981.

Bauer, Gretchen, and Hannah Britton, *Women in African Parliaments*, Lynne Rienner, 2006.

Bauer, Peter, *Dissent on Development: Studies and Debates in Development Economics*, Harvard University Press, 1976.

Bayart, Jean-François, *L'Etat en Afrique: la politique du ventre*, Fayard, 1989. (English version, *The State in Africa: The Politics of the Belly*, Longman, 1993.)

Bell, Clive, Shantayanan Devarajan, and Hans Gersbach, "The Long-Run Economic Costs of AIDS: Theory and an Application to South Africa," World Bank, Policy Research Working Paper 3152, 2003.

Berg, Andrew, and Anne Krueger, "Trade, Growth, and Poverty: A Selective Survey," IMF, 2003.

Bhagwati, Jagdish, *Free Trade Today*, Princeton University Press, 2001.

Bhattacharya, Amar, Peter Montiel, and Sunil Sharma, "How Can Sub-Saharan Africa Attract More Private Capital Inflows?" *Finance & Development*, June 1997.

Birdsall, Nancy, "Seven Deadly Sins: Reflections on Donor Failings," in William Easterly (ed.), *Reinventing Aid*, MIT Press, forthcoming 2007.

Birmingham, David, *Kwame Nkrumah: Father of African Nationalism*, Ohio University Press, 1998.

Bloom, David, and Jeffrey Sachs, "Geography, Demography, and Economic Growth in Africa," *Brookings Papers on Economic Activity*, 1998.

Boone, Peter, "The Impact of Foreign Aid on Savings and Growth," London School of Economics, Centre for Economic Performance Working Paper No. 677, 1994.

Bose, Anuradha, and Peter Burnell (eds.), *Britain's Overseas Aid Since 1979: Between Idealism and Self-Interest*, Manchester University Press, 1991.

Boyce, James, and Léonce Ndikumana, "Is Africa a Net Creditor? New Estimates of Capital Flight from Severely Indebted Sub-Saharan African Countries, 1970–96," *Journal of Development Studies*, Vol. 38, No. 2, 2001.

———. "Public Debts and Private Assets: Explaining Capital Flight from Sub-Saharan African Countries," *World Development*, Vol. 31, No. 1, 2003.

Bratton, Michael, and Nicolas van de Walle, *Democratic Experiments in Africa: Regime Transitions in Comparative Perspective*, Cambridge University Press, 1997.

Brautigam, Deborah, and Steven Knack, "Foreign Aid, Institutions, and Governance in Sub-Saharan Africa," *Economic Development and Cultural Change*, Vol. 52, No. 1, 2004.

Burnside, Craig, and David Dollar, "Aid, Policies, and Growth," *American Economic Review*, Vol. 90, No. 4, 2000.

Callaghy, Thomas, and John Ravenhill (eds.), *Hemmed In: Responses to Africa's Economic Decline*, Columbia University Press, 1993.

Callaghy, Thomas, "The State and the Development of Capitalism in Africa: Theoretical, Historical, and Comparative Reflections," in Donald Rothchild and Naomi Chazan (eds.), *The Precarious Balance: State and Society in Africa*, Westview Press, 1988.

Chabal, Patrick, and Jean-Pascal Daloz, *Africa Works: Disorder as Political Instrument*, James Currey, 1999.

Chauvin, Nicolas, and Aart Kraay, "What Has 100 Billion Dollars Worth of Debt Relief Done for Low-Income Countries?" World Bank, 2005.

Chenery, Hollis, and Alan Strout, "Foreign Assistance and Economic Development," *American Economic Review*, Vol. 56, No. 4, 1966.

Claessens, Stijn, Enrica Detragiache, Ravi Kanbur, and Peter Wickham, "HIPC's Debt: Review of the Issues," *Journal of African Economies*, Vol. 6, No. 2, 1997.

Clapham, Christopher, Greg Mills, Anna Morner, and Elizabeth Sidiropoulos (eds.), *SADC Regional Integration in Southern Africa: Comparative International Perspectives*, South African Institute of International Affairs, 2001.

Clapham, Christopher, *Private Patronage and Public Power: Political Clientalism in the Modern State*, St. Martin's Press, 1982.

Clark, Ann Marie, "Non-Governmental Organizations and Their Influence on International Society," *Journal of International Affairs*, winter 1995.

Clemens, Michael, "Do Visas Kill? The Effects of African Health Worker Emigration," Center for Global Development, 2006.

Clemens, Michael, Steve Radelet, and Rikhil Bhavnani, "Counting Chickens When They Hatch: The Short-Term Effect of Aid on Growth," Center for Global Development, CGD Working Paper 44, 2004.

Cline, William, *Trade Policy and Global Poverty,* Center for Global Development, 2004.

Cohen, Herman, *Intervening in Africa: Superpower Peacemaking in a Troubled Continent*, St. Martin's Press, 2000.

Collier, Paul, and Anke Hoeffler, "Greed and Grievance in Civil War," World Bank, 2001.

———, *Breaking the Conflict Trap: Civil War and Development Policy*, World Bank, 2003.

Collier, Paul, and Jan Willem Gunning, "Why Has Africa Grown Slowly?" *Journal of Economic Perspectives*, Vol. 13, No. 3, 1999.

Collier, Paul, "The Failure of Conditionality," in Catherine Gwin and Joan Nelson (eds.), *Perspectives on Aid and Development*, Overseas Development Council, 1997.

———, "The Role of the State in Economic Development: Cross-Regional Experiences," *Journal of African Economies*, Vol. 7, No. 2, 1998.

Commission for Africa, *Our Common Interest,* 2005.

Commission on Weak States and U.S. National Security, *On the Brink: Weak States and U.S. National Security*, Center for Global Development, 2004.

Crocker, Chester, *High Noon in Southern Africa: Making Peace in a Rough Neighborhood*, W. W. Norton, 1993.

Crocker, Chester, Fen Olser Hampson, and Pamela Aall (eds.), *Turbulent Peace: The Challenges of Managing International Conflict*, United States Institute of Peace, 2001.

Cumming, Gordon, *Aid to Africa: French and British Policies from the Cold War to the New Millennium*, Ashgate, 2001.

Dangarembga, Tsitsi, *Nervous Conditions*, Women's Press, 1988.

Danielou, Morgane, Patrick Labaste, and Jean-Michel Voisard, "Linking Farmers to Markets: Exporting Malian Mangoes to Europe," World Bank, Africa Region Working Paper 60, 2003.

De Long, Bradford, and Barry Eichengreen, "The Marshall Plan: History's Most Successful Structural Adjustment Program," National Bureau of Economic Research, 1991.

de Soto, Hernando, *The Other Path*, Harper Collins, 1989.

———, *The Mystery of Capital,* Basic Books, 2000.

de Waal, Alex, "How Will HIV/AIDS Transform African Governance?" *African Affairs*, Vol. 102, No. 406, 2003.

Demery, Lionel, and Christiaan Grootaert, "Correcting for Sampling Bias in the

Measurement of Welfare and Poverty in the Côte d'Ivoire Living Standards Survey," *World Bank Economic Review*, Vol. 7, No. 3, 1993.

Devarajan, Shantayanan, Margaret Miller, and Eric Swanson, "Goals for Development: History, Prospects and Costs," World Bank, 2002.

Diamond, Jared, *Guns, Germs, and Steel: The Fates of Human Societies*, W. W. Norton, 1999.

Diamond, Larry, and Marc Plattner (eds.), *Democratization in Africa*, Journal of Democracy, 1999.

Dollar, David, *Assessing Aid: What Works, What Doesn't, and Why*, World Bank, 1998.

Dollar, David, and Jakob Svensson, "What Explains the Success or Failure of Structural Adjustment Programs?" *Economic Journal*, Vol. 11, No. 466, 2000.

Easterly, William, *The Elusive Quest for Growth*, MIT Press, 2001.

——, "Think Again: Debt Relief," *Foreign Policy*, November 2001.

——, "How Did Heavily Indebted Poor Countries Become Heavily Indebted? Reviewing Two Decades of Debt Relief," *World Development*, Vol. 30, No. 10, 2002.

Easterly, William, and Ross Levine, "Africa's Growth Tragedy: Policies and Ethnic Divisions," *Quarterly Journal of Economics*, Vol. 112, No. 4, 1997.

Einhorn, Jessica, "The World Bank's Mission Creep," *Foreign Affairs*, September 2001.

Elbadawi, Ibrahim, and Nicholas Sambanis, "Why Are There So Many Civil Wars in Africa? Understanding and Preventing Violent Conflict," *Journal of African Economies*, Vol. 9, No. 3, 2000.

Elbadawi, Ibrahim, Benno Ndulu, and Njuguna Ndung'u, "Debt Overhang and Economic Growth in Sub-Saharan Africa," in Zubair Iqbal and Ravi Kanbur (eds.), *External Finance for Low-Income Countries*, IMF, 1997.

Elliott, Kimberly, *Delivering on Doha: Farm Trade and the Poor*, Center for Global Development, 2006.

Emery, James, "Governance and Private Investment in Africa," in Nicolas van de Walle, Nicole Ball, and Vijaya Ramachandran (eds.), *Beyond Structural Adjustment: The Institutional Context of African Development*, Palgrave Macmillan, 2003.

Engelbert, Pierre, "The Contemporary African State: Neither African nor State," *Third World Quarterly*, Vol. 18, No. 4, 1997.

——, "Pre-Colonial Institutions, Post-Colonial States, and Economic Development in Tropical Africa," *Political Research Quarterly*, Vol. 53, 2000.

——, "Solving the Mystery of the AFRICA Dummy," *World Development*, Vol. 28, No. 10, 2000.

——, *State Legitimacy and Development in Africa*, Lynne Rienner, 2000.

English, E. Philip, and Harris Mule, *The Multilateral Development Banks: The African Development Bank*, Lynne Rienner, 1996.

Esty, Daniel, *Greening the GATT: Trade, Environment, and the Future*, Institute for International Economics, 1994.

Fanon, Franz, *The Wretched of the Earth*, Penguin, 1963.

Farmer, Paul, et al., "Community-Based Approaches to HIV Treatment in Resource-Poor Settings," *Lancet*, Vol. 358, 2001.

Fearon, James, "Primary Commodity Exports and Civil War," *Journal of Conflict Resolution*, Vol. 49, No. 4, 2005.

Fearon, James, and David Laitin, "Ethnicity, Insurgency, and Civil War," *American Political Science Review*, Vol. 97, No. 1, 2003.

Fischer, Stanley, et al., *Should the IMF Pursue Capital Account Convertibility?* Princeton University, Essays in International Finance No. 207, 1998.

Foden, Giles, *The Last King of Scotland*, Vintage, 1999.

Fox, Matthew, et al., "The Impact of HIV/AIDS on Labour Productivity in Kenya," *Tropical Medicine and International Health,* Vol. 9, No. 3, 2004.

Frankel, Jeffrey, and David Romer, "Does Trade Cause Growth?" *American Economic Review*, Vol. 89, No. 3, 1999.

Freeman, Richard, and David Lindauer, "Why Not Africa?" National Bureau of Economic Research, NBER Working Paper 6942, 1999.

Friedman, Milton, "Foreign Economic Aid," *Yale Review*, summer 1958.

George, Susan, *A Fate Worse Than Debt,* Grove Press, 1988.

Gibb, Richard, "Southern Africa in Transition: Prospects and Problems Facing Regional Integration," *Journal of Modern African Studies*, Vol. 36, No. 2, 1998.

Glaeser, Edward, Rafael La Porta, Florencio Lopez-de-Silanes, and Andrei Shleifer, "Do Institutions Cause Growth?" National Bureau of Economic Research, NBER Working Paper 10568, 2004.

Goldstein, Markus, and Christopher Udry, "Agricultural Innovation and Resource Management in Ghana," International Food Policy Research Institute, 1999.

Gordon, David, "Conditionality in Policy-Based Lending in Africa: USAID Experience," in Paul Mosley (ed.), *Development Finance and Policy Reform*, St. Martin's Press, 1992.

Gourevitch, Philip, *We Wish to Inform You That Tomorrow We Will Be Killed with Our Families: Stories from Rwanda*, Farrar Straus and Giroux, 1998.

Graham, Edward, *Fighting the Wrong Enemy: Antiglobal Activists and Multinational Enterprises*, Institute for International Economics, 2000.

Greene, Graham, *The Heart of the Matter*, first published in 1948.

Gunning, Jan Willem, and Paul Collier, *Trade Shocks in Developing Countries: Africa*, Oxford University Press, 2000.

Gwin, Catherine, et al., *Miracle or Design? Lessons from the East Asian Experience*, Overseas Development Council, 1994.

Haacker, Markus (ed.), *The Macroeconomics of HIV/AIDS,* IMF, 2004.

Haddad, Lawrence, and Ravi Kanbur, "How Serious Is the Neglect of Intra-Household Inequality?" *Economic Journal*, Vol. 100, 1990.

Haggard, Stephan, and Robert Kaufman, *The Politics of Economic Adjustment*, Princeton University Press, 1992.

Hancock, Graham, *Lords of Poverty*, Atlantic Monthly Press, 1992.

Hanmer, Lucia, Robert Lensink, and Howard White, "Infant and Child Mortality in Developing Countries: Analysing the Data for Robust Determinants," *Journal of Development Studies*, Vol. 40, No. 1, 2003.

Hansen, Henrik, and Finn Tarp, "Aid Effectiveness Disputed," *Journal of International Development,* Vol. 12, No. 3, 2000.

Harff, Barbara, "No Lessons Learned from the Holocaust? Assessing Risks of Genocide and Political Mass Murder Since 1955," *American Political Science Review*, Vol. 97, No. 1, 2003.

Harford, Tim, and Michael Klein, *The Market for Aid*, World Bank, 2005.

Hargreaves, James, and Judith Glynn, "Educational Attainment and HIV–1 Infection in Developing Countries: A Systematic Review," *Tropical Medicine and International Health,* Vol. 7, No. 6, 2002.

Heilbroner, Robert, *The Worldly Philosophers: The Lives, Times and Ideas of the Great Economic Thinkers*, first published in 1953.

Heller, Peter, "Pity the Finance Minister: Issues in Managing a Substantial Scaling Up of Aid Flows," IMF, Working Paper 180, 2005.

Herbst, Jeffrey, "The Structural Adjustment of Politics in Africa," *World Development,* Vol. 18, No. 7, 1990.

———, *The Politics of Reform in Ghana, 1982–1991*, University of California, 1992.

———, *States and Power in Africa: Comparative Lessons in Authority and Control*, Princeton University Press, 2000.

Hertel, Thomas, and Alan Winters (eds.), *Poverty and the WTO: Impacts of the Doha Development Agenda,* World Bank, 2005.

Hochschild, Adam, *King Leopold's Ghost*, Houghton Mifflin, 1998.

Hoekman, Bernard, and Michael Kostecki, *The Political Economy of the World Trading System: From GATT to WTO*, Oxford University Press, 2001.

Holman, Michael, *Last Orders at Harrods*, Interlink, 2005.

Holt, Victoria, and Moira Shanahan, "African Capacity-Building for Peace Operations: UN Collaboration with the African Union and ECOWAS," Henry Stimson Center, 2005.

Homer-Dixon, Thomas, *Environment, Scarcity, and Violence*, Princeton University Press, 2001.

Hope, Kempe Ronald, "From Crisis to Renewal: Towards a Successful Implementation of the New Partnership for Africa's Development," *African Affairs*, Vol. 101, 2002.

Hulme, David, and Michael Edwards, *NGOs, States, and Donors: Too Close for Comfort?* St. Martin's Press, 1997.

Human Security Centre, *Human Security Report*, University of British Columbia, 2005.

Hyden, Goran, *No Shortcuts to Progress: African Development Management in Perspective*, University of California Press, 1983.

Iqbal, Zubair, and Mohsin Khan (eds.), *Trade Reform and Regional Integration in Africa*, IMF, 1998.

Iweala, Uzodinma, *Beasts of No Nation*, Harper Collins, 2005.

Jackson, Robert, and Carl Rosberg, *Personal Rule in Black Africa: Prince, Autocrat, Prophet, Tyrant,* University of California Press, 1982.

Jackson, Robert, *Quasi-States, Sovereignty, International Relations, and the Third World,* Cambridge University Press, 1990.

Jain, Pankaj, and Mick Moore, "What Makes Microcredit Programmes Effective? Fashionable Fallacies and Workable Realities," Institute of Development Studies, IDS Working Paper 177, 2003.

Jeffries, Richard, "The State, Structural Adjustment, and Good Government," *Journal of Commonwealth and Comparative Politics*, Vol. 31, No. 1, 1993.

Johnson, Chalmers, *MITI and the Japanese Miracle: The Growth of Industrial Policy, 1925–1975*, Stanford University Press, 1983.

Joseph, Richard (ed.), *State, Conflict, and Democracy in Africa*, Lynne Rienner, 1999.

Joseph, Richard, *Democracy and Prebendal Politics in Nigeria: The Rise and Fall of the Second Republic*, Cambridge University Press, 1987.

Kanbur, Ravi, "Aid, Conditionality, and Debt in Africa," in Finn Tarp (ed.), *Foreign Aid and Development: Lessons Learnt and Directions for the Future*, Routledge, 2000.

———, "Economic Policy, Distribution, and Poverty: The Nature of Disagreements," *World Development*, Vol. 29, No. 6, 2001.

Kapur, Devesh, John Lewis, and Richard Webb, *The World Bank: Its First Half Century,* Brookings Institution Press, 1997.

Kapuscinski, Ryszard, *Emperor*, Vintage, 1989.

Karl, Terry Lynn, *The Paradox of Plenty: Oil Booms and Petro-States*, University of California Press, 1997.

Kaufmann, Daniel, and Aart Kraay, "Growth Without Governance," World Bank, 2002.

Kenny, Charles, "Why Are We Worried About Income? Nearly Everything That Matters Is Converging," *World Development,* Vol. 33, No. 1, 2005.

Kenny, Charles, and David Williams, "What Do We Know About Economic Growth? Or, Why Don't We Know Very Much?" *World Development*, Vol. 29, No. 1, 2001.

Kenyatta, Jomo, *Facing Mt. Kenya*, Vintage Press, 1962.

Khalfan, Ashfaq, Jeff King, and Bryan Thomas, "Advancing the Odious Debt Doctrine," Centre for International Sustainable Development Law, 2003.

Killick, Tony, "Politics, Evidence, and the New Aid Agenda," *Development Policy Review*, Vol. 22, No. 1, 2004.

———. *Aid and the Political Economy of Policy Change*, Routledge, 1998.

King, Robert, and Ross Levine, "Finance and Growth: Schumpeter Might Be Right," *Quarterly Journal of Economics*, Vol. 108, No. 3, 1993.

Kraay, Aart, and Claudio Raddatz, "Poverty Traps, Aid, and Growth," World Bank, Policy Research Working Paper 3631, 2005.

Kraay, Aart, and Vikram Nehru, "When Is Debt Sustainable?" World Bank, 2004.

Krasner, Steven, "Sharing Sovereignty: New Institutions for Collapsed and Failing States," *International Security*, Vol. 29, No. 2, 2004.

Kremer, Michael, "Pharmaceuticals and the Developing World," *Journal of Economic Perspectives*, Vol. 16, No. 4, 2002.

Kremer, Michael, and Seema Jayachandran, "Odious Debt," *Brookings Review*, Vol. 21, No. 2, 2003.

Krueger, Anne, "Why Trade Liberalisation Is Good for Growth," *The Economic Journal*, 1998.

Krugman, Paul, "Financing vs. Forgiving a Debt Overhang," *Journal of Development Economics,* Vol. 29, No. 2, 1988.

Kwasi Tieku, Thomas, "Explaining the Clash and Accommodation of Interests of Major Actors in the Creation of the African Union," *African Affairs*, Vol. 103, 2004.

Lal, Deepak, *The Poverty of Development Economics,* MIT Press, 2000.

Lancaster, Carol, *Transforming Foreign Aid: US Assistance in the 21st Century*, Institute for International Economics, 2000.

Landell-Mills, Pierre, "Governance, Cultural Change, and Empowerment," *Journal of Modern African Studies*, Vol. 30, No. 4, 1992.

Landes, David, *The Wealth and Poverty of Nations: Why Some Are Rich and Some Poor*, W. W. Norton, 1998.

Lanjouw, Jean, "Intellectual Property and the Availability of Pharmaceuticals in Poor Countries," Center for Global Development, CGD Working Paper 5, 2002.

Lavelle, Kathryn, *The Politics of Equity Finance in Emerging Markets*, Oxford University Press, 2004.

Lemarchand, René, *Burundi: Ethnic Conflict and Genocide*, Cambridge University Press, 1994.

Leonard, David, and Scott Straus, *Africa's Stalled Development: International Causes and Cures*, Lynne Rienner, 2003.

Levine, Ruth, *Millions Saved: Proven Successes in Global Health*, Center for Global Development, 2004.

Lewis, Maureen, "Addressing the Challenge of HIV/AIDS: Macroeconomic, Fiscal, and Institutional Issues," Center for Global Development, CGD Working Paper 58, 2005.

———, "Governance and Corruption in Health Care Delivery," Center for Global Development, CGD Working Paper 78, 2006.

Lewis, Peter, "Economic Reform and Political Transition in Africa: The Quest for a Politics of Development," *World Politics*, Vol. 49, No. 1, 1996.

Leys, Colin, *The Rise and Fall of Development Economics*, University of Indiana, 1996.

Lindauer, David, and Lant Pritchett, "What's the Big Idea? The Third Generation of Policies for Economic Growth," *Economia*, fall 2002.

Mallaby, Sebastian, "NGOs: Fighting Poverty, Hurting the Poor," *Foreign Policy*, September 2004.

———, *The World's Banker*, Penguin Press, 2004.

Mamdani, Mahmood, *Citizen and Subject: Contemporary Africa and the Legacy of Late Colonialism*, Princeton University Press, 1996.

———, *When Victims Become Killers: Colonialism, Nativism, and the Genocide in Rwanda*, Princeton University Press, 2001.

Mandela, Nelson, *The Struggle Is My Life,* International Defence & Aid Fund for Southern Africa, 1986.

———, *Long Walk to Freedom. The Autobiography of Nelson Mandela,* Little Brown, 1994.

Marechera, Dambudzo, *The House of Hunger*, Heinemann, 1993.

Maren, Michael, *The Road to Hell: The Ravaging Effects of Foreign Aid and International Charity*, Free Press, 2002.

Mathews, Jessica, "Power Shift," *Foreign Affairs*, January 1997.

Mbire, Barbara, and Michael Atingi, "Growth and Foreign Debt: The Ugandan Experience," African Economic Research Consortium, AERC Research Paper 66, 1997.

McCarthy, Colin, "The Southern African Customs Union in Transition," *African Affairs*, Vol. 102, 2003.

McKinnon, Ronald, *Money and Capital in Economic Development*, Brookings Institution, 1973.

Meltzer, Alan, et al., *Report of the International Financial Institution Advisory Commission*, 2000.

Michailof, Sergio, Markus Kostner, and Xavier Devictor, "Post-Conflict Recovery in Africa: An Agenda for the Africa Region," World Bank, Africa Region Working Paper 30, 2002.

Migdal, Joel, *Strong Societies and Weak States: State-Society Relations and State Capabilities in the Third World*, Princeton University Press, 1988.

Mills, Anne, and Kara Hanson, "Expanding Access to Health Interventions in Low and Middle-Income Countries: Constraints and Opportunities for Scaling Up," special edition of *Journal of International Development*, Vol., 15, No. 1, 2003.

Mistry, Percy, "Africa's Record of Regional Co-Operation and Integration," *African Affairs*, Vol. 99, 2000.

Moore, Barrington, *Social Origins of Dictatorship and Democracy: Lord and Peasant in the Making of the Modern World*, Beacon Press, 1966.

Moore, Mike, *A World Without Walls: Freedom, Development, Free Trade, and Global Governance*, Oxford University Press, 2003.

Moran, Theodore, Edward Graham, and Magnus Blomström (eds.), *Does Foreign Direct Investment Promote Development?* Institute for International Economics, 2005.

Mosley, Paul, "How to Confront the World Bank and Get Away with It: A Case Study of Kenya," in Chris Milner and A. J. Rayner (eds.), *Policy Adjustment in Africa*, Macmillan, 1992.

Moss, Todd, *Adventure Capitalism: Globalization and the Political Economy of Stock Markets in Africa*, Palgrave Macmillan, 2003.

———, "Briefing: The G8's Multilateral Debt Relief Initiative and Poverty Reduction in Sub-Saharan Africa," *African Affairs*, Vol. 105, No. 419, 2006.

Murray, Rachel, *Human Rights in Africa: From the OAU to the African Union*, Cambridge University Press, 2004.

Museveni, Yoweri, *Sowing the Mustard Seed: The Struggle for Freedom and Democracy in Uganda*, Macmillan, 1997.

Naipaul, V. S., *A Bend in the River*, Knopf, 1979.

Narayan, Deepa, *Voices of the Poor,* Vols. 1–3, World Bank, 2000.

Ndulu, Benno, and Stephen O'Connell, "Governance and Growth in Sub-Saharan Africa," *Journal of Economic Perspectives*, Vol. 13, No. 3, 1999.

Nelson, Joan, "Promoting Policy Reforms: The Twilight of Conditionality?" *World Development*, Vol. 24, No. 9, 1996.

Ng, Francis, and Alexander Yeats, "Open Economies Work Better: Did Africa's Protectionist Policies Cause Its Marginalization in World Trade?" World Bank, 1996.

Nitzschke, Heiko, and Kaysie Studdard, "The Legacies of War Economies: Challenges and Options for Peacemaking and Peacebuilding," *International Peacekeeping*, Vol. 12, No. 2, 2005.

Nkrumah, Kwame, *Ghana: Autobiography of Kwame Nkrumah,* first published in 1957.

North, Douglass, *Institutions, Institutional Change, and Economic Performance*, Cambridge University Press, 1990.

Nugent, Paul, *Big Men, Small Boys, and Politics in Ghana*, Pinter, 1995.

———, *Africa Since Independence: A Comparative History*, Palgrave Macmillan, 2004.

Nyerere, Julius, *Nyerere on Socialism*, Oxford University Press, 1985.

OECD, *Open Markets Matter: The Benefits of Trade and Investment Liberalisation,* 1998.

Pakenham, Thomas, *The Scramble for Africa, 1876–1912*, Random House, 1991.

Paton, Alan, *Cry the Beloved Country,* first published in 1948.

Patrick, Stewart, "Weak States and Global Threats: Fact or Fiction?" *Washington Quarterly,* Vol. 29, No. 2, 2006.

Pattillo, Catherine, Hélène Poirson, and Luca Ricci, "External Debt and Growth," IMF, Working Paper 69, 2002.

Pearson, Lester, et al. *Partners in Development: Report of the Commission on International Development,* Praeger Publishers, 1969.

Perkins, Dwight, Steven Radelet, and David Lindauer, *Economics of Development,* W. W. Norton, 6th edition, 2006.

Pérouse De Montclos, Marc-Antoine, *Diasporas, Remittances, and Africa South of the Sahara: A Strategic Assessment,* Institute for Security Studies, 2005.

Power, Samantha, *A Problem from Hell: America and the Age of Genocide,* Harper, 2003.

Prahalad, C. K., *The Fortune at the Bottom of the Pyramid: Eradicating Poverty Through Profits,* Wharton School Publishing, 2004.

Pritchett, Lant, and Lawrence Summers, "Wealthier Is Healthier," *Journal of Human Resources,* Vol. 31, No. 4, 1996.

Prunier, Gerard, *The Rwanda Crisis: History of a Genocide, 1959–1994,* Hurst and Company, 1995.

———, *Darfur: The Ambiguous Genocide,* Cornell University Press, 2005.

Przeworski, Adam, and Fernando Limongi, "Political Regimes and Economic Growth," *Journal of Economic Perspectives,* Vol. 7, No. 2, 1993.

Przeworski, Adam, et al., *Democracy and Development: Political Institutions and Well-Being in the World, 1950–1990,* Cambridge University Press, 2000.

Radelet, Steve, *Challenging Foreign Aid,* Center for Global Development, 2003.

Ramachandran, Vijaya, and Manju Kedia Shah, "Minority Entrepreneurs and Private Sector Growth in Sub-Saharan Africa," *Journal of Development Studies,* Vol. 36, No. 2, 1999.

Regan, Patrick, and Daniel Norton, "Greed, Grievance, and Mobilization in Civil Wars," *Journal of Conflict Resolution,* Vol. 49, No. 3, 2005.

Reno, William, *Warlord Politics and African States,* Lynne Rienner, 1998.

Ricardo, David, *Principles of Political Economy and Taxation,* first published in 1817.

Rodrik, Dani, "Getting Institutions Right," Mimeo, Harvard University, 2004.

———, "Understanding Economic Policy Reform," *Journal of Economic Literature,* March 1996.

Rodrik, Dani, and Francisco Rodríguez, "Trade Policy and Economic Growth: A Skeptic's Guide to the Cross-National Literature," National Bureau of Economic Research, 1999.

Rogerson, Andrew, "The International Aid System 2005–2010: Forces for and Against Change," Overseas Development Institute, ODI Working Paper 235, 2004.

Rosenstein-Rodan, Paul, "International Aid for Undeveloped Countries," *Review of Economics and Statistics,* Vol. 43, No. 2, 1961.

Ross, Michael, "What Do We Know About Natural Resources and Civil War?" *Journal of Peace Research,* Vol. 41, No. 3, 2004.

Rostow, Walt, *The Stages of Economic Growth: A Non-Communist Manifesto,* Cambridge University Press, 1960.

Rothchild, Donald, *Ghana: The Political Economy of Recovery,* Lynne Rienner, 1991.

Rush, Norman, *Mating,* Vintage, 1991.

Sachs, Jeffrey, "Resolving the Debt Crisis of Low-Income Countries," *Brookings Papers on Economic Activity,* 2002.

——, "Ending Africa's Poverty Trap," *Brookings Papers on Economic Activity,* 2004.

——, *The End of Poverty,* Penguin Press, 2005.

Sachs, Jeffrey, and Andrew Warner, "Economic Reform and the Process of Global Integration," *Brookings Papers on Economic Activity,* 1995.

Sander, Cerstin, and Samuel Munzele Maimbo, "Migrant Labor Remittances in Africa: Reducing Obstacles to Developmental Contributions," World Bank, Africa Region Working Paper 64, 2003.

Schatzberg, Michael, *The Dialectics of Oppression in Zaire,* Indiana University Press, 1991.

——, "Power, Legitimacy, and Democratisation in Africa," *Africa,* Vol. 63, No. 4, 1993.

Schott, Jeffrey, *The WTO After Seattle,* Institute for International Economics, 2000.

Sen, Amartya, *Development As Freedom,* Knopf, 1999.

Senghor, Leopold, *The Collected Poetry of Leopold Senghor,* trans. Melvin Dixon, University of Virginia Press, 1998.

Serieux, John, and Yiagadeesen Samy, "The Debt Service Burden and Growth: Evidence from Low Income Countries," North-South Institute, 2001.

Shaw, Edward, *Financial Deepening in Economic Development,* Oxford University Press, 1973.

Shillington, Kevin, *Ghana and the Rawlings Factor,* Palgrave Macmillan, 1992.

Simmons, P. J., "Learning to Live with NGOs," *Foreign Policy,* fall 1998.

Singer, Hans, *International Development Co-Operation: Selected Essays by H. W. Singer on Aid and the United Nations System,* Palgrave Macmillan, 2001.

Singer, P. W., *Children at War,* Pantheon, 2005.

Smith, Adam, *An Inquiry into the Nature and Causes of the Wealth of Nations,* first published in 1776.

Stedman, Stephen, Donald Rothchild, and Elizabeth Cousens (eds.), *Ending Civil Wars: The Implementation of Peace Agreements,* Lynne Rienner, 2002.

Strauss, John, and Duncan Thomas, "Health, Nutrition, and Economic Development," *Journal of Economic Literature,* Vol. 36, No. 2, 1998.

Subramanian, Arvind, et al., "Trade and Trade Policies in Eastern and Southern Africa," IMF, 2000.

Tangri, Roger, *The Politics of Patronage in Africa: Parastatals, Privatization, and Private Enterprise in Africa,* Africa World Press, 2000.

Tarp, Finn (ed.), *Foreign Aid and Development: Lessons Learnt and Directions for the Future,* Routledge, 2000.

Taylor, Ian, *NEPAD: Toward Africa's Development or Another False Start?* Lynne Rienner, 2005.

Theobald, Robin, "Patrimonialism," *World Politics*, Vol. 34, No. 4, 1982.

Thompson, Leonard, *A History of South Africa*, Yale University Press, 2001.

Todaro, Michael, *Economic Development*, Addison-Wesley, 9th edition, 2005.

Tripp, Aili Mari, *Women and Politics in Uganda*, University of Wisconsin Press, 2000.

Uche, Chibuike, "The Politics of Monetary Sector Cooperation Among the Economic Community of West African States Members," World Bank, Policy Research Working Paper 2647, 2001.

UK Department for International Development, *Eliminating World Poverty: A Challenge for the 21st Century*, DFID white paper, 1997.

——, "Why We Need to Work More Effectively in Fragile States," DFID, 2005.

UN Economic Commission for Africa, *Assessing Regional Integration in Africa*, United Nations, 2004.

UNAIDS, *Report on the Global AIDS Epidemic*, 2004.

Vail, Leroy, *The Creation of Tribalism in Southern Africa*, University of California Press, 1989.

van de Walle, Nicolas, *African Economies and the Politics of Permanent Crisis, 1979–1999*, Cambridge University Press, 2001.

——, "Africa's Range of Regimes," *Journal of Democracy*, Vol. 13, No. 2, April 2002.

Wade, Robert, *Governing the Market*, Princeton University Press, 1990.

Wainaina, Binyavanga, "How to Write About Africa," *Granta*, January 2006.

Wangwe, Samuel, "NEPAD at Country Level," Economic and Social Research Foundation, 2002.

Warren, Bill, *Imperialism: Pioneer of Capitalism*, Verso Books, 1981.

Weinstein, Jeremy, "Autonomous Recovery and International Intervention in Comparative Perspective," Center for Global Development, CGD Working Paper 57, 2005.

White, Howard, Tony Killick, and Steve Kayizzi-Mugerwa, *African Poverty at the Millennium: Causes, Complexities, and Challenges,* World Bank, 2001.

Widner, Jennifer (ed.), *Economic Change and Political Liberalization in Sub-Saharan Africa*, Johns Hopkins University Press, 1994.

Williamson, John, "What Washington Means by Policy Reform," in *The Progress of Policy Reform in Latin America*, Institute for International Economics, 1990.

World Bank, *Accelerated Development in Sub-Saharan Africa: An Agenda for Action*, 1981.

——, *Sub-Saharan Africa—From Crisis to Sustainable Growth: A Long-Term Perspective Study*, 1989.

——, *The East Asian Miracle: Economic Growth and Public Policy*, 1993.

——, *World Development Report 1997: The State in a Changing World*, 1996.

——, *Can Africa Claim the 21st Century?* 2000.

——, "World Bank Group Work in Low-Income Countries Under Stress: A Task Force Report," 2002.

——, *A Guide to the World Bank*, 2003.

——, *World Development Report 2004: Making Services Work for Poor People*, 2003.

——, *World Development Report 2005: A Better Investment Climate for Everyone,* 2004.

————, "Working Together to Achieve the Millennium Development Goals: Additions to IDA Resources, Fourteenth Replenishment," 2005.

Wrong, Michela, *In the Footsteps of Mr. Kurtz: Living on the Brink of Disaster in Mobutu's Congo*, Perennial Publishers, 2002.

Young, Crawford, *The Politics of Cultural Pluralism*, University of Wisconsin, 1976.

————, *The African Colonial State in Comparative Perspective*, Yale University Press, 1994.

Zartman, William (ed.), *Collapsed States*, Lynne Rienner, 1995.

Journals

African Affairs, Royal Africa Society.
Development Policy Review, Overseas Development Institute.
Economic Development and Cultural Change, University of Chicago.
Finance & Development, IMF.
Journal of Democracy, National Endowment for Democracy.
Journal of Development Studies, Taylor and Francis.
Journal of Economic Perspectives, American Economic Association.
Journal of Modern African Studies, Cambridge University Press.
World Bank Research Observer, World Bank.
World Development, Elsevier Science.

Regular Reports

Africa Confidential, Blackwell Publishing, fortnightly.
Africa South of the Sahara, Routledge, annual.
African Economic Outlook, OECD and the African Development Bank, annual.
African Stock Market Handbook, UNDP, occasional.
AIDS Epidemic Updates, UNAIDS, occasional.
"Comprehensive Report on U.S. Trade and Investment Policy Toward Sub-Saharan Africa and Implementation of the African Growth and Opportunity Act," US Trade Representative, annual.
EIU Country Profiles, The Economist Intelligence Unit, annual.
EIU Country Reports, The Economist Intelligence Unit, quarterly.
Freedom in the World, Freedom House, annual.
Human Development Report, UNDP, annual.
Human Security Report, Human Security Center, launched in 2005.
Investment Climate Assessments, World Bank, occasional for selected countries.
Staff Country Reports, IMF, annually for each member country.
World Development Report, World Bank, annual.
World Economic Outlook, IMF, annual.
World Investment Report, UNCTAD, annual.

Databases

African Development Indicators, World Bank, annual.
Direction of Trade Statistics, IMF, annual.

Doing Business, World Bank, annual.
Global Development Finance, World Bank, annual.
Governance Matters, World Bank, biannual.
Human Development Index, UNDP, annual.
International Financial Statistics, IMF, monthly.
ODA Flows, OECD/DAC, annual.
World Development Indicators, World Bank, annual.

Index

About the Book

IN THE ONGOING BATTLE AGAINST GLOBAL POVERTY, THE countries of Africa continue to present the greatest challenge. *African Development* offers a comprehensive yet highly accessible introduction to the issues, actors, and institutions involved across the diverse continent.

Each issue chapter is organized around three fundamental questions: Where are we now? How did we get to this point? What are the current debates? Vivid profiles introduce the student to ten well-known "big men" and ten equally important but lesser known African leaders. The reader will also find out why the "Washington Consensus" may be less than a consensus, the difference between the red box and the blue box in global trade negotiations, and why no one should believe the poverty numbers in Cote d'Ivoire.

The text also includes an overview of each of the multitude of agencies working in Africa and the ABCs of development jargon, helping the reader to decipher the bewildering array of euphemisms and acronyms commonly used. Other useful features include chapter-by-chapter suggestions for further reading and a comprehensive index.

Todd J. Moss is a senior fellow at the Center for Global Development in Washington, DC and an adjunct professor at Georgetown University. He is the author of *Adventure Capitalism: Globalization and the Political Economy of Stock Markets in Africa.*